eXtensions

essays in
english studies from
Shakespeare to the
Spice Girls

*For Mick,
thanks for your generous
friendship,
love, Dianne*

**Edited by Sue Hosking
and Dianne Schwerdt**

Wakefield
Press

Wakefield Press
Box 2266
Kent Town
South Australia 5071

First published 1999

Designed and typeset by Clinton Ellicott, Wakefield Press, Adelaide
Printed and bound by Hyde Park Press, Adelaide

Apects of Lucy Potter's essay 'Re-reading *Hamlet*' were first published in a
focus edition of *Australasian Drama Studies* (October 1998) under the title
'*Hamlet* and the Scene of Pedagogy'.

National Library of Australia
Cataloguing-in-publication entry

Extensions: essays in English studies from Shakespeare to the Spice Girls.

ISBN 1 86254 498 0.

1. Literature – History and criticism. I. Schwerdt, Dianne O. (Dianne Ona).

808

A R T S A

Wakefield Press thanks Wirra Wirra Vineyards and Arts South Australia
for their continued support.

Contents

Re-Writings

Reading Film and Popular Culture

Introduction

Sue Hosking and
Dianne Schwerdt

U ntil quite recently, anyone who decided to study 'English' knew what to expect. The 'greatness' of certain books (the canon) of English literature was taken for granted. The 'greatest' books were regarded as exemplars of 'high art', produced and appreciated by the finest sensibilities. The critic's job was to interpret how great writers had used their considerable and indisputable skills to convey universal truths about the human condition. We may still choose to study 'the greats' of English literature: it would be absurd not to. When we do study canonical works, however, we now approach them for different reasons and with an extensive 'toolkit' of reading practices and methodologies that enable us to find a multitude of new meanings which reflect significantly, often startlingly, both on the past and the present.

The evidence wherever 'English' is studied today is that the discipline has been transformed – fragmented and multiplied into many versions. We may now concern ourselves not only with literary texts but with a variety of texts, applying and extending our understanding of narrative and genre, among other things, to film, television and everyday life: advertising, sport, fashion and pop music, for example. The boundaries between academic disciplines are breaking down. 'English Studies' now shares concerns and ways of thinking about the world with other disciplines within and beyond the humanities (Politics, History, Geography, Anthropology, Philosophy, Psychology,

Performance Arts, Media Studies, Environmental Studies, Physics, Psychiatry, Pathology and other disciplines in Medicine, to name a few). This broadens our horizons: we can step into different areas to see how new perspectives alter and expand our thinking about what we read, or view, or experience in a textual sense.

While the discipline of 'English' may have been fragmented it has also been energised by the explosion of knowledges that characterises the postmodern world in which we live. We are now acutely aware of the relativity of truths and values. Thinking about Shakespeare's *The Tempest*, for example, we recognise, as David Smith does in his essay 'New and Old Worlds', that Prospero's dismissal of Caliban as a 'mis-shapen knave' may be representative of a ruler's view, but it is not the only view. That Caliban can be seen as an exploited original (ab-original) inhabitant of an island is a perception that is crucial to postcolonial studies, which in the last thirty years or so have focused on the imbalances of power in master–slave or coloniser–colonised relationships. Assumptions about the authority of empire and the centrality of canonical texts have been questioned and the dominance of 'English' disputed in the wake of proliferating written and spoken 'englishes' around the world.

For almost a decade the English Department at the University of Adelaide has taught a first-year course that has a postcolonial focus and is concerned with the multiplicity of 'literatures in English' rather than the hegemony of 'English Literature'. At the same time, the course emphasises the intertextuality or interrelatedness of all manner of 'texts', whether literary, visual or cultural.[1] Cultural studies has extended our understanding of what 'texts' are, so we can 'read' a variety of things from film versions of Shakespeare to football. Mandy Treagus suggests that today we may reveal more about the way we think as a culture in our responses to the 'plot' of four quarters of football, than in our reading of a novel. However, whatever we respond to, and how we 'read', depends upon so many variable factors: our social position (class), our racial origin (ethnicity), whether we are male or female (gender) or gay (sexuality). The more we read, the more we bring to texts, and the more we understand how texts interconnect in complex ways.

The discipline that we (at the University of Adelaide) continue to call 'English', foremost among the humanities, provides the opportunity for intensive study and reflection on human interactions. This is an occupation that is crucially important if we are to retain balance in a world where economic rationalism and complex technologies encroach on our lives to the extent where as human beings we may begin to wonder how much we really matter in the scheme of things. Contributors to this collection of essays all share and demonstrate this intense preoccupation with human interactions and their representations. What is remarkably diverse, however, is the range of subject matter considered and the different kinds of critical approaches employed. The net is cast beyond the canon in explorations of texts from current theoretical positions. The essays provide intertextual and comparative readings, consider ways in which texts exist 'in conversation' with other texts, introduce and work with notions of race, class and gender and how they are represented in texts, as well as ways in which they shape the production of texts. All of this is offered in accessible, straightforward writing that introduces challenging concepts and demonstrates how they might be applied. The terminology of literary theory is important for our purposes: new practices and concepts require new vocabulary. We have, however, made a conscious effort to employ this new vocabulary in a way that is useful and explanatory. Our main aim has been to demonstrate, rather than define, new reading practices.

Our book begins with Shakespeare, the best known and most revered author in the history of English literature (though these days not most read or viewed). The first essay considers contradictions and ambivalences in *The Tempest*, and draws attention to ways in which 'political values in the play might be differently prioritised'. Lucy Potter, using feminist and poststructuralist approaches, focuses on Ophelia, demonstrating that *Hamlet* is 'not at all the play it seems to be'. The collection as a whole provides grouped re-readings of drama (Shakespeare), poetry and fiction, reflecting the way in which English literature traditionally has been divided into genres. Yet within these familiar genre categories, the essays all raise ideas and ask questions that once would not have concerned critics. Smith suggests that *The Tempest* seems to be concerned with the new world, as it is thought of today, with a clutch of 'connotations to do with colonialism, the Americas and the West Indies'. His essay looks at both new and old worlds in the play, highlighting the multiple perspectives that have attracted different interpretations with very different systems of political prioritising. The approach that views Caliban as exploited provides a framework for other essays in this collection: notably in the group headed 'Re-writings'. Philip Butterss also draws on *The Tempest* in his study of masculinities, which we have grouped with feminist approaches to fiction under 'Gendered Readings'. Butterss argues that *The Tempest* can be read generally as 'a tale concerning the proper performance of masculinity', with

Prospero having to re-learn how to exercise power and authority so that he can be a fit masculine ruler. In this reading, Caliban becomes an example of marginalised masculinity. Already then, it should be apparent that the sub-groupings we have used outline only one of a series of flexible relations in which the essays might be linked – generically, thematically, ideologically – in terms of race, politics or gender – or all of these – or more.

Philip Waldron and Megan Fyffe both offer close readings of poems. Their essays are linked as studies in the genre of poetry. Yet they could be grouped with essays that are concerned with gender, and Fyffe's essay connects with others that focus on aspects of the Gothic genre. Through a detailed analysis of two Romantic poems, Waldron demonstrates some of the central preoccupations and characteristics of Romanticism. His scholarly analysis of two poems which are very significant in literary history demonstrates the continuing importance of cultural custodianship within the discipline of 'English'. Blake's poem reflects on the city of London, and is spoken by a figure which 'may or may not be identifiable with the voice of William Blake' but which is certainly male, abroad in the streets of a major city. By way of contrast, Fyffe reads three poems by Emily Dickinson, a poet who rarely set foot outside her father's house and who scarcely published in her lifetime. The challenge of this essay is to refute the assumption that a housebound spinster, who sewed her poems together with needle and thread and stored them under a window-seat in her bedroom, would have no knowledge of the world and its workings. Waldron, reading Blake's 'London', and Fyffe, reading Dickinson's 'She Rose to His Requirement' (#Poem 732), come to similar conclusions, though by very different means. Their readings therefore invite comparisons between, for example, different kinds of social protest evident in certain works by Blake and Dickinson. Waldron points out that Blake makes use of the conceit of the 'marriage hearse' to draw attention to the connections between prostitution, syphilis and the infection of the bride 'so that one major rite of passage (the marriage) becomes its opposite (the funeral)'. Fyffe, likewise, focuses on the equation between weddings and funerals, but her feminist reading practice offers a completely different critique; she suggests that Dickinson challenged society's endorsement of marriage because the loss of female subjectivity that was inevitable when a woman became someone's wife was equivalent to death. At the same time the essay on Dickinson, like other essays in this collection, reveals contradictions that are apparent in the texts (poems) under discussion. Contradictions, inconsistencies, absences: these can tell us a great deal about ideologies of the times in which texts were produced. The fact that we notice these contradictions now tells us how our thinking and attitudes have changed (though not necessarily progressed) over time. Searching for and analysing these kinds of tensions in texts is a significant methodology in contemporary criticism.

A number of the essays in this collection explore issues of gender. Most are concerned with women: how they have been ignored or contained or diminished in canonical texts, or sometimes by critical readings of those texts, and how women writers and feminist critics have sought to redress this situation through strategically different writing and reading practices. By way of contrast, Philip Butterss 'reads the masculine' in four texts (three of which are subjects of different kinds of analysis in this collection) in his essay 'What it Means to be a Man'. Feminism, as Butterss points out, has had significant effects on men and 'the idea of masculinity ... is currently undergoing considerable change'. Men are having to rethink and renegotiate their identities. Studies in masculinity, though relatively new, are becoming an important focus for research in universities, complementing the work of feminists.

Rosemary Moore and Amanda Nettelbeck investigate aspects of women's writing. Taking a psychoanalytic feminist approach to *Jane Eyre*, Rosemary Moore argues that Jane's experience of being a woman in a man's world results in a split in her characterisation that is 'central to the unfolding of meaning in her story'. Furthermore the profoundly conflicting emotions Jane Eyre experiences are seen to 'link questions of sexuality and gender with writing'. Jane's quest for self-knowledge, in a sense, is every woman's quest. To know herself, Jane, like all women, must confront the ways she is represented in her time as a woman over a wide variety of discourses – 'medical, psychological, social, moral and religious'. Amanda Nettelbeck is particularly interested in the Gothic mode, which has special significance in women's writing. The conventions of Gothic horror have been used differently by men and women. For women, whether writing in the nineteenth or twentieth centuries, the Gothic is particularly appealing because, as Nettelbeck points out, it enables women writers and readers to explore the 'anxieties of closure and, perhaps, repression that underlie women's everyday domestic life'.

Among the many boundaries that are now in the process of breaking down in our discipline is that between critical readers and writers. Marc Vickers, writing about Joseph Conrad's *Heart of Darkness*, admits that all texts require the active participation of readers in order for meanings to be constructed. However, he suggests that Conrad's novel makes unusual demands, to the extent that all readers 'are forced, in their minds at least, to write, or re-write, the novel' if it is to have any meaning at all. Writers, of course, are critical readers. Nowhere is this more evident than among post-colonial writers who undertake to re-write or answer back to canonical texts. The African writer, Chinua Achebe, having read *Heart of Darkness* and other books like it about Africa, wrote his own novel, *Things Fall Apart*, partly as a critique of what he perceived as nine-teenth-century Europe's racism, which does not allow African people a voice. Dianne Schwerdt, writing on *Things Fall Apart*, and Sue Hosking, discussing work by Jack Davis and Archie Weller, are both concerned with postcolonial texts that participate in the recon-struction of once-colonised worlds. The essay on Aboriginal writing insists that there are different ways of re-inscribing and re-centring alternative identities, arguing against the negativity of concepts of 'half-caste' people and 'inauthentic' writing in favour of recognition of the (re-)creative potential of hybridity. The postcolonial texts dis-cussed are all impressive in their own right. When they are consid-ered in the context of colonial assumptions encoded in canonical texts, they politicise our (re-)readings of earlier texts. Anyone who is familiar with Achebe's work obviously will respond to Conrad's novel differently from someone who is not. The essays in this collection point to and extend the dialogue or conversation between texts, clearly demonstrating the operation of intertextuality. This is a crucial concept in contemporary criticism, whether in the sense of certain works re-writing or answering back to others, or responding to absences, or in the sense of narratives functioning within a par-ticular genre (for example the Gothic genre, which may create less obvious intertextual relationships, such as between Elizabeth Jolley's *The Well* and *The X-Files*).

The Gothic genre, which interests several of our contributors, provides a useful nexus in this collection, demonstrating the signifi-cance of genre studies and intertextuality. The Gothic genre (which always has been the province of popular culture, even in its literary origins) has adapted well to television and film, the major forms of contemporary narrative entertainment, where it now survives and continues to evolve most significantly. Treagus and Butterss discuss Gothic aspects of *The X-Files* and *The Piano*, respectively, and in her discussion of *The Silence of the Lambs*, Joy McEntee shows how film may be 'read' as a continuation of a line of literary works. The film character Hannibal Lecter is a thoroughly modern monster, yet in conveying his monstrosity *The Silence of the Lambs* echoes literary conventions of nineteenth-century Gothic novels: for most of the film Lecter inhabits a space that is more subterranean dungeon than contemporary prison cell and he appears to have supernatural (or unnatural) powers that enable him to feed on minds as well as bodies. Furthermore, as McEntee points out, the stylised labyrinths of Jame Gumb's 'architecturally chaotic basement', in which the film's denouement takes place, 'make the connections between nineteenth-century and twentieth-century settings quite explicit'.

A number of essays in this collection demonstrate the significance of cultural studies and cultural studies approaches to texts. Like other contributors to this collection who set out to introduce readers to crucial concepts and terms in contemporary criticism and theory, writers whose essays deal with film, television and popular culture lead us gently into these areas. Cultural studies approaches, however, are not exclusive to the subject matter explored in the final section: interests in Aboriginalities and masculinities, for example, cannot be contained in narrow areas and inevitably spill into other domains. Indeed, in 'English Studies' today many of us believe that it is more useful to develop our awareness of the permeability of boundaries, rather than their permanence.

Within any given culture, stories are crucial to ways in which we know ourselves as human. 'English' (including cultural studies) is much more than simply the study of stories. Nevertheless, we are all captivated by narrative and textual representations of our imagined worlds and our imagined selves. The worlds and selves of texts can never be 'real'; what is involved in their construction is fascinating and fertile ground for critical and theoretical analysis, and tells us a great deal about what it is to be human. How do representations unfold? How are narratives or story fragments told? How are impressions of the world conveyed? What do they signify? What power structures are reinforced or critiqued in texts? What subtexts exist, consciously or otherwise, to destabilise assumptions – about what it is to be 'normal', or a woman, or a girl, or a man, or a ruler, or an Aboriginal or an African? Who tells the stories? Who reads them? What happens when we bring contemporary reading practices to bear on texts that were written in the past?

One of the ways in which we may come to an understanding of how thinking has changed over time is by tracing how the expression of a particular type or form of literature or genre of story varies. We seek to understand what *The X-Files* tells us today about what we think as a cultural community, what we value, what we fear as we move into the new millennium. In this kind of investigation it helps to know how the stories of *The X-Files*, expressed through the medium of television, differ from the most significant forms of horror stories – Gothic novels – originating in the late eighteenth and nineteenth centuries. Literary studies, therefore, inform cultural studies. Likewise, when it comes to discussing the Spice Girls, what their popularity in contemporary (girl) culture tells us is significantly better understood in the context of literary representations of girls across the broad span of modernity since the eighteenth century and as far back as the Renaissance. At the same time, as Catherine Driscoll reminds us, the current escalation of ways in which 'girls themselves represent being girls' makes us think again about the significance of girls and daughters in canonical literary texts in English, including Shakespeare's plays.

Reading Potter's essay on *Hamlet*, in relation to Driscoll's essay on the Spice Girls, we can see that although the 'texts' under consideration are very different, the approaches to those texts have something in common. Informed by contemporary feminist examinations of women and gender, Potter re-reads *Hamlet* concentrating not on the character who has traditionally been accepted as central to the tragedy, but rather on Ophelia, a young woman and a daughter, virtually dismissed by the influential critic A.C. Bradley at the beginning of the twentieth century as intellectually 'not remarkable' (*Shakespearean Tragedy*, 112). Demonstrating how Ophelia, rather than Hamlet, fulfils the expectations of the play's plot – that is, she takes absolute action while Hamlet remains paralysed by his conscience – Potter accumulates textual evidence to argue that it is possible to see Ophelia as the *Subject* of the tragedy, rather than its passive victim. Why bother with this kind of reading? Emphatically, we bother because such readings have not always been possible. It is important to redress the kind of thinking that dismissed female characters like Ophelia as irrelevant to the concept of tragedy, or female writers, like Emily Dickinson (described by John Crowe Ransom in the 1960s as a 'little home-keeping person'), as incapable of serious thought. Likewise, it is important to acknowledge that African people and Aboriginal Australians, like many other colonised people whose histories and cultures have been eclipsed by those of Europe, are not voiceless, and nor are they content to remain the unheard inheritors of marginality.

In our postmodern world (a world which Waldron suggests might more appropriately be described as post-Romantic) we are increasingly aware that labels or descriptive categories cannot satisfactorily accommodate the multiplicity of versions – of truth, identity, history – that co-exist. Having examined a selection of literary texts in his essay on masculinity, Butterss concludes that 'masculinity should not be seen as a fixed and obvious category'. Hosking writes about two versions of 'Aboriginality' from a 'spectrum of possibilities' and Schwerdt draws attention to 'versions of the colonial experience', quoting the Ibo proverb 'Where one thing stands another will stand beside it'. What is being signalled here is the importance of recognising that there is almost always another way of seeing the same thing. Our study of texts in this volume draws specific attention to the multiplicity of viewpoints available to us. We are constantly reminded that being able to read texts from a variety of positions and use a range of reading strategies effectively broadens and diversifies our approach to any one text or group of texts.

This collection indicates some of the ways in which 'English Studies' has been extended in the last decades of the twentieth century. In one sense the essays stand alone; in another, they are parts of a proliferating discipline, standing side by side but existing in flexible relations that might be grounded in different ways – each potential permutation contributing to the infinite variety of what we do, who we are and what we stand for.

Note

1. See Russell McDougall and Sue Hosking 'The Trials, Tribulations and Ironies of Teaching Post-colonialism as 'English I' in an Australian University' in *Teaching Post-Colonialism and Post-Colonial Literatures*. Eds. Anne Collett, Lars Jensen and Anna Rutherford. Aarhus: Aarhus UP, 1997: 174–196.

Works Cited

Bradley, A.C. *Shakespearean Tragedy: Lectures on Hamlet, Othello, King Lear, Macbeth*. London: Macmillan and Co., 1904.

Ransom, John Crowe. 'A Poet Restored'. *Emily Dickinson: A Collection of Critical Essays*. Ed. Richard B. Sewall. Englewood Cliffs, New Jersey: Prentice-Hall, 1963.

(Re-)Reading Shakespeare

New and Old Worlds
in The Tempest

David Smith

T*he Tempest* made its first published appearance in the *First Folio* of 1623, the first collected edition of Shakespeare's plays. It was the very first play in the edition, in fact, and headed a group classified as Comedies. In more recent times the play has been re-defined a little hesitantly as a Romance. However, the term Romance is not all that satisfactory, either; it is a term which tends to obscure both the play's comic elements *and* its tragic elements.

The fact that *The Tempest*'s genre has never satisfactorily been defined is part of the fascination of this strange, puzzling play, whose contradictions, ambivalences, mix of sentiments and moods may be seen to be epitomised in a moment in Act V, scene one, where Miranda and her husband-to-be, Ferdinand are 'discovered' playing chess. In the theatre the two are usually positioned at the back of the stage and Miranda's father, Prospero, somewhat like a stage-manager – just one of his many roles in the play – draws a curtain aside to reveal them. The couple look up to see gazing at them Ferdinand's father, the King Alonso, Alonso's brother, Sebastian, Prospero's brother, Antonio, and Gonzalo the Councillor. Miranda arises from the chessboard, surveys this motley bunch of men – Alonso, who has conspired in the past in the usurpation and banishment of her father, Antonio and Sebastian who have in the course of the play gone very close to murdering Alonso and Gonzalo in their sleep – and says with awed astonishment:

How many goodly creatures are there here!
How beauteous mankind is! O brave new world
That has such people in't! (V,i,182–184)

Theatrical productions often increase the irony by having her gaze directly at the murderous Antonio and Sebastian as she speaks. Standing to one side, her father, Prospero, who has arranged this whole scene, comments sardonically: ''Tis new to thee' (V,i,185). This is a moment which encapsulates the strange mix of elements in the play, drawing attention as it does both to its tragi-comedy (the audience almost invariably laughs uneasily at this point) and also to its clash of abstractions: here we see the conflict between idealism and (to put it at its most extreme) cynicism, and the tug between reconciliation and forgiveness on the one hand and revenge and bitterness on the other.

But the scene can be made to yield further illumination. In the first place, whatever Miranda's intentions in using those words 'O brave New World', their presence may remind the reader of the fact that the play *does* seem at certain key points to be implicitly concerned with the new world as it is customarily thought of today, with its historical and geographical clutch of connotations to do with colonialism, the Americas and the West Indies.

In addition, the reader may be reminded of the *Brave New World* of the British writer Aldous Huxley, who in 1932 was to utilise the mix of reactions that Miranda's phrase inspires by appropriating it as the title for his dystopian novel about a future world in the seventh century A.F. (A.F. standing for After [Henry] Ford). Huxley's New World takes to extremes one element of Prospero's vision in the play: his drive for order, his stress on not giving way to the passions. His world is one that is sanitised, ordered and deodorised (and incidentally deathly boring), a world where the so-called 'uncivilised' – the 'savages' – are kept on reservations, banished along with the few remaining tattered copies of Shakespeare's plays. It was clearly the ambivalence of Miranda's phrase (and the ambivalence of its context), together with the fact that it lent itself to multiple perspectives, that attracted Huxley, who has in turn added his own layer of meaning to it.

Huxley is certainly not the only one to have appropriated aspects of the text being considered in this essay. Its kaleidoscopic aspects, its sudden changes in perspective, lend themselves to this kind of appropriation.

Any consideration of *The Tempest* must try to do justice to what

David Hirst has called the 'recurrent and violent shifts of perspective' (18) which take place throughout the play. In addition, criticism must take into account the play's opaqueness, with the central character in particular distanced from the reader or spectator; even his soliloquies, as Anne Righter has put it, are 'strangely externalised utterances' (11). The play is so opaque that some recent critics, such as Stephen Orgel, have concentrated more on the absences in the play than the presences ('Prospero's Wife', 1ff). Finally the reader needs to be particularly responsive to the ways in which political values in the play might be differently prioritised. It is relevant to note here another group of critics – a number of them creative writers from Africa and the West Indies, such as George Lamming, Derek Walcott and Edward Brathwaite – who have in the last thirty years or so appropriated aspects of *The Tempest* partly, as Rob Nixon has argued, 'to meet contemporary political and cultural needs' (559). In the process these writers, whatever else they have achieved, have shown that any consideration of power in the play has to take full account of Caliban's place in the power structure.

Power is, after all, very much amongst the play's central concerns. The drama opens, appropriately enough, with a violent storm, with nature, in other words, at its most powerful. It is a scene which, by long tradition, has been presented in the theatre as naturalistically as possible (so naturalistically in fact that for a time in the eighteenth and nineteenth centuries it was customary to stage the scene at the beginning of the second act, so late-comers would not miss it).

It is important first to note (and here those perspectives start shifting) that this naturalistic tempest setting is later to be transformed into a whole sequence of sea-images: of sea as resurrection, as change, epitomised by Ariel's song to Ferdinand about the supposed drowning of his father, 'Full fadom five thy father lies;/Of his bones are coral made;/Those are pearls that were his eyes:/Nothing of him that doth fade,/But doth suffer a sea-change/Into something rich and strange' (I,ii, 399–404). These water-images are in turn inverted, reversed and burlesqued in the comic scenes of the sub-plot involving Stephano, Trinculo and Caliban. This inversion and burlesque is effected partly through the medium of Stephano's never-ending wine (his 'celestial liquor' [II,ii,118] as Caliban enthusiastically puts it), and partly through the manner in which these drunken co-conspirators end up 'dancing up to th[eir] chins' (IV,i,183) in the cess-pit near Prospero's cell.

The second point to note about this opening scene is that amidst the din and storm there are some very important verbal exchanges. Issues touched upon in the first few shouted exchanges include the question of power. Interrelated with this are questions of authority, of people's roles, of the opposition between a hierarchical and rigidly structured society and one where there is natural order, and the upsetting of the natural order. All these issues are highlighted in the dialogue between Gonzalo and the Boatswain:

> Gonzalo. *Nay, good, be patient.*
> Boatswain. *When the sea is. Hence! What cares these roarers for the name of King? To cabin: silence! trouble us not.*
> Gonzalo. *Good, yet remember whom thou hast aboard.*
> Boatswain. *None that I more love than myself. You are a counsellor: if you can command these elements to silence, and work the peace of the presence, we will not hand a rope more; use your authority; if you cannot, give thanks you have lived so long, and make yourself ready in your cabin for the mischance of the hour, if it so hap. (I,i,15–26)*

The boatswain asserts a 'natural' order against the civil hierarchical order represented by Gonzalo and the King. It is both a natural order of the elements, and a natural human order: that is to say, an order based on merit, on natural superiority, rather than one based on class or rank. The latter indeed is the kind of order that Antonio and Sebastian try to assert when they enter; their curses, it is interesting to note, are far more vicious and degraded than any to which Caliban later gives vent.

So in this opening scene questions of authority, questions of nature and the natural order and interrelationships based on power, are all raised, against that ironic backdrop of the raging tempest. It is ironic because – and this only becomes fully apparent in the theatre – inevitably some of these shouted interchanges are lost to the noise of the wind, language buffeted and made impotent, as it were, by the power of the elements. In some productions about the only words heard above the simulated roar and power of the wind and lightning have been the repeated cries of 'Master'.

There is to be further irony in scene two when we learn that the apparently death-threatening tempest, a natural event, is in fact fully under the control of Prospero's Art: and we become aware that we have witnessed an illusion within an illusion. The seamen were calling out for the ship's master; the real master however is, as Ariel is soon to let us know, the 'great master' Prospero. But the reader will also do well to remember that for those on the boat the tempest was real: point of view is crucial.

Point of view, and the changing of perspectives, is something that Prospero is quick to invoke as he tells his daughter Miranda how they came to the island:

> *By foul play, as thou say'st, were we heav'd thence,*
> *But blessedly holp hither. (1,ii,62–63)*

So the actions which led to their arrival on this island were both 'foul' and 'blessed', a dichotomy which could be said to exist in the actions of the play itself. One part of the drama *does* pull towards 'blessedness': towards idealism, forgiveness, reconciliation and sanctity. Another part pulls in other directions, not necessarily towards foul play or sin but certainly away from the purity that one side of Prospero is trying to insist upon. (There is a splendid moment relevant to this dichotomy in Act IV, scene one when Prospero, after telling Ferdinand to 'Sit ... and talk with [Miranda] ...' (32), turns away and then a few lines later with his sudden schoolmasterly hectoring – 'Look thou be true; do not give dalliance/Too much the rein ...' – implies that the lovers, once his back is turned, are doing rather more than simply sitting.)

Although Prospero at this stage of the play (I, ii) is projecting a basically benign image, he does betray the fact that while he might well be in control of his Art, and apparently just in control of the subjects around him, he is at times only barely in control of himself. As he touches upon the perfidy, the wickedness of his brother Antonio, here as elsewhere in the play his disjointed, broken syntax betrays the turbulence he is barely repressing:

> *My brother, and thy uncle, call'd Antonio, –*
> *I pray thee, mark me, that a brother should*
> *Be so perfidious! – he whom next thyself*
> *Of all the world I lov'd, and to him put*
> *The manage of my state; as at that time*
> *Through all the signories it was the first,*
> *And Prospero the prime duke, being so reputed*
> *In dignity, and for the liberal Arts*
> *Without a parallel; these being all my study,*
> *The government I cast upon my brother,*
> *And to my state grew stranger, being transported*

And rapt in secret studies. Thy false uncle –
Dost thou attend me? (I,ii,66–78)

This disjointed syntax indicates, as suggested above, the tight control
he is keeping over himself, but, as that last line foregrounds, it also
indicates the tight control or authority he is exercising over his
daughter. As he exercises this patriarchal authority so his recollec-
tion of the past is once again centrally occupied with those questions
of political authority and power implicit in the first scene: his *relinquishing* of authority, his brother's *usurpation* of authority. To extend
the point, the scenes that follow are awash with images of power,
dominance and authority and, interrelated with these, images of
freedom and imprisonment.

We are presented with a whole series of different kinds of power
relationships. In addition to those between Prospero, Caliban and
Ariel, and between Caliban, Stephano and Trinculo, there is the relationship already mentioned between father and daughter (Prospero
and Miranda), between siblings (Alonso and Sebastian) and between
strutting peacocked males (Sebastian and Antonio). There is also –
not that this exhausts the permutations – the relationship between
Ferdinand and Miranda. This relationship, with its rather more
metaphorical, certainly more fanciful (and certainly less physically
hurtful) use of such terms as 'power', 'servants' and 'bondage', seems
to be suggesting other possibilities, other power structures.

Also explored are questions of liberty, and the relativity of liberty.
As Prospero quickly reminds Ariel – when the latter shows signs of
restlessness and a desire for liberty – his imprisonment before this
was far more irksome. Imprisoned by Sycorax in a pine tree Ariel
could not even move; now he can go anywhere he likes as long as
where he likes is where Prospero bids him go. Following this piece of
casuistry we have spun before us a kaleidoscope of different images
of liberty and imprisonment: the sailors imprisoned on the ship, the
imprisonment of Caliban, and Ferdinand's imprisonment first by
Prospero, and then, in a rather different way, by Miranda.

Within the romance plot of Miranda and Ferdinand – which at
times seems like a play within a play – imprisonment becomes a state
of mind or simply a play on words. In Act III, scene one, for example,
Ferdinand talks of being a 'slave' (66) to Miranda's service, and of his
prospective marriage to her as welcome 'bondage' (89) – all this is in
direct ironic juxtaposition with Caliban in the previous scene (II, ii)
proclaiming virtually the reverse, proclaiming his freedom when he
really seems to be under a new form of bondage: ''Ban, 'Ban,

Cacaliban/Has a new master: – get a new man!/Freedom, high-day!
high-day, freedom! freedom, high-day, freedom!' (II,ii,184–187).

This relationship of Ferdinand and Miranda can be looked at in
several ways. It is possible to view Miranda and Ferdinand's use of
what is after all conventional literary courtly love terminology – they
sound sometimes as though they have strayed out of some highly
artificial Elizabethan love sonnet – as obscuring the issue; in a sense
their part in the discourse of imprisonment and bondage serves to
mystify the very real slavery and imprisonment of Caliban.

David Dabydeen and Nana Wilson-Tagoe argue rather differently,
suggesting that Miranda and Ferdinand offer 'an alternative vision of
human possibilities'. According to them the 'love between Ferdinand
and Miranda redefines the power relationship. *Romantic slavery* ...
stands in positive contrast to the *Political slavery* that characterises
the relationship between Prospero, Sebastian, Alonso and Antonio'
(6). It is possible, however, to argue that the whole exploration of
power and power relationships and slaves and masters in *The
Tempest* is rather more subtle and complex than Dabydeen and
Wilson-Tagoe's bipolar model allows for.

Consider for example how we are shown, as Caliban demonstrates when he attaches himself to Stephano and Trinculo, that real
slavery ('real' as distinct from that embodied in conventional love
epithets) *does not* rely upon force necessarily, that it *can* indeed be a
state of mind. In the so-called comic sub-plot Caliban demonstrates
what is virtually a slave mentality. '[I'll be] thy foot-licker' (IV,i,219) he
says in what is arguably one of the most disturbing lines in the play.
There is surely a sense conveyed here that Caliban *needs* a new
master to give him a sense of freedom. 'Has a new master: – get a new
man' (II,ii,185).

It is unequivocally *as* a slave that Caliban is first introduced;
Prospero with some satisfaction pronounces him as 'My slave'
(I,ii,308). In Prospero's opening account of Caliban's function that is
what he would seem to be: literally, the slave of Prospero and
Miranda. However, the mutual interdependence that Prospero
touches upon in this account of him, namely the fact that they *need*
Caliban, is an interesting one:

We cannot miss him: he does make our fire,
Fetch in our wood, and serves in offices
That profit us. What, ho! slave! Caliban!
Thou earth, thou! speak!
Caliban. *(Within) There's wood enough within.* (I,ii,313–316)

What is also interesting here is that the first direct command Caliban is given in the drama is an exhortation to speak. And the first line he speaks is off-stage. Moreover, he speaks in blank verse – which is normally granted by Shakespeare to his more serious characters: Stephano and Trinculo, for example, speak in the comic sub-plot in the lower register of prose.

What are we to make of Caliban? His name would seem to be an anagram of cannibal, the word cannibal itself being apparently derived from 'Carib', the first tribal Indian name known to Europe. In the 1623 Folio Caliban appears in the cast of characters as a 'salvage and deformed slave'. There is little question about his being a slave. The text is also insistent about his being deformed: insistent, but strangely imprecise. Prospero, for example, calls him a 'mis-shapen knave' (V,i,268), but the only really descriptive references of him are to his fish-like features. 'Monster' is actually his most frequent epithet; he is called that some forty or so times in the text. He is also variously called 'moon-calf', 'this thing of darkness', 'thou earth' and 'hag-seed'. From this confusion of epithets, surely, no clear image emerges.

Caliban's first speech – as distinct from his off-stage voice – is basically a slather of curses, though less crude than Sebastian's or Antonio's. His second speech, however, is very much more troubling. It is a speech which has become the springboard for those numerous commentators and theatre producers who see Caliban very much in the light of the exploited aboriginal, the original inhabitant of the island who has been displaced and rendered a slave by Prospero:

> *This island's mine, by Sycorax my mother,*
> *Which thou tak'st from me. When thou cam'st first,*
> *Thou strok'st me, and made much of me; wouldst give me*
> *Water with berries in't; and teach me how*
> *To name the bigger light, and how the less,*
> *That burn by day and night . . . (I,ii,333–338)*

It is worth noting that Prospero makes no attempt to rebut Caliban's claim of land-rights, but instead indignantly denies that he is treating Caliban as a slave for no reason. According to him Caliban 'didst seek to violate/The honour of my child' (I,ii,349–50). Again it is worth noting that Caliban makes no attempt to deny that either: in fact, quite the reverse.

> *O ho, O ho! Would't had been done!*
> *Thou didst prevent me; I had peopled else*
> *This isle with Calibans. (I,ii,351–353)*

No noble savage is being pictured here; rather we are presented with a very lustful, indeed virtually mythically lustful creature who with almost lip-smacking pleasure imagines populating the island by way of the violated body of Miranda. Another dimension to the picture of Caliban emerges as he goes on to complain that he is not simply literally imprisoned by Prospero and Miranda, but also metaphorically imprisoned by their culture and by the most powerful thing he knows, namely language:

> *You taught me language; and my profit on't*
> *Is, I know how to curse. The red plague rid you*
> *For learning me* your *language! (I,ii,365–367. My emphasis.)*

Later in the same scene Ferdinand is to talk of *my* language very possessively when he first meets Miranda, astonished as he is that she speaks his language. (At this stage he thinks, the King being dead, that he is the King.)

> *My language! heavens!*
> *I am the best of them that speak this speech,*
> *Were I but where 'tis spoken. (I,ii,431–433)*

Later in the play, in one of the scenes between Caliban, Stephano and Trinculo, Stephano expresses his astonishment that Caliban should speak 'our' language (Stephano, being a commoner, is not quite so possessive as Ferdinand): 'Where the devil should he learn our language?' (II,ii,67). As if to reinforce his linguistic self-awareness, Caliban is very positive that it is Prospero's books they should seek: it is the books that give Prospero power and the words in the books that keep Caliban enslaved. As he says to Stephano 'Remember/First to possess his books; for without them/He's but a sot, as I am' (III,ii,89–91).

Paul Brown has persuasively argued in this connection that 'the "gift" of language [by Prospero] inscribes a power relation [with Caliban as the] linguistic subject of the master language ... Whatever Caliban does with this gift [of language] announces his capture by it' (61). To put the argument in more comprehensive terms, it could be said that every time Caliban opens his mouth he is in a sense witness to the fact that he is enslaved by Prospero's culture.

The other aspect of Caliban which needs to be examined here is expressed or implied in part in that grudging acknowledgement of Caliban by Prospero in the final scene of the play: 'this thing of darkness I/*Acknowledge mine*' (V,i,275–276. My emphasis). What *is* Prospero acknowledging? Simply possession? Responsibility? The answer may be found by adopting – as the play adopts – a somewhat indirect approach.

Already cited in this essay is one instance of many of Prospero's tight control over himself: namely his barely repressed bitterness and instinct for revenge distorting his syntax in that early scene with Miranda. Another example could be taken from the final scene where his tight control seems to be barely holding out against bitterness, as when for instance he 'forgives' his brother:

> *For you, most wicked sir, whom to call brother*
> *Would even infect my mouth, I do forgive*
> *Thy rankest fault, – all of them ... (V,i, 130–132)*

It is tempting to add that if this is Prospero in a forgiving mood, then Prospero in an unforgiving mood would not be a very pleasant thing to contemplate.

What is reasonably certain is that Prospero is very tightly and often barely controlling certain inner instincts. Stephen Orgel's extension of this argument, namely that Caliban 'does in fact embody a whole range of qualities that we see in Prospero, but that [Prospero] consistently denies in himself: rage, passion, vindictiveness; perhaps deepest and most disruptive, sexuality' is, however, perhaps putting the matter too strenuously (Introduction, 28). Prospero's urge for restraint (his anxious enjoinders on Ferdinand and Miranda to observe chastity before marriage and fidelity after it) is hardly, surely, the repressed face of Caliban's attempted rape of Miranda or Caliban's expressed lustful desire to 'people the isle with Calibans'.

What is unarguable, however, is that along with Caliban's monstrousness and dangerousness there is a certain elemental vitality: an imaginative apprehension of things. For example his speech about the music of the island in Act III, scene two ('the isle is full of noises/Sounds and sweet airs, that give delight, and hurt not ...' [131–141]) is surely one of the most moving in the play, and certainly puts him in a very different light from the view of him we are customarily given by Prospero. Caliban has then, to repeat, an imaginative apprehension which certainly casts an unattractive light on the so-called civilised Antonio and Sebastian and for that matter on

Stephano and Trinculo and certainly gives him rather more stature than those about him are willing to grant him. We should not minimise Caliban's savagery and we should not forget that in terms of the water resurrection imagery in the play he – along with Stephano and Trinculo – spends the last part of the play stinking of 'horse-piss' (IV,i, 199). At the same time however we should also remember that it is the dominant culture – the culture represented in the play, the culture whose language is spoken, whose books are talked about, whose art this is, the culture of Prospero, Alonso and Stephano – which sees Caliban as alien, and variously tries to ridicule, dismiss, repress, change, reform, enslave and even banish him. And it is about the nature of this same culture that Caliban's representation poses basic questions.

Having raised the issue of Prospero and his passion, it is surely relevant to return in the final stages of this essay to Prospero, and specifically to his project, which forms the subject matter of much of the play. 'Now does my project gather to a head' he says confidently at the beginning of Act V. It may well be queried, however, whether the certainty of that image of 'gathering' applies to the whole of his actions during the course of the drama. What *did* Prospero mean by the term 'project' when he first used it? Here the text is disquietingly reticent; here we certainly have abundant evidence instead of what Stephen Orgel calls absences or gaps, and what Anne Righter calls the opaqueness of the play. On the evidence of the text we might say that Prospero is not sure himself about his project. Certainly he wants to right the wrongs done him and restore things back to what he sees as their rightful order. But with how much vengeance he set out (as distinct from wanting to forgive and reconciliate), it is impossible to say. Nevertheless it is certainly worth citing in this connection David Hirst's comment that it is extraordinarily difficult to act forgiveness! ('To bully, to terrify, to make the guilty repent, to regain his dukedom, [these] are actions an actor can *play*; to forgive [on the other hand] is passive and will not sustain a performance or give it purpose' [Hirst, 57].)

What is reasonably certain is that the events that follow the commencement of the project are as educative for Prospero as for the others. He re-enacts his own usurpation in the Sebastian/Antonio scenes and these scenes (and the spontaneous attempted usurpation burlesqued in the Stephano/Trinculo/Caliban scenes) are a fresh reminder to him that his vision of a tightly controlled order – in which abundance is tempered by chastity and reason – *is* a vision, a vision which importantly excludes passion: whether that be the passion of

Venus or the passion of Caliban and Sebastian and Antonio or for that matter, the passion of Prospero. We hear much of the virtues of reason (usually from Prospero) in the final part of the play, but one of the central ironies of the drama is that it is only by *infecting* reason (I,ii,208) through his magic that Prospero is able to restore what he sees as reason, as the rightful order. So, 'This thing of Darkness/ I acknowledge mine', in this sense is a grudging but genuine acknowledgement by Prospero of what he has tried to deny, even as in a sense he represses it by forgiving.

It would be appropriate to conclude these remarks by returning to that episode with which this essay began: namely the scene where Miranda and Ferdinand are discovered at the back of the stage playing chess. But this time it is relevant to listen to the conversation they are 'discovered' having:

> Miranda. *Sweet lord, you play me false.*
> Ferdinand. *No, my dearest love,*
> *I would not for the world.*
> Miranda. *Yes, for a score of kingdoms you should wrangle,*
> *And I would call it fair play. (V,i,172–174)*

This sounds like nothing more than a bit of tender billing and cooing, and that indeed is what it is in part. If the speech is listened to more closely, however, it may be speculated that Miranda and Ferdinand in this tender flirtatious game of chess are signalling their possible entrance into the world of their elders: the world of cheating, deceiving and wrangling. They may, in other words, be stepping out of their romance play.

And Caliban? The last time he is heard on stage he is rather dubiously talking of being 'wise hereafter,/And seek[ing] for grace' (V,i, 294–295), a rather obsequious speech which is followed, it is safe to assume, by much bowing and scraping – but then nobody has taken the trouble to tell Caliban that Prospero and his avenging spirits are shortly to depart! The island will shortly become Caliban's island, unless, that is to say, they take Caliban with them to exhibit him in Milan as an exotic native or unless, as has happened so often in history, Ariel picks up that broken wand or staff that has been discarded by Prospero ... But that is another story ...

Works Cited

Brown, Paul. '"This thing of darkness I acknowledge mine": *The Tempest* and the discourse of colonialism' in *Political Shakespeare: New Essays in Cultural Materialism*. Eds. Jonathan Dollimore and Alan Sinfield. Manchester: Manchester UP, 1985: 48–71.

Dabydeen, David and Nana Wilson-Tagoe. *A Reader's Guide to West Indian and Black British Literature*. Surrey: Dangeroo Press, 1987.

Hirst, David L. *The Tempest: Text and Performance*. London: Macmillan, 1984.

Nixon, Rob. 'Caribbean and African Appropriations of *The Tempest*'. *Critical Inquiry* 13 (1987): 557–578.

Orgel, Stephen. 'Prospero's Wife'. *Representations* 8 (1984): 1–13.

Orgel, Stephen. Introduction. *The Tempest* by William Shakespeare. Oxford: Oxford UP, 1987: 1–87.

Righter, Anne. Introduction. *The Tempest* by William Shakespeare. Harmondsworth: Penguin, 1968: 7–51.

Shakespeare, William. *The Tempest*. Ed. Frank Kermode. London: Methuen, 1962. (All quotations from this edition.)

Further Reading

Black, James. 'The Latter End of Prospero's Commonwealth'. *Shakespeare Survey* 43 (1991): 29–41.

Brotton, Jerry. '"This Tunis, sir, was Carthage": Contesting Colonialism in *The Tempest*'. *Post-Colonial Shakespeares*. Eds. Anita Loomba and Martin Orkin. London: Routledge, 1998: 23–42.

Donaldson, Laura. 'The Miranda Complex: Colonialism and the Question of Feminist Reading'. *Decolonising Feminisms: Race, Gender, and Empire-Building*. London: Routledge, 1992: 13–31.

Greenblatt, Stephen. 'Learning to Curse: Aspects of Linguistic Colonialism in the Sixteenth Century'. *First Images of America: The Impact of the new World on the Old*, vol. 2. Ed. Fredi Chiappelli. Los Angeles: University of California Press, 1976: 561–580.

Kott, Jan. '*The Tempest*, or Repetition'. *Mosaic* 10 (1977): 9–36.

Ophelia
Centre Stage

Lucy Potter

This essay re-reads *Hamlet* by placing Ophelia on centre stage. The shift of focus away from the play's male protagonist produces a new interpretation of *Hamlet* that gives Ophelia, the woman, a more important relationship to tragedy than she has hitherto enjoyed. The project is both exciting and necessary: exciting because such a re-reading has not always been possible and necessary if we are to take an idea of tragedy that includes a positive appreciation of woman into the next century. It is evident from these comments that a feminist approach guides the arguments made in this essay.

The crucial argument of much feminist criticism is that 'the personal is political' (Callaghan 2). It is, then, on the concept of the person that much of feminism's valuable work in the area of English Renaissance drama is based. In this context, the choice of *Hamlet* as the play to be re-read is important because it allows the essay to challenge a history of Shakespearean criticism that has evaluated and valued the play in terms of the *main* protagonist commemorated in the title. A brief reminder of how the female characters in *Hamlet* are treated in the more traditional criticism which this essay challenges emphasises why such a challenge is necessary.

At the beginning of the twentieth century, A.C. Bradley delivered a series of lectures which, when published, influenced a generation of Shakespearean criticism. Bradley's work places Ophelia and Gertrude on the edges of *Hamlet* in two main ways: what is said about them and how they are perceived in relation to Bradley's understanding of tragedy. An examination of Ophelia is unwillingly undertaken in the hope that her character will not be 'desecrated' by analysis (161); she remains intellectually 'not remarkable', her madness is 'the kindest stroke that could fall on her' and the picture of her death is 'purely beautiful' (112,164–165). In her turn, Gertrude 'loved to be happy, like a sheep in the sun', the good in her nature must struggle 'through [a] heavy mass of sloth' and 'Like other faulty characters in Shakespeare's tragedies, she dies a better woman than she lived' (167). The 'faulty character' Gertrude is not considered in terms of the play as a tragedy. Ophelia is granted some status in terms of the play as an aesthetic construction, a beautiful work of art, because her love and fate have elements of 'pathetic beauty' (160). However, Ophelia's contributions to the play's aesthetics actually work to exclude her from the play as a tragedy because elements of 'pathetic beauty' are different from elements of 'deep tragedy' (160). These opinions carry more weight (in a negative sense) because *Hamlet* is Shakespeare's *best tragedy* according to Bradley's critical hierarchy and, therefore, superior to the other tragedies he discusses: *Othello*, *Macbeth* and *King Lear*. The authority of Bradley's opinions as they were voiced at Oxford University in 1904 should not be underestimated, nor should the subsequent influence of his work. Admittedly, Bradley's comments on Ophelia and Gertrude have been deliberately chosen by this essay for how shocking they are to our perspective at the end of the twentieth century and many of the critics influenced by Bradley are not as scathing in their comments about the play's female characters. However, the influence of Bradley's work is still evident today; in particular, the hierarchy of Shakespearean tragedy he established. *Hamlet* continues to be popular on school reading lists and the play has been publicly privileged by two commercial film reproductions in the last ten years (Mel Gibson's version and that of Kenneth Branagh). Bradley's influence may also be discerned in Shakespearean criticism that *values* female characters in dramatic genres other than tragedy; the importance of women in Shakespeare's plays is often felt in the context of romance or comedy where their dramatic function is to bring about social and political reconciliation through marriage.

To underestimate the authority and influence of Bradley's work would diminish the advances already made during this century by feminist theory and practice. Bradley's work and its influence are interrogated by feminism through its focus on gender as a 'significant dynamic' in English Renaissance tragedy (Callaghan 3). The focus challenges the assumption that tragedy is about the fall of a man made 'great' by virtue of his birth, his military prowess or his moral sensibilities and that the woman exists to make the fall of such a man more tragic. From this basis, the feminist critic can begin to find evidence of inconsistencies and contradictions in characterisation, and discrepancies between character and action which make visible the moments when characters resist or evade the roles assigned to them by the play. A new relationship between tragedy and its female characters is suggested as a consequence of such examinations, one that gives woman a more positive role than the one allowed her by the traditional assumptions of '"Great Man" tragedy' (Callaghan 2).

The re-reading of *Hamlet* may be placed in the context of other feminist examinations of Shakespeare's plays by its use of gender as 'a crucial concept of analysis' (Callaghan 3). A person's gender, unlike their sex, is not biologically verifiable and gender is therefore understood as a cultural construction. The first part of the essay collects evidence from *Hamlet* of how the play constructs the categories of *man* and *woman* in terms of how they are different from each other. These categories are represented in the middle of the essay as a table that lists a series of opposites. The second part of the essay demonstrates that the gender categories established by the play are not stable constructions by examining some inconsistencies in the play's representation of Hamlet. This allows the essay to argue that matters in *Hamlet* are not always what they seem to be and to suggest that the *Subject* of this tragedy is not necessarily the character in the play's title. Throughout these discussions, the term *agency* is used; in the context of the essay this has the simple meaning of a character's ability to act.

The re-reading of Hamlet's character as inconsistent is important with respect to how the essay understands the concept of the person. As Catherine Belsey has noted, Hamlet is 'the most discontinuous of Shakespeare's heroes. Alternately mad, rational, vengeful, inert, [and] determined' (41). He is also represented by the play as interacting with a variety of human states including the emotional, spiritual, social, familial, political, sexual and rational. This makes Hamlet a *complex* individual in one sense but a fragmented character in another because each human state makes claims on his personality that are not necessarily compatible. For example, Hamlet's responsibilities as a royal heir conflict with his private desires. Hamlet recognises this fact: 'The time is out of joint – O cursed spite,/That ever I was born to set it right', as does Laertes: 'His greatness weigh'd, his will is not his own,/[For he himself is subject to his birth:]' (I,v,188–189; I,iii,17–18; parentheses in original). Both quotations also state that Hamlet is *subject to* external forces at work in his life, which is to say that he does not control the creation of himself as a person within the play. Moreover, as a character in a play, Hamlet's sense of himself as a person is ultimately conferred by the playwright who brings him into existence. Again, Hamlet is *subject to* a force outside his control. At no time can Hamlet be the author either of his identity or his history. The extent of Hamlet's subjection argues that he is not an individual who exercises free will but a *subject* who exists through the external forces by which he is subjected. Since there are many of these forces at work, Hamlet's identity can also never be the unified whole implied by the term *individual*: his identity is necessarily fragmented, discontinuous and often contradictory. The definition of the person as a *subject* repeats some of the basic ideas about the concept of the person argued by the theoretical approach known as Poststructuralism. This essay demonstrates its use of elements of a poststructuralist approach through the words subject, subjectivity, subject-position(s) and through its use of the verb to subject. To avoid confusion, when spelt with a capital letter, the word Subject refers not to any poststructuralist idea but to the character who is the topic of the tragedy.

Early in Act V, Hamlet says to Horatio, 'There's a divinity that shapes our ends,/Rough-hew them how we will' (V,ii,10–11). The words follow hard on Hamlet's knowledge of Ophelia's death (V,i,269–271) and work to define the part Hamlet will soon play in the multiple deaths that are evidently necessary to 'set right' a time that is 'out of joint' (I,v,188–189). The words also show Hamlet's acceptance of a controlling force outside himself. As such, his words translate into action that not only presses the play towards its end but indicates a Hamlet different from, even opposite to, the character who upbraids himself for remaining 'unpregnant of [his] cause' (II,ii,568). Indeed, Hamlet seems to have suffered a sea-change; his movement from raging impotence to resolute and effective action is coded in his report of the events at sea which secure his return to Denmark (V,ii,12–62). Horatio is quick to recognise and celebrate the emergence of this other Hamlet: 'Why, what a king is this!' (V,ii,63).

The 'divinity that shapes our ends' speech therefore refuses an interpretation of the play based on the coherence of Hamlet's identity because it demonstrates that more than one Hamlet exists in the play. It might be said that there are multiple Hamlets in the play or that Hamlet is a plural subject. The play itself supports an under-

standing of Hamlet as a plural subject because it offers him a variety
of subject-positions. In other words, there are many different people
that Hamlet can be in this play: he can be heir, son/stepson, friend,
courtier, soldier, scholar, lover, philosopher, murderer/avenger,
madman (Ophelia's reports at II,i,74–97 and III,i,150–161), actor (he
admits to feigning madness II,ii,378–379; III,iv,187–188), producer/
playwright/director (of 'The Mousetrap'), Subject of Horatio's narrative (V,ii,379–386), Subject of the Shakespearean play-text. Although
neither list is meant to be exhaustive, Ophelia is offered a fraction of
the subject-positions the play makes available to Hamlet: daughter,
sister, lover, madwoman and suicide victim. The highly sexualised
category of courtesan may either replace that of lover or be added to
the list as the female equivalent of courtier. It is apparent from this
comparative exercise that the availability and range of Hamlet's and
Ophelia's subject-positions is a matter of the difference between
men and women.

   This is not to say that either Hamlet or Ophelia choose or will-
ingly accept any of the positions the play offers them. However,
since the focus of this essay is woman, not man, the matter of *choice*
is examined in relation to Ophelia and Gertrude.

   All of Act I, scene three is devoted to Laertes and Polonius
advising Ophelia how to act towards Hamlet's tenders of affection.
Laertes, concerned that Hamlet's public responsibility as a prince
'circumscribes' his actions as a private man, warns Ophelia against
'opening' her 'chaste treasure ... To [Hamlet's] unmast'red importu-
nity' (I,iii,22,31–32). Laertes advises caution: 'Fear it, Ophelia, fear it,
my dear sister;/And keep you in the rear of your affection,/Out of the
shot and danger of desire' (I,iii,33–35). Polonius takes up the theme
but rather than preaching prudence he tells Ophelia how to make her
'chaste treasure' more valuable: 'From this time/Be somewhat
scanter of your maiden presence;/Set your entreatments at a higher
rate/Than a command to parle' (I,iii,120–123). Polonius' advice, like
that of Laertes, is actually a prescriptive lesson he 'teach[es]' Ophelia
(I,iii,105,45). Ophelia's *choice* is not of her own making; in fact, it is
forced choice. By her promise to 'keep' the 'effect' of Laertes' 'lesson'
and 'obey' the tenets of her father (I,iii,45,136), the play casts Ophelia
as non-agentic (unable to act). Any action Ophelia might make does
not emanate from her but is prescribed and authorised by others. In a
context where she is not allowed to argue her opinions, it is not surprising that Ophelia does not know 'what [she] should think' (I,iii,104).

   The dramatic process which writes Ophelia as a non-agent denies
that any action of hers in relation to Hamlet will (can) be

autonomous. Hence, it is with some ease that Hamlet continues to subject Ophelia by offering her a choice of action which is actually no choice at all because the alternatives have, in fact, been chosen by him:

> ... *Get thee to a*
> *nunn'ry, farewell. Or if thou wilt needs marry, marry*
> *a fool, for wise men know well enough what monsters*
> *you make of them. To a nunn'ry, go; and quickly too.*
> *(III,i,136–139)*

Ophelia goes mad instead and commits suicide. Her death can nevertheless be interpreted as an extension of the role Hamlet seeks to subject her to in these lines. The nun's body is hidden by her habit and the use of her voice is prescribed by the dictates of her order; the body of the dead Ophelia, her voice forever silenced, is buried. Although the essay uses this interpretation for its purposes, it is important to note that in the sixteenth century a 'nunnery' could also mean a brothel (*O.E.D.* 1.b.). Nevertheless, whether she be nun or prostitute, Hamlet seeks to dictate Ophelia's behaviour: that is, to subject her.

As a suicide *victim*, Ophelia loses all the subject-positions connected to her sex and becomes 'One that *was* a woman' (V,i,135; my emphasis). She is buried with 'maimed rites' and, were it not for a 'great command' she would 'in ground unsanctified have lodged' because 'her death was doubtful' (V,i,219,227–229). Presumably it is Claudius who gives the command for no one else in the play has the king's power to 'o'ersway the order' of the church (V,i,228). It is, then, as a result of a male command that Ophelia is *saved* from becoming, quite literally, a nobody buried in an unmarked and unsanctified grave:

> *Yet here she is* allow'd *her virgin crants,*
> *Her maiden strewments, and the bringing home*
> *Of bell and burial. (V,i,232–234; my emphasis)*

The play is also at pains to represent Gertrude as non-agentic, as a character who does not (cannot) act. In Act III, Hamlet assaults his mother with verbal 'daggers' that 'enter' her ears, 'turn'st [her] eyes' and 'cleave' her heart (III,ii,396; III,iv,95,89,156). Gertrude describes Hamlet's words performing actions and pressured by their agentic properties she is forced into asking the plaintive question 'What shall I do?' (III,iv,180). Using a riddle, Hamlet commands her to be sexually abstinent and keep secret from Claudius the truth about Hamlet's 'madness':

> *Not this, by no means, that I bid you do:*
> *Let the bloat king tempt you again to bed,*
> *Pinch wanton on your cheek, call you his mouse,*
> *And let him, for a pair of reechy kisses,*
> *Or paddling in your neck with his damn'd fingers,*
> *Make you to ravel all this matter out,*
> *That I essentially am not in madness,*
> *But mad in craft . . . (III,iv,181–188)*

Hamlet's commands not only determine what Gertrude's subsequent actions will be but make those actions necessary if the play's plot is to continue as he wants it to. The degree to which Gertrude's actions are not her own can only increase through an awareness that they are not only prescribed by Hamlet but moulded to fit his master plan. By admitting in the same speech that he is 'But mad in craft', Hamlet also suggests that his own 'madness' is not the same as the 'apoplex'd' sense he sees in his mother (III,iv,73); in other words, Hamlet makes it seem that Gertrude's 'apoplex'd' sense is real but that his own 'madness' is not.

When Gertrude's question is read alongside Ophelia's statement that she knows not what to think, three connected arguments can be suggested: that women are constructed as non-agents in *Hamlet*; that 'male characters in [this tragedy] demarcate the suitable boundaries of female behaviour' (Callaghan 121); that male control of the female characters is masked as patriarchal supervision. In the context of Hamlet's idea that a divinity 'shapes *our* (my emphasis) ends', male control of female subject-positions seriously questions precisely whom 'our' might include.

The play's representations of Ophelia and Gertrude as non-agents encourages the audience to think that the play's plot is driven by the actions of the male protagonist(s). The thought is the product of a comparison which the play both sets up and encourages between the women who act according to how they are instructed to act and the men who do the instructing. By these processes, agency denotes gender difference in *Hamlet* because it is a category around which distinctions between men and women are formed.

In the process of constructing the female characters, the play has linked the concepts of agency and rationality and defined both as male prerogatives. It is a connection proposed early in the play through Hamlet's description of Gertrude as 'a beast that wants discourse of reason' (I,ii,150), advanced through Ophelia's confession that she does not know what to think and Gertrude's 'apoplex'd' sense, and cemented in the representation of Ophelia's madness in Act IV, scene five. Since agency is a masculine prerogative, rationality must also be a faculty Hamlet is seen to possess. The play accomplishes this task largely through the soliloquy in which Hamlet argues the question 'To be, or not to be' (III,i,55–87) and exercises the faculty that distinguishes man:

> ... *What [a] piece of work is a*
> *man, how noble in reason, how infinite in faculties,*
> *in form and moving, how express and admirable in*
> *action, how like an angel in apprehension, how like a*
> *god! the beauty of the world; the paragon of animals;*
> *and yet to me what is this quintessence of dust?*
> *Man delights not me – nor woman neither, though by*
> *your smiling you seem to say so.*
> *(II,ii,303–310; parentheses in original)*

Beginning as a compliment to 'a man', the passage undoes its praise by segregating 'woman' from the wider category, 'Man', into which it slides in the passage's conclusion. Therefore, the word 'Man' is not used here as a common-gender noun and 'woman' is excluded from the range of qualities Hamlet associates with 'Man' in general. As 'a man', it seems that Hamlet possesses the rational faculty that Gertrude and Ophelia lack. By association, Hamlet has also defined rationality as a divine quality.

It should be noted that some editions of the play do not specify 'a man' at the beginning of the passage so that it reads 'What a piece of work is man'. This observation is made to draw attention to the fact that editorial decisions can change the meaning of a text.

Although Hamlet aborts his praise of 'Man', the passage has advanced a definition of Hamlet's subjectivity in terms of how it is different from that of the play's female characters. In the larger context of the play, the speech also defines rationality as a condition of agency. In turn, Hamlet's rationality is represented as a by-product of his interiority, or conscience. The argument, as Hamlet presents it, goes like this: if Gertrude was not less than 'a beast that wants discourse of reason' she 'Would have mourn'd longer' (I,ii,150–151); as it stands, her grief is merely a conventional performance that betrays her interior emptiness. Hamlet is more 'particular' about death than Gertrude (I,ii,75) because he possesses the rational faculty his mother lacks:

> *Seems, madam? nay, it is, I know not 'seems.'*
> *'Tis not alone my inky cloak, [good] mother,*
> *Nor customary suits of solemn black,*
> *Nor windy suspiration of forc'd breath,*
> *No, nor the fruitful river in the eye,*
> *Nor the dejected haviour of the visage,*
> *Together with all forms, modes, [shapes] of grief,*
> *That can [denote] me truly. These indeed seem,*
> *For they are actions that a man might play,*
> *But I have that within which passes show;*
> *These but the trappings and the suits of woe.*
> *(I,ii,76–86; parentheses in original)*

In other words, Hamlet's interiority seems to be more authentic than his exteriority because, apparently, his conscience cannot be performed or staged like other 'forms of grief'. By suggesting that it is Gertrude and not himself who performs 'actions that a man might play', Hamlet makes the reality of his existence more substantial than Gertrude's. By comparison, the reality of Gertrude's existence is an illusion of the person created by a performance. Hamlet *is*, Gertrude *seems* to be and thereby begins Hamlet's obsession with finding the *real* woman behind the false, painted face of performance, locking her up and dictating the behaviour of her sexual body:

> *I have heard of your paintings well enough.*
> *God hath given you one face, and you make yourselves*
> *another. You jig and amble, and you [lisp], you nick-*
> *name God's creatures and make your wantonness*
> *[your] ignorance. Go to, I'll no more on't, it hath*
> *made me mad. I say, we will have no more marriage.*
> *Those that are married already (all but one) shall live,*
> *the rest shall keep as they are. To a nunn'ry, go.*
> *(III,i,142–149; parentheses in original)*

The need for patriarchal control of the female that the passage urges draws Hamlet into the sphere of action, forging the bonds between interiority, rationality and agency and promoting the representation of Hamlet as more fully a person than either of the female protagonists. Hamlet carries with him the transcendental, god-like qualities associated with 'Man' and therefore, when he goes to work on Gertrude with his words, it is as an avenging angel come to 'scourge and minister' (III,iv,175) to a world made fallen by the 'trespass' of woman:

> *Lay not that flattering unction to your soul,*
> *That not your trespass but my madness speaks;*
> *It will but skin and film the ulcerous place,*
> *Whiles rank corruption, mining all within,*
> *Infects unseen . . . (III,iv,145–149)*

The 'unweeded garden' (I,ii,135) Denmark has become is, of course, a metaphorical Garden of Eden after Eve's transgression. Gertrude's alignment with the first woman, who also succumbed to temptation in the absence of male supervision, suggests that her behaviour is *natural*. The suggestion is augmented by Hamlet when he advises Gertrude to be sexually abstinent on the grounds that 'use *almost* can change the stamp of nature' (III,iv,168; my emphasis). In fact, Gertrude has always been sexually voracious according to Hamlet. Her 'appetite' can be contained but not changed by the man to whom she is married: 'she would hang on [Hamlet's father]/As if increase of appetite had grown/By what it fed on, and yet, within a month –' (I,ii,143–145). In this way, the play makes it appear that the difference between men and women is biologically verifiable and, therefore, a matter of difference that is as fixed and immutable as a person's sex. In this way, the play constructs the category of *man* through a series of opposites that may be illustrated as follows.

MALE	FEMALE
(masculine)	(feminine)
ACTIVE	PASSIVE
RATIONAL	IRRATIONAL
(mind/interiority)	(body/exteriority)
HEAVEN	HELL
(order/light)	(chaos/dark)

Gertrude's reference to her soul's 'black and [grained] spots' (III,iv,90; parentheses in original) completes the association of woman with the terms on the right hand side of the list.

With Eve as the quasi-historical precedent for the type of woman she is, Gertrude may be interpreted as a representation of a *realist* model of femininity due to her character's likeness to the first woman and because what she *really* is underlies what she seems to be. While she lives, Ophelia is also associated with this model: as Hamlet says, echoing Laertes, 'be thou as chaste as ice, as pure as/snow, thou shalt not escape calumny' (III,i,135–136: 'Virtue itself scapes not calumnious strokes' I,iii,38). However, once Ophelia is dead and forever unable to be 'a breeder of sinners' (III,i,121), she becomes the representative of an *idealist* model of femininity that has the Virgin Mary as its archetype. The Virgin Mary is *ideal* because, as the mother of God, she answers to the highest conception of what a woman should be. The point of identifying the *realist* and *idealist* models operating in *Hamlet* is to suggest this play's affinity with others of the same period that contrast female stereotypes, 'one saintly, submissive, faithful, forgiving and silent, and the other predatory, dominating, usually lustful, destructive, and voluble' (Belsey 165; Gertrude 'questions' Hamlet 'with wicked tongue,' III,iv,12). For example, Hero in *Much Ado About Nothing*, Hermione in *The Winter's Tale* and Cordelia in *King Lear* are all prototypical of the dead Ophelia: Hero's chastity is proved (by male report) only after her death is feigned (V,i,230–252); Hermione, suspected of adultery, must pose as a (sexually impermeable, silent) statue to be reconciled with her husband after twenty years (V,iii); Cordelia's 'voice was ever soft,/Gentle and low' (V,iii,273–274); note the past tense). On the other hand, the *realist* model of femininity can be seen at work in *Othello* through that play's representation of Desdemona's transformation from 'a maiden, never bold' into a 'perjur'd woman' and 'a whore' (I,iii,94; V,ii,63,132). Desdemona's speech and her sexual desire are linked when she argues her wish to accompany Othello to Cyprus: 'if I be left behind,/A moth of peace, and he go to the war,/The rites for why I love him are bereft me' (I,iii,255–257). This verbal and very public display of her sexuality leads Brabantio to accuse her of deception, an accusation Desdemona herself later verifies and one that sets the plot in motion (I,iii,293; II,i,122–123). Although Desdemona is innocent of the charge of adultery, the play never quite manages to extricate her from the *realist* model of femininity it uses to write her character. When Desdemona identifies herself as her own murderer, she re-asserts the ideas of duplicity and deception that propel the play's action from the moment she appears on stage. Her *lie* is part of her last speech (V,ii,124–125) and thus she stays the woman whose association with the 'practices of cunning hell' are inscribed forever in the etymology of her name, Des*demon*a (I,iii,102). It should be noted through these few references that female characters representing the *idealist* model of femininity tend to survive only in non-tragic dramatic forms.

Having demonstrated that *Hamlet* constructs its male protagonist in terms of his difference from Ophelia and Gertrude, it remains to argue that a number of inconsistencies appear in the process which make the play's representation of Hamlet unstable. Accordingly, the lists in the table of opposites should no longer be considered as mutually exclusive.

The first notable inconsistency in the play's construction of Hamlet's subjectivity may be discerned from Gertrude's agonised cry that Hamlet cease his remonstrations against her:

> *O Hamlet! speak no more;*
> *Thou turn'st my [eyes into my very] soul,*
> *And there I see such black and [grained] spots*
> *As will [not] leave their tinct.*
> *(III,iv,88–91; parentheses in original)*

Clearly, the sudden appearance of Gertrude's conscience in these lines is an effect of Hamlet's speech. In fact, there is no difference between how Hamlet's and Gertrude's consciences are constructed because both are products of Hamlet's words. However, at the very moment the play threatens to allow a slide between gender categories by giving Gertrude the conscience that defines Hamlet, his difference from her is re-established when he encourages Gertrude to continue her conventional performance: 'Assume a virtue, if you have it not' (III,iv,160). Despite the potential for similarity glimpsed in this scene, the play rules that Gertrude's interiority can never be inherent or autonomous because it is an effect of Hamlet's speech and it remains inauthentic because she does not resist performing 'actions that a man might play'. She plays a role written for her by Hamlet so that events may proceed as he has planned. The play's construction of Gertrude's conscience as forever inauthentic deflects the audience's attention away from the fact that Hamlet's conscience is produced in precisely the same way as Gertrude's, through speech. The play has in fact shifted a fundamental inconsistency in its representation of Hamlet on to Gertrude; Hamlet makes it seem that it is only Gertrude's conscience that is performed. It is important to note in this context that performance is a major theme in *Hamlet*: it is a play that contains a play-within-a-play, a speech from another play re-presented (II,ii,434–518), a protagonist who feigns madness and whose subject-positions include play-wright, producer and director (III,ii,1–45).

The discovery that Hamlet's conscience is produced in precisely the same way as Gertrude's weakens Hamlet's claim on the masculine concept to which it is attached, the rational mind. Ophelia is the key to finding out that the play is not consistent in its representation of Hamlet as rational. In the first instance, she describes to Polonius the appearance before her of a mad Hamlet:

> *My lord, as I was sewing in my closet,*
> *Lord Hamlet, with his doublet all unbrac'd*
> *No hat upon his head, his stockings fouled,*
> *Ungart'red, and down-gyved to his ankle,*
> *Pale as his shirt, his knees knocking each other,*
> *And with a look so piteous in purport*
> *As if he had been loosed out of hell*
> *To speak of horrors – he comes before me.*
> *(II,i,74–81)*

There is no reason to doubt that in this representation Hamlet is truly mad. The horrors of which he does not speak are the 'carnal, bloody, and unnatural acts' Horatio vows to re-tell in Act V (ii,379–86) and Hamlet himself confesses that the 'real' woman, whom he attempts to *see* in this same scene with Ophelia (II,i,84–97), has 'made [him] mad'. Moreover, according to the table of opposites, Hamlet's madness is verifiable through Ophelia's association of it with hell. Polonius believes Hamlet is mad and Gertrude and Claudius suspect it (II,i,99–103,108; III,i,188–189). All this evidence of Hamlet's irrationality argues that he slides into the right hand list in the table of opposites, the female side. However, the play halts this slippage and, therefore, any interpretation of Hamlet via his association with the qualities used to define the category of woman. The mad Hamlet appears to Ophelia off-stage and not in front of the audience; Hamlet's later acts of feigned madness produce doubt that he was ever truly mad; the soliloquies busily construct a rational Hamlet; the judgement of the only eye-witness is discredited when she herself goes mad. In this way, the play relocates the irrational in Ophelia, shifting an inconsistency in the representation of Hamlet's subjectivity on to the woman for the second time.

Unlike Gertrude, Ophelia resists this process and there is no small irony in the fact that her resistance follows hard on Hamlet's 'To be or not to be' soliloquy:

O, what a noble mind is here o'erthrown!
The courtier's, soldier's, scholar's, eye, tongue, sword,
Th' expectation and rose of the fair state,
The glass of fashion and the mould of form,
Th' observ'd of all observers, quite, quite down!
And I, of ladies most deject and wretched,
That suck'd the honey of his [music] vows,
Now see [that] noble and most sovereign reason
Like sweet bells jangled out of time, and harsh;
That unmatch'd form and stature of blown youth
Blasted with ecstasy. O, woe is me
T' have seen what I have seen, see what I see!
(III, i, 150–161; parentheses in original)

In terms of the play's performance (that is, depending on how much Gertrude, Claudius and Polonius are allowed to hear of this scene as a whole) it is possible to stage (and read) Ophelia's recognition of Hamlet's irrationality as a soliloquy no different in its dramatic function from the more famous one that begins the scene or to render the 'To be or not to be' speech as no soliloquy at all. Either interpretation would support the slides between gender categories which the scene permits because the soliloquy would no longer be a formal device particular to the construction and revelation of Hamlet's identity.

Ophelia goes mad only after she recognises Hamlet's irrationality. She is left musing on this profundity after Hamlet leaves her to disassociate himself from the term 'ecstasy' through his conversation with Gertrude: '[Ecstasy?]/My pulse as yours doth temperately keep time,/And makes as healthful music. It is not madness/That I have utt'red' (III,iv,139–142; parentheses in original). The fact that Hamlet defines his sanity here in terms of a similarity to Gertrude should not be played down for it allows Gertrude to slide, momentarily, into the list of qualities that define man.

As Ophelia, Gertrude and Hamlet slide between the lists in the table of opposites, cracks in the foundations of rationality as a marker of masculine identity begin to widen. As a consequence, the idea that rationality is a pre-requisite for the ability to act becomes unstuck. Ironically, it is Hamlet who gives notice that rationality is a problematic basis for agency: firstly, when he does not act on the 'grounds more relative' than those his father's ghost provides, which *prove* Claudius' guilt (II,ii,604; III,ii,286–287); secondly, when his rational mind fails to provide true evidence on which to act, as his misreading of Claudius at prayer demonstrates (III,iii,73–96). Most importantly, Hamlet reasons that agency and conscience are mutually exclusive terms:

> *Thus conscience does make cowards [of us all],*
> *And thus the native hue of resolution*
> *Is sicklied o'er with the pale cast of thought,*
> *And enterprises of great pitch and moment*
> *With this regard their currents turn awry,*
> *And lose the name of action . . .*
> *(III,i,82–87; parentheses in original)*

Through these inconsistencies, Hamlet himself contradicts the play's representation of his character as agentic: he admits that he is a 'coward' whose conscience 'turns awry' the 'currents' of action. Hamlet has reasoned that the ability to act is possible only if 'the pale cast of thought' does not interfere, for to think about action is to recognise that conscience makes that action impossible. According to the processes of his own thought, Hamlet is inevitably a 'coward'. As the end of the play demonstrates, the action that finally allows Hamlet to avenge his father's death is not of his own making; it is the product of a plot by a man who has proved his lack of conscience not only in the act of murder but in his subsequent failure to confess his sins: 'Pray can I not,/Though inclination be as sharp as will' (III,iii,38–39).

Evidence that agency and conscience are mutually exclusive terms has already been gathered. With the words cited above, Hamlet also defines rationality and agency as mutually exclusive terms. Thus, Hamlet disconnects the list of qualities which the play has joined together to define the category of man. In the process, the table of opposites is rendered entirely unstable and the woman is allowed access to the action that Hamlet has refused.

The play's plot is driven throughout by a command to act and the character who fulfils the expectations of this role is not Hamlet but Ophelia. In being mad, Ophelia is free from the conscience that troubles Hamlet and makes him unable to act and her suicide is action in its most absolute sense. Her suicide is also an escape from the patriarchal supervision that subjects her while she is alive and an action that allows her to rewrite the meanings that the play has assigned to her as a passive woman. As the action of an irrational woman, Ophelia's suicide thereby completes the exposure of the instability of the system of differences through which the play strives to construct the categories of man and woman.

In her madness and suicide, Ophelia has realised the subject-positions refused by Hamlet, who spends his time convincing the audience and other characters in the play that he is 'But mad in craft' and not performing the action demanded of him. This last slide between the lists in the table of opposites is the play's final irony because, in the absence of Hamlet's action, Ophelia steps in to fulfil his role and becomes the Subject of the tragedy called *Hamlet*. Indeed, *Hamlet* is not at all the play it seems to be.

Works Cited

Belsey, Catherine. *The Subject of Tragedy: Identity and Difference in Renaissance Drama*. London: Methuen, 1985.

Bradley, A.C. *Shakespearean Tragedy: Lectures on Hamlet, Othello, King Lear, Macbeth*. London: Macmillan and Co., 1904.

Callaghan, Dympna. *Women and Gender in Renaissance Tragedy: A Study of King Lear, Othello, The Duchess of Malfi and The White Devil*. London: Harvester Wheatsheaf, 1989.

Shakespeare, William. *The Riverside Shakespeare*. 2nd ed. Ed. G. Blakemore Evans. Boston: Houghton Mifflin, 1997.

The Oxford English Dictionary. 18 vols. 2nd ed. Oxford: Clarendon Press, 1989.

Further Reading

Barker, Francis. *The Tremulous Private Body: Essays on Subjection*. London: Methuen, 1984.

Belsey, Catherine. 'Literature, History, Politics'. *Literature and History* 9 (1983): 17–27.

Davies, Bronwyn. 'The Concept of the Person: a Feminist, Poststructuralist Analysis'. *Postmodern Critical Theorising* 30 (1991): 42–53.

Leech, Clifford. *Tragedy*. London: Methuen, 1969.

Neely, Carol Thomas. 'Constructing the Subject: Feminist Practice and the New Renaissance Discourses'. *English Literary Renaissance* 18 (1988): 5–18.

Tennenhouse, Leonard. *Power on Display: The Politics of Shakespeare's Genres*. New York: Methuen, 1986.

Poetry:
Close Readings

Romanticism:
Two Poems

Philip Waldron

Historians have long felt that fundamental changes in sensi-bility and ideas in Europe, Russia, and America evolved in the late eighteenth and early nineteenth centuries to leave the world a radically different place. These fundamental revisions – rebellion against authority, religious questionings, emphasis on the judgement and rights of the individual, the growth of democracy, new ideas about the nature of education, assertion of the value of the insights of the child, belief that the analytic powers of reason were not enough to save us – and other changes in values and valuing, retain their power even now. Indeed one might perhaps wonder if 'post-Romantic' might not be a more apt description of our own period than the currently fashionable 'post-Modernist'.

The 'Romantic revolution' is, for the purposes of literary history, normally taken to refer to a period something like 1789–1824. We might nominate 1789 because it is the year of the French Revolution which seemed, at least initially, to embody the hopes and aspira-tions of the period and because it is the year that saw the appearance of Blake's *Songs of Innocence*. With the deaths of Keats in 1821, Shelley in 1822 and Byron in 1824 the great efflorescence of Romantic poetry faded. Coleridge was to survive until 1834 and Wordsworth until 1850, but their greatest poetry had, in the main, been written in their youth.

In this essay I want to illustrate some of the central preoccupations and characteristics of the Romantic poets from a close reading of two major poems: Blake's 'London' (1794) and Coleridge's 'Frost at Midnight' (1798). In each of these poems, brief as they are, we find preoccupations typical of the Romantic period including the primacy of the individual as against the institutional, the value of childhood, the existence of the supernatural, the superiority of the natural to the urban, solitude as an ideal, an emphasis on the crucial importance of education, and (above all) the inadequacy of reason without imagination.

Blake's 'London' is a good illustration of the fact that the passionate feelings and commitments of the Romantics did not preclude the possibility of tight formal control.

LONDON

I wander thro' each charter'd street,
Near where the charter'd Thames does flow,
And mark in every face I meet
Marks of weakness, marks of woe.

5   In every cry of every man,
In every Infant's cry of fear,
In every voice, in every ban,
The mind-forg'd manacles I hear.

How the Chimney-sweeper's cry
10 Every black'ning Church appalls;
And the hapless Soldier's sigh
Runs in blood down Palace walls.

But most thro' midnight streets I hear
How the youthful Harlot's curse
15 Blasts the new-born Infant's tear,
And blights with plagues the Marriage hearse.

Reading this poem gives rise to a series of questions. What sort of description of London is given? Is that description literal or symbolic? What is wrong with London? Can it be put right? Is the poem structured, or is it just a catalogue of ills? If there is a structure, what holds that structure together? Given the documentary nature of the content of the poem, is there any point in it being a poem rather than an essay or pamphlet?

What sort of description of London is given? Any answer to this question must consider the nature of the voice of the poem. The poem is spoken by a figure walking through London at the end of the eighteenth century. This figure may be a putative self, constructed for the purposes of the poem, and it may or may not be identifiable with the voice of William Blake. Certainly, we are unlikely to doubt that the poem reflects an outrage felt by the poet but the very fact that the voice speaks in verse discourages any strongly realistic reading, for the rhythms of speech have become subsumed in the artifice of the poem, especially metre and rhyme. We do not so much read a description of London as listen to a voice as we follow imaginatively in the footsteps of a wanderer. In the first stanza the experience of the wanderer is visual as he observes ('marks') signs ('marks') of human weakness and misery. The streets, organised by the charters and contracts of trade and commerce, are populated by a humanity which, without exception, reveals its misery to the wanderer. The other three stanzas of the poem, however, communicate an aural rather than visual description as the wanderer listens to London rather than looks at it. 'London' is thus not a picture of London but an evocation of the sound of the city as it falls upon the ears of a wandering figure.

Indeed, eighteenth-century London, though much smaller than now, must have been a very noisy place with its cabs, carriages and horses. It would have constantly rung with the street cries and songs of people hawking wares, selling food, and advertising services at the tops of their voices. Again, the wanderer finds misery wherever he turns: 'every cry of every man', 'every Infant's cry', 'every voice' contains within it the sounds of bondage ('manacles') and fear. The historical details of London, tying the setting of the poem to a particular period, are apparent. The cry of the chimney-sweeper 'appalls' every church with the encrustation of soot which, in the manner of graffiti, inscribes each place of worship with a sign commemorating the chimneys that daily incarcerate the wretched child. The soldier, returned from recent war in Europe, laments in vain to the Palace he has served. But the most terrible sound is the young prostitute's 'curse' as she holds her 'new-born Infant' to her. The 'charter'd streets' have now become 'midnight streets' and the visual is totally eliminated by a world of darkness. London has become a sound-world.

However, such an account of the poem, although (I think) accurate, is grossly inadequate because it is restricted to the literal. It is not simply that the poem has a literal level and a symbolic level and that therefore a literal reading misses some of the richness and implications of 'London'. At some points of the poem, a literal reading is impossible as detail becomes impenetrable. A literal reading of 'mind-forg'd' is not possible. How can we hear the manacles in every infant's cry if infants' cries do not sound remotely like the clanking of manacles? How can a cry appall or shame a church – let alone run down a Palace wall as if it possessed mass and was therefore subject to gravity? How could a curse blast a tear? What is a marriage hearse? Blake's account of London, in spite of accurate historical elements such as the existence of the chimney-sweep and the harlot or prostitute, uses these elements as a ground for a poem that is itself symbolic. The point, however, is not that the symbolic is less real than the literally true, but rather that Blake is dealing with truths perceived by the imagination rather than by the senses. For most readers, the first stanza sounds echoes of the two great 'marks' of the Bible: the mark of Cain (*Genesis*) and the mark of the Beast or Anti-Christ (*Revelation*). If we hear these echoes 'London' immediately becomes not merely a poem about late eighteenth-century London, a document of social protest, but also a poem about temporal manifestations of eternal horrors – the murder of one's brother-man and the revelation of the nature of unchanging and essential evil. With this more than literal response it becomes less strange that the wanderer should hear manacles rattling through the street cries and infant whimpers of fear. The manacles are 'mind-forg'd' because ultimately the imprisoning misery of the inhabitants of London derives not from political, economic, and religious abuses but from the states of mind or failures of imagination that create or forge those abuses.

Blake believed that it was not enough to change the world. Humanity needs a more radical, internal revolution of the self which will change the way we *see* the world and therefore the way in which we create it. The manacles of oppression derive from the mind and cannot be broken by merely physical change such as the re-organisation of social power. Cruelty exists because of the organisation of the self, and the organisation of society is only the symptom of an underlying disease. This is not to suggest that Blake is indifferent to the plight of the individual chimney-sweep or of the unfortunate soldier, but that a revolution of the external world is insufficient if the vices of the mind and of the imagination are to survive to produce new abuses. The difficulties offered to the reader by the curse that blasts the infant's tear, and by the marriage hearse, are rather different. These tropes derive from a compression whereby the effects of the harlot's syphilis, communicated congenitally to her child and by infection to her client, result in eye damage, blindness, and eventual death. The 'Marriage hearse' is one of the great conceits of English poetry: sexual repression results in prostitution, the infection of the client and eventually of the (falsely) virtuous bride so that one major rite of passage (the marriage) becomes its opposite (the funeral) as the wedding carriage transmutes to the funeral hearse. Prostitutes exist because of the 'mind-forg'd manacles' of a false chastity which denies the existence, and frustrates fulfilment, of sexual desire so that repression of the self leads to oppression of the prostitute with the eventual consequence of a slow and horrible death.

What then of my other questions? Is the poem structured or is it just a catalogue? If it is a structure, what holds that structure together? Is there some reason for 'London' being a poem, with the artifice that implies? The poem does have a structure: a cumulative structure in which the details of London become progressively more disturbing and distressing. The generally perceived 'every man' narrows to the individual sufferings of the sweeper, the soldier and, above all, the harlot. That her 'curse' is the culminating horror is indicated by Blake's phrasing in the first line of the last stanza, ('but most thro' midnight streets I hear'). The cries of London become a blasting curse bearing the contemporary plague of syphilis.

This basic structure is held together by a series of verbal and other echoes. The reader hears not only the different cries of the poem but also the repetition of key words: 'charter'd' (twice), 'mark' (three times), 'every' (seven times), 'cry' (three times). A tissue of sound binds the poem. Through the centre of this poem walks the wanderer, a thread and receptor to whom the perceptions of sight and sound attach. Without the speaking wanderer 'London' would be less vivid and less affecting, but additionally our sharing an unfolding of horror as it is progressively revealed to the wanderer unifies the poem. The thread of the commercial appears in the first line ('charter'd streets') with legal, contractual, economic implications and persists to the trade in sexual misery which is the harlot's curse as much as her disease.

The poem is a clear example of the falseness of some common assertions about Blake: that he was interested in ideas but not really a conscious artist, that he was insensitive to form, even that he was incoherent. Such accusations have been levelled against the other Romantics too, sometimes seen as a group of emoting eccentrics, befuddled by enthusiasms and passions and actually not very bright. 'London', we can see, is a highly fashioned poem[1] – which brings us to our final question. Why write a *poem* about (among other things) the oppression of the individual by the institutions of the Church, Palace, marriage and the roots of that oppression? Indeed, why write poems at all? Can they do important things that prose cannot?

Hopefully, that question has been more or less answered already. The conceit of the marriage hearse, the binding of the unit by echo, both internally within the lines by the echoes of repeated vocabulary and also by rhyme itself are details inseparable from 'London' being a poem. Rhyme and metre are, at least at first sight, the two obvious elements of poetry that set it apart from prose. As elements of pattern and design they arouse expectations which can be reinforced or broken. An example of this is the rhyming of lines one and three of Blake's last stanza. The poem is written in quatrains (i.e. four line stanzas with an a b a b rhyming structure), and we know therefore that the last word of line three must rhyme with 'hear'. That word we consciously or unconsciously assume is 'ear' – which is after all what one hears with. But it is not the new-born infant's ear, but its 'tear' that suffers the wintry blast of the harlot's curse. Without rhyme the horror of that dramatic surprise could not exist and the corresponding horror of the reader could not be so powerfully aroused.

'London' is, obviously, an urban poem. Literature has contrasted town and country since before Christ and the Romantic period was not the first that produced poets (and other people) who felt that the organisation of urban, civilised society came at excessive cost. Christianity, for example, asserts this with the story of the Garden of Eden, the concept of the loss of natural innocence, and belief in our expulsion into what we now know as life, with the calamities attendant upon our corruption and perversity. Although an idealising of the natural seems to exist as far back as surviving writing enables us to recollect, it is nevertheless true that an especially strong emphasis on 'nature' and 'the natural' developed particularly with the writings of Rousseau[2] in the mid-eighteenth century, culminating in the poetry of the English Romantics.

One poem that rests upon and illustrates a felt superiority of the natural world is Coleridge's 'Frost at Midnight'.

> FROST AT MIDNIGHT
> The Frost performs its secret ministry,
> Unhelped by any wind. The owlet's cry
> Came loud – and hark, again! loud as before.
> The inmates of my cottage, all at rest,
> 5   Have left me to that solitude, which suits
> Abstruser musings: save that at my side

My cradled infant slumbers peacefully.
'Tis calm indeed! so calm, that it disturbs
And vexes meditation with its strange
10   And extreme silentness. Sea, hill, and wood,
This populous village! Sea, and hill, and wood,
With all the numberless goings-on of life,
Inaudible as dreams! the thin blue flame
Lies on my low-burnt fire, and quivers not;
15   Only that film, which fluttered on the grate,
Still flutters there, the sole unquiet thing.
Methinks its motion in this hush of nature
Gives it dim sympathies with me who live,
Making it a companionable form,
20   Whose puny flaps and freaks the idling Spirit
By its own moods interprets, everywhere
Echo or mirror seeking of itself,
And makes a toy of Thought.
But O! how oft,
How oft, at school, with most believing mind,
25   Presageful, have I gazed upon the bars,
To watch that fluttering stranger! and as oft
With unclosed lids, already had I dreamt
Of my sweet birthplace, and the old church tower,
Whose bells, the poor man's only music, rang
30   From morn to evening, all the hot Fair-day,
So sweetly, that they stirred and haunted me
With a wild pleasure, falling on mine ear
Most like articulate sounds of things to come!
So gazed I, till the soothing things, I dreamt,
35   Lulled me to sleep, and sleep prolonged my dreams!
And so I brooded all the following morn,
Awed by the stern preceptor's face, mine eye
Fixed with mock study on my swimming book:
Save if the door half opened, and I snatched
40   A hasty glance, and still my heart leaped up,
For still I hoped to see the stranger's face,
Townsman, or aunt, or sister more beloved,
My playmate when we both were clothed alike!
Dear Babe, that sleepest cradled by my side,
45   Whose gentle breathings, heard in this deep calm,
Fill up the interspersèd vacancies
And momentary pauses of the thought!

> My babe so beautiful! it thrills my heart
> With tender gladness, thus to look at thee,
> 50   And think that thou shalt learn far other lore,
> And in far other scenes! For I was reared
> In the great city, pent 'mid cloisters dim,
> And saw nought lovely but the sky and stars.
> But thou, my babe! shalt wander like a breeze
> 55   By lakes and sandy shores, beneath the crags
> Of ancient mountain, and beneath the clouds,
> Which image in their bulk both lakes and shores
> And mountain crags: so shalt thou see and hear
> The lovely shapes and sounds intelligible
> 60   Of that eternal language, which thy God
> Utters, who from eternity doth teach
> Himself in all, and all things in himself.
> Great universal Teacher! He shall mold
> Thy spirit, and by giving make it ask.
> 65   Therefore all seasons shall be sweet to thee,
> Whether the summer clothe the general earth
> With greenness, or the redbreast sit and sing
> Betwixt the tufts of snow on the bare branch
> Of mossy apple tree, while the nigh thatch
> 70   Smokes in the sun-thaw; whether the eave-drops fall
> Heard only in the trances of the blast,
> Or if the secret ministry of frost
> Shall hang them up in silent icicles,
> Quietly shining to the quiet Moon.

'Frost at Midnight' turns upon contrasts and oppositions in addition to those of the natural and the urban. Coleridge contrasts his own life with the hoped for future of the babe (his son Hartley) who sleeps in his cradle. This contrasting of past personal disaffection with hope for a more complete and satisfying life for the infant in the years to come generates a good deal of changing of tense as Coleridge reflects on the past, muses upon the present scene, and envisages the future as the poem ranges across time and accordingly alters its perspectives. 'Frost at Midnight' begins in the present but immediately shifts to the past before returning to the present:

> The owlet's cry
> Came loud – and hark, again! loud as before.

Coleridge stresses that he has been left alone with the peacefully slumbering child by the other inmates of the cottage, who have gone to bed. Again there is a shift in tense, from the perfect ('have left me') to the present ('which suits abstruser musings') where the poem remains for lines 6–22. The second verse paragraph (lines 23–43) is entirely in the past tense as Coleridge reminisces about his school days. The third paragraph (lines 44–64) opens in the present, as Coleridge gazes upon the sleeping babe and listens to its 'gentle breathings', before moving to the future as he contrasts the desired and imagined eventual education of the child ('thou shalt learn far other lore' 50) with the interpolated past ('For I was reared/In the great city ...' 51–52) returning immediately to the future ('But *thou*, my babe! shalt wander like a breeze' 54) as Coleridge foresees the child's future contact with the timeless truths promulgated by God ('eternal language' 60) through the natural world. The remainder of the poem (lines 65–74) is written solely in the future tense. The poet looks to the fulfilment of the babe as he grows in a natural and there-fore (for Coleridge) religious environment, becoming equipped to deal successfully with the vicissitudes of time and experience ('there-fore all seasons shall be sweet to thee ...' [65]) and finding future happiness regardless of circumstance.

'Frost at Midnight', then, is not written about a single subject from a single standpoint, but ranges in memory or imagination across two lifetimes, one largely past and one in the future. At first reading the poem may seem to be set in a particular place (a room in a cottage) at a particular time (late one winter's night) but as we look carefully at the details of change of tense we realise that the poem deals with a period from about 1782, when Coleridge entered Christ's Hospital school in London, to an only loosely determinate date, say halfway through the nineteenth century, when Hartley will reach full and healthy maturity.[3] The point is not that 'Frost at Midnight' lacks a focus, but rather that the focus is internal and therefore shifts as the mind continually turns back upon itself. The faculty which here confers its own form upon experience in the absence of a single external subject is described elsewhere by Coleridge as 'the shaping spirit of Imagination,'[4] the implication being that form comes from within subjective experience rather than from tradition as in, for example, the sonnet. As the subject of 'Frost at Midnight' shifts and changes the imagination makes its own connections and asserts its own sets of relevances to create a very fluid poem that is able to touch on many of the Romantic preoccupations adumbrated at the beginning of this essay. These preoccupations are not clearly separable – for example, ideas about the value of childhood are obviously tied to educational ideas – but rather illuminate aspects of each other within the poem, a little like different facets of a single crystal.

The clearest single focus contrasting Coleridge's past experience with the hoped for future of Hartley is that of education. Coleridge's own education at Christ's Hospital was miserable. Charles Lamb, Coleridge's friend, relates that senior schoolboys, or monitors, used to wake up the younger boys during the night for the pleasure of beating them. Reared in a boarding school in the 'great city' London, Coleridge feared the 'stern preceptor's face' (i.e. the schoolmaster's), imprisoned ('pent') in the urban, and denied communication with the natural world save for the sky and the stars. Hartley will not be educated by an authority figure – a schoolmaster with all the physical brutality the eighteenth century conferred on that figure – but will learn very different things ('far other lore/And in far other scenes!' [50–51]). This child will be taught by a God who articulates a nonverbal language intelligible through a perception of beauty in nature, both aural and visual ('lovely shapes and sounds intelligible' [59]). Freed from the prison of the schoolroom, Hartley will wander 'like a breeze' through the lakes, stones, and mountain crags. Nature here has its own unity and internal reflections as the clouds 'image in their bulk' (52) the world beneath them. The 'stern preceptor' of Coleridge's boyhood will be replaced by the 'Great universal Teacher'. God will form the inner self and being ('shall mold/Thy spirit'), protecting Hartley from the anxiety and insecurity that Coleridge felt throughout his life. This reflects a basic tenet of Romanticism: that a childhood dominated by authority figures such as parents, teachers, priests, beadles and so on invested with a hostility and contempt for the values of childhood, and later for the sexual stirrings of adolescence, will lead to an irretrievable blighting of adulthood. Indeed, such an attitude is still very common. Much of 'Frost at Midnight' turns upon the belief, to use Blake's categories, that a stifled and subverted innocence in childhood will lead inevitably to the development of a wretched and even vicious adult unable to cope with the later world of experience.

This opposition is a version of the war permanently waged between the individual and the institution. During much of Western history the assertion of the primacy of the individual has been a social and religious heresy. Christianity, for example, affirms values such as submission, humility, and selflessness through the Church and its central text, the Bible. The Romantics proclaimed that individual vision not only had its own value, but that the true visionary had insights that gave access to a wisdom denied the great mass of humanity. This wisdom was antagonistic to the great inhibiting and oppressive institutions such as the Church, the law, the Monarchy, the government, educational bodies and so on. The great political manifestation of such ideas was the French Revolution though this disappointed many (including Wordsworth) by erecting a new series of oppressive institutions in place of the old, betraying its original ideals. The freeing of Hartley from school and city is a liberation from institutionalisation and lies at the root of the emphasis on nature in 'Frost at Midnight'. The Romantics valued nature both for what it lacked (institutionalisation) and what it offered (here, the 'eternal language' of God). Nature could be both a retreat from the world of experience and a sacred text created by the self, by the 'shaping spirit of Imagination'.

This leads us to another characteristic of Romanticism: the emphasis on the supernatural. Nature ultimately is important because it reveals a world beyond and above itself, which we can call 'supernature'. The term 'supernatural' need not refer merely to fairies, goblins, God, ghosts and suchlike, but can be used to indicate belief in an area of experience other than sense experience and the analysis of that experience by reason. For example, to believe that a dream might offer an insight is to believe that supernatural experience has value. And, indeed, all the Romantic poets stress the importance and relevance of dream, as well as of other visionary experience. Such a belief can be called anti-rational in that it implies that there is more to the mind than reasoning, without the further implication that reason is of no value. In any case, the Romantics demonstrated an almost obsessive interest in the supernatural both in the everyday and more philosophical uses of that word.

Coleridge's own 'The Ancient Mariner' is perhaps the best known example of a common manifestation. In 'Frost at Midnight' he binds, in part, the shifting patterns of the mind which constitute his poem by referring to the supernatural implications of the phenomenon of the stranger. As a fire dies to its lowest level a film of soot can sometimes be seen fluttering in a fireplace. This was sometimes called a 'stranger' because of a superstition that it was a sign that an unexpected visitor was about to arrive. The film is observed as the 'sole unquiet thing' (15–16) in the room where Coleridge muses, an 'echo or mirror' (22) of gentle rumination as the 'Spirit ... makes a toy of Thought', sinking towards sub-rational regions. Coleridge is writing of a supernature, itself enclosed by the 'hush of nature' (17). The superstitious folk story of the significance of the film as the '*stranger*' (26, 41) stimulates recall of how the schoolboy Coleridge used to watch it fluttering in the grate ('upon the bars'), hoping it might transmute to the face of his aunt or sister (Coleridge's father died when he was eight) bringing the lost world of his first childhood to the school-room. He hopes that that sort of loneliness will not be the lot of Hartley. A bridge between present adult musing and solitude and past childhood loneliness is initiated by the phenomenon of the sooty film fluttering again, now, in the cottage fire grate. This stimulation of the memory of related but different past experience is psychologically plausible, but it is also a structuring device enabling the reader to see connections and parallels between patterns of experience. The 'shaping spirit of Imagination' finds form in experience: it does not arbitrarily impose it.

The stillness of 'Frost at Midnight', disturbed only by the fluttering stranger, brings us to another Romantic emphasis: the importance of solitude. Stress on the importance of individual experience has its concomitant stress on being alone, free from social and other distraction. It is no small matter that the other inmates of the cottage have left Coleridge 'to that solitude, which suits abstruser musings'. The mind finds many of its most fruitful insights while turned inward upon itself, and this cannot happen if there are distractions such as those of society, conversation, or even sound or spectacle. This is to be distinguished from that loneliness experienced when the desolate self finds itself to be insufficient.

'Frost at Midnight' closes with the imaginative evocation of a nature that transcends time. Composed of elements of both summer and winter, it is a world that contains the beauty of greenness as well as that of snow and frost. The observation is sharp and vivid: the redbreast perched between the cold tufts of snow and the 'sun-thaw' as radiant heat causes the thatch to smoke even though the air temperature remains cold are strikingly realistic details. And yet the scene is a product of the imagination, a transformation of temporal sense experience: the falling of the drops of water thawing on the thatch, only heard in odd moments when the wind abates, is a future possibility, as is their freezing to silent icicles beneath the moon.

No one would claim Blake's 'London' and Coleridge's 'Frost at Midnight' to be formally similar poems. 'London' functions within a tight structure of rhyme and metre. 'Frost at Midnight' is written in blank verse and attempts an interior monologue in conversational style. It is not loose in the sense of being artistically casual but it is shaped more completely from within a personal voice than Blake's four quatrains. Yet the poems share related preoccupations and values, as we have seen. To read these two poems is to glimpse a little of the variety and richness of Romanticism, and to see something of its continuing relevance.

Notes

1. As it happens, extensive drafts and revisions of 'London' survive in manuscript and from them we can see that a great deal of careful rewriting took place before Blake was satisfied. This seems to have been typical. For all their talk of 'inspiration' the Romantics worked hard and long on their composition.
2. See Rousseau's writings, especially *Emile*.
3. Actually, Hartley had a wretched life, his latter days being spent wandering around the English Lake District communing with nature with the aid of a bottle in his pocket. He died of bronchitis in 1849 without fulfilling what had been a good deal of early promise as an intellectual and as a poet.
4. See Coleridge's great poem 'Dejection: An Ode' (1802) line 86. That poem gives an account and analysis of Coleridge's emotional and spiritual damage. As with 'Frost at Midnight' the poem finishes with the hoped for future happiness of a loved one (Sara Hutchinson) in contrast to a personal dejection.

Emily Dickinson:
'Homeless at home'

M e g a n   F y f f e

Emily Dickinson's greatest poetic output occurred in the decade
of the 1860s – a time when the 'cult' of domesticity was developing. The contrast between the (female) home and the (male) world
was the central convention of domesticity, producing a contradictory
and complex concept of ideal womanhood. The ideology expounded
by women's magazines, religious literature and gift annuals deemed
women predestined for the home because of their superior morality
and encouraged people to link the home and the outside world to
specific sex roles. Within the home the woman's sole focus was to
please others, providing a nurturing refuge for her husband and
children. In short, women were instructed to make the home their
world (Ryan 19–43). In this way woman and home became inextricably interdependent on one another for meaning. Women relied on
a home for an identity and a house only became a home with the
presence of a woman. This led to the peculiar situation where women
came to be defined *as* the domestic space; they not only maintained
but also embodied that space. Titles of women's journal articles
such as 'Woman, A Being To Come Home To' (Ferguson 271) suggest
the interchangeability of 'woman' and 'home'. Although the woman is
still denoted as a being, it is unclear whether the woman *makes* or *is*
the space of the home. Indeed, Julia Kristeva suggests that 'when
evoking the name and destiny of women, one thinks more of the
space generating and forming the human species than of *time*,

becoming, or history' (Kristeva 33). Denoted as domestic space, women thus could never be part of linear time or history, which belonged to men.

A number of contradictions were embedded in this carefully constructed domestic ideology of separate spheres. Nineteenth-century patriarchal society 'used the concept of "woman's sphere" to esteem female importance while containing it' (Cott 158). Women were invested with incomparable power over the order of the world while remaining isolated from it in their domestic sphere. Women in the home were said to bring about moral and social reforms and secure society against ruin. Publications like *The Lily* (a women's rights journal founded by Amelia Bloomer in the 1850s), carefully manipulated women to make them believe they had both power and virtue: 'Without home ... the world would be a chaos, without order ... or social regulation, without public or private virtue' (quoted in Ryan 111). However, no matter how crucial their activities were, they were still performed in a narrow and isolated social space. In addition their activities were not considered work because they appeared unsystematised and non-urgent in relation to the activities of men in the 'real' work force (Cott 61). So the cult of domesticity was based on a web of contradictions. Women were simultaneously empowered and disempowered through passivity and submission to a domestic destiny. Elevated as protectors of morals, it was less possible for women to transgress moral boundaries, defined by those who were really in power. At the same time, while women's labour was glorified, it was devalued because it took place in the private rather than the public sphere. Women were at once dignified monarchs of morality and insignificant servants of society.

Not only was the domestic ideology of the time self-contradictory, it was also undermined by the image of the home as a place of polarised alienation and 'nameless dread' (DeLamotte 15). Women were supposed to be protecting and protected from the outside world, but the home was not always a comforting haven. In Gothic literature the terrors and injustices experienced by heroines occur in what appears in the world as a comfortable place – an enclosed home (DeLamotte 27). The voice of the wife in Dickinson's poems often has accents of the Gothic. She speaks of fleeing 'gasping from the House' (#609) which encapsulates an unnamed terror; she speaks of suffering within 'Incarceration – Home' (#1334). Either way Dickinson reinforces Kate Ferguson Ellis's warning: 'The safety of the home is *not* a given, nor can it ever be permanently achieved' (Ellis xvi). Although the Gothic appears to be inverting the 'normal' safety of home into a place of 'abnormal' injustice and terror, the reality may be that it is working as a site of resistance to the dominant ideological position. The woman is not 'at home' in the home and yet she cannot escape it. This contradictory social position of women as 'homeless at home' is central to Dickinson's life and poetic exploration of the home.

The Dickinson household certainly replicated the contradictory domestic ideological view of women. Emily's father, Edward Dickinson, believed that 'Modesty and sweetness of disposition, and patience and forbearance and fortitude, are the cardinal virtues of the female sex ... These will atone for the want of brilliant talents, or great attainments' (Dickinson 100). Yet Edward also supported the advancement of women in schooling and society. He published a kind of manifesto of his attitude toward women and their role in life under a pseudonym in the short-lived Amherst newspaper *New England Inquire* which proclaimed the 'natural abilities of the sexes are ... not *inferior* to the other, but *exactly equal*' (Dickinson 101).

The contradictory views of Emily Dickinson's father were reflected in his treatment of her. Given an education almost identical to that of her brother Austin, until the age of eighteen, she was sent to Mount Holyoke Seminary and Amherst Academy and her father seems to have chosen her to be his intellectual companion when it became clear that his wife was deficient in this area (Dickinson *Letters* 191). However, Edward 'espoused two mutually contradictory attitudes – that women should be excellently educated, but that upon completing school, they should forget their education and entirely commit themselves to providing domestic comfort' (Wolff 121). When Emily began to mature she was taken out of school and expected to take her place in society. Even though it was Emily, not Austin, who obviously possessed the imagination and intellect for greatness she was told to renounce her intellectual pursuits for domesticity. The fact that Dickinson was educated as if she were a boy only served to impress upon her that she was merely a guest in the male realm of intellectuality. At the time, women were constantly reminded that they would never truly finish their education until they had mastered the art of homemaking (Welter 34). The advice for female minds like Dickinson's was that they could be 'literary' but only within the confines of the home: 'As for genius, make it a domestic plant. Let its roots strike deep in your house' (Anon. quoted in Welter 35). This affirmation of women's intellect and writing appears to be motivated by a desire to confine rather than liberate it. Dickinson's father also demonstrated this contradictory behaviour.

One of Emily's letters reveals her father's confusing oscillation between encouragement and suppression of her intellect: 'Father ... buys me many Books – but begs me not to read them – because he fears they joggle the Mind' (261). Since she chose to write Dickinson could not fit into Edward's contradictory female mould; in fact she often declared war against her father's attempt to enforce the division of the male and female spheres: 'Father's real life and *mine* sometimes come into collision' (*Letters* 65).

It is not surprising that Emily Dickinson's life reflects a contradictory attitude toward domestic life and wifehood. Joanne Dobson has noted that Dickinson's outer life appears congruent with the conservative norms for domestic femininity. She argues that 'the momentum of Dickinson's life ... led her in the opposite direction (from her contemporaries) – from a socially active childhood and youth to a virtual self-imprisonment within her home' (Dobson, '"Prickly Art" of Housekeeping' 232). Indeed, home became increasingly important to Emily Dickinson as a place that she referred to as a 'holy thing' (*Letters* 59) – high praise considering Dickinson's dubious view of religious reverence. She shared her mother's dislike for travelling for long periods of time. After returning home from Mount Holyoke for a Thanksgiving vacation she wrote to her brother Austin: 'Never did Amherst look more lovely to me and gratitude rose in my heart to God, for granting me such a safe return to my *own* DEAR HOME' (*Letters* 58). Dickinson began to abstain from attending social gatherings from as early as 1848, and she gradually reduced her company to a few close friends and her family. In the last years of her life she became completely homebound, probably to a phobic degree (Wolff 167).

There is much evidence to suggest that while Emily Dickinson lived within her father's house she was a domestic woman immersed in the workings of the household. When her mother fell ill in May 1850 Emily was involved for about two weeks in an intense period of domestic labour. In her letters over the years she makes reference to a variety of chores she was expected to perform (Dobson, 'Prickly Art' 233). As an unmarried woman in a well-to-do household with a servant to attend to most of the heavier housework Emily could have chosen to relinquish the domestic role. Her sister Lavinia took charge of most of the housework (except during their mother's illness) in order to free up Emily's time to write. Lavinia recognised that Emily 'had to think – she was the only one of us who had to do that' (Bingham 413). In spite of this Emily took domestic work seriously and her diligence was respected by her family and friends who particularly admired her baking and desserts (Gilbert 38).

Although Dickinson displayed a devotion to her home and performed domestic tasks, her attitude to domesticity is not one of
complete and easy compliance. She conveys her aversion to housework and the demands on her time in her emphatic response to her
role during her mother's sickness: 'my two hands but two – not four,
or five as they ought to be – and so *many* wants – and me so *very*
handy' (*Letters* 30). Later she expressed extreme exasperation and
contempt for the numerous duties she was expected to perform:
'God keep me from what they call *households*' (*Letters* 36). Dickinson
cheekily acknowledged and avoided the societal requirement that
she be chained to the kitchen: 'Wouldn't you love to see me in these
bonds of great despair, looking around my kitchen, and praying for
kind deliverance – God forbid – ' (*Letters* 36).

In light of this contradiction Dobson's suggestion that Emily
Dickinson's self-enforced seclusion was a 'natural extreme of compliance to contemporary codes of feminine behaviour' ('Prickly Art'
232) seems ill-informed. Dickinson's domestic orientation cannot be
explained as deliberately submissive, regulating her behaviour to
suit social norms and allay anxieties about her 'unladylike' writing.
Dobson's view suggests a return to the image of Emily Dickinson
best represented by John Crowe Ransom's 1956 description of her as
a 'little home-keeping person' whose life was 'a humdrum affair of
little distinction' (62). As Sandra Gilbert notes, this way of thinking
implies that 'the very substance of most female lives is so trivial, so
"humdrum", that it could not possibly inspire or energise great art'
(38). Emily Dickinson's poetry reveals this belief to be false.

The very fact that Dickinson devoted herself to writing conflicts
with the image of Dickinson as a subservient domestic woman. In the
nineteen sixties Alan Tate insisted that 'Cotton Mather would have
burnt her for a witch' (27). In the late seventies Adrienne Rich
observed that for Dickinson to 'say "yes" to her powers was not
simply a major act of nonconformity in the nineteenth century; even
in our time it has been assumed that Emily Dickinson, not patriarchal
society, was "the problem"' (183). The kind of confrontational, rebellious and intense poetry Dickinson wrote was considered inappropriate for women in the nineteenth century because it pressed 'too
close against the barriers of repression; and the nineteenth century
woman had much to repress' (Rich 175). More recently Camille Paglia
has asserted that Dickinson sloughs off her passive female body and
sexualises pleasure and pain in her poems, suggesting that had
people read her poems they would have discovered a 'visionary

sadist, a fictive sexual persona of towering force' (673). These views consistently contradict that of Dickinson as a mere domesticated spinster who rarely left her father's house. In fact, they portray a woman at the other end of the spectrum from the submissive, pious, pure and domestic 'True Woman'. This other woman embodies the contradiction of the home; she contests the prescribed role for women while still remaining 'at home'.

Emily Dickinson managed to keep herself free from the hold of a marriage house; she voiced her horror as many of her friends succumbed to married life, which Dickinson saw as more of a death. She wrote to her friend Emily after her wedding:

> *Dear Emily ... hidden by your veil you stood before us all and made those promises ... And now five days have gone, Emily, and long and silent, and I begin to know that you will not come back again. There's a verse in the Bible, Emily, I don't know where it is, nor just how it goes can I remember, but it's a little like this – 'I can go to her, but she cannot come back to me'.* (Letters 146)

In a letter to Susan Gilbert (a close friend and later her sister-in-law), Dickinson expresses concern and fear that marriage is as devastating as it is enviable:

> *How dull our lives must seem to the bride, and the plighted maiden, whose days are fed with gold, and who gathers pearls every evening; but to the* wife, *Susie, sometimes the* wife *forgotten, our lives perhaps seem dearer than all others in the world; you have seen flowers at morning,* satisfied *with the dew, and those same sweet flowers at noon with their heads bowed in anguish before the mighty sun ... Oh Susie, it is dangerous, and it is all too dear, these simple trusting spirits, and the spirits mightier, which we cannot resist! It does so rend me, Susie, the thought of it when it comes, that I tremble lest at sometime I, too, am yielded up.* (Letters 93)

In her poetry Dickinson's representation of the home is as strikingly contradictory as her experience of it. Her view of marriage, as the deliverance of a woman into the house of her husband where she must assume the role of wife, is expressed as the ultimate sacrifice. Poem #732 considers the wedding ceremony as a handing over of everything important in exchange for an empty title:

She rose to His Requirement – dropt
The Playthings of Her Life
To take the honorable Work
Of Woman, and of Wife –

If ought She missed in Her new Day,
Of Amplitude, or Awe –
Or first Prospective – Or the Gold
In using, wear away,

It lay unmentioned – as the Sea
Develop Pearl, and Weed,
But only to Himself – be known
The Fathoms they abide –

There is a clear and irreversible change taking place in the first stanza; the subject of the poem is rising from her lowly social position as an unmarried girl to that of 'Woman, and of Wife –'. She receives a title, legitimation and the accompanying rise in social status as a wife, a role that is 'honorable' within her community. At this point in the poem the speaker's view could be mistaken for one endorsing marriage as a necessary stage in any girl's life in order for her to put aside her childish and unfulfilling single state and become a 'true woman'. This reading of Dickinson's marriage poems is advocated by Richard Chase who considers the idea of wedlock as delighting Dickinson's speakers because it elevates commoner to queen and child to woman (157). Dickinson is certainly utilising the nineteenth-century notion that marriage gave women some kind of power, particularly in society. However, Chase ignores the bitterly ironic attitude present in poems such as #732. For every benefit of marriage there is a corresponding disadvantage and often the deficit (in this case the relinquishment of all personal power) is greater than a hollow advantage.

A positive reading of this poem is thrown into confusion by the words: 'His Requirement'. Although we do not receive a visual image of the husband we feel the presence of a male figure presiding over the metamorphosis of his female. We hear his commanding voice in the word 'Requirement' which injects a somewhat sinister element of unequal power into the proceedings. As soon as the bridegroom has been admitted into the poem wedlock loses its charm. Marriage becomes an act of force with the female submitting to a controlling authoritarian who is exercising his right to take possession of her (Zeigler 65). In Poem #273 we witness the gruesome relinquishing of

female virtue implied in Poem #732: 'He put the Belt around my life –
/I heard the Buckle snap – '. We hear the 'sharp, crackling finality' of
the woman's bondage to the embodiment of male authority (Clark
Griffith 177). The image of an earthly husband figure is often conflated with or replaced by a reading of the male figure as God initiating a marriage/sacrifice of an earthly soul to his command. It
appears that Dickinson held similar opinions about both heavenly
and earthly masters and as her poems frequently explore several
(often contradictory) images and motivations her marriage poems
can lend themselves to a number of readings.

With the image of the dominating male altering the tone of the
poem, marriage is portrayed as a drastic event. Indeed, if the wife
does acquire a regal position she is locked into this state, never to
return to the freedom of her unmarried life. There is an absolute
cleavage of the girl from the wife's life. She can merely look back upon
that state through the 'soft Eclipse' of marriage (Poem #199). We
come to realise the full extent of this transition when we investigate
what the wife sacrifices in order to pass into her new life. The speaker
suggests that women lose everything of importance: 'Amplitude' or
the largeness of life and a broad range of possibilities and 'Awe' or the
wonder and ecstasy of living. Whatever the woman could have made
of her life, be it 'Pearl' (success and fulfilment) or 'Weed' (mistakes
and disappointments), is lost and the direction and control of her life
is handed over to her husband. In Dickinson's poetry 'Pearl' is often
analogous with something precious, particularly writing or female
creativity and this makes the loss even more grievous. Dickinson
cleverly emphasises both the magnitude of such immolation and the
quiet taboo used in society to cloak it. Life's opportunities are portrayed as passed over, muted and swamped by the 'Sea' of society's
endorsement of marriage; a woman's potential is left 'unmentioned'
in the wake of this force. The suffocation and loss of a woman's subjectivity and agency in marriage are deadly in their unspoken finality.
In effect, 'a wedding is virtually a funeral' (Kirkby 69).

Dickinson vigorously questions the way women are expected to
submit to being 'Born – Bridalled – Shrouded/In a Day – ' (Poem
#1072). The male figure is implicated as the instigator and regulator
of this process. However, the bride herself is left in an ambiguous
position of guilt and innocence. The speaker acknowledges that the
woman is somehow compelled to answer the male's 'Requirement';
however, it is also made clear that the bride propels herself into
such an arrangement. In Poem #1072 the bride even displays a
masochistic delight in 'Stroking the Melody' of her prized 'Victory' in

gaining a husband. By admitting ambiguity into the true nature of such a victory and by presenting the underlying vision of the bride's life as it could have been without marriage (filled with 'Awe' and 'Amplitude'), the speaker questions whether marriage must be 'the way' (Poem #1072) for all women. Women enter marriage in order to avoid becoming social nobodies; however, Dickinson questions whether women have considered that to be a 'Somebody' for the appeasement of 'an admiring Bog' is a worse fate (Poem #288).

Poem #187 is confronting in its aggressive articulation of the nature of the housewife's lot in life:

> *How many times these low feet staggered –*
> *Only the soldered mouth can tell –*
> *Try – can you stir the awful rivet –*
> *Try – can you lift the hasps of steel!*
>
> *Stroke the cool forehead – hot so often –*
> *Lift – if you care – the listless hair –*
> *Handle the adamantine fingers*
> *Never a thimble – more – shall wear –*
>
> *Buzz the dull flies – on the chamber window –*
> *Brave – shines the sun through the freckled pane –*
> *Fearless – the cobweb swings from the ceiling –*
> *Indolent Housewife – in Daisies – lain!*

This poem presents an image of a woman exhausted by the unending chores of the house. The unnoticed heroics of wives and their self-sacrificial, thankless work is magnified to the point where the woman is literally staggering from the extreme effort needed to do the work women's magazines of the day described as 'peaceful' (Cott 67). This conjures up a frightening comparison with Jesus staggering under the weight of the cross as he carried it to his death at Golgotha. It is not only the magnitude and difficulty of the work which causes the housewife to stagger, but also the 'enforced trivia' (Kirkby 71).

We are not hearing the lament of the housewife herself for we discover in the final line that she is in fact dead: 'in Daisies – lain'. The speaker is actually conducting a post-mortem of the housewife's life, and the post-mortem reveals a number of paradoxes. On one hand the housewife's death is a final release from the strain of her house labours. She will never have to wear a thimble again nor worry about the cobwebs or flies within her home. Her 'Indolent' state may mean

she is finally 'free from pain' (Wolff 207). Yet there is a strong sense
that although the housewife no longer sweats and staggers under the
demands of the house there is little chance of relief or release from
bondage, even in death. Not only is she shackled inside the house
during life but in death she is hideously restrained within her coffin.
The description of her body is clinical. The corpse is assessed in the
manner of a surgeon conducting a post-mortem; it is dissected in
death into detached pieces: 'forehead', 'hair' and 'fingers'. There is
evidence to suggest that the housewife's confinement is unnatural.
Her body is incarcerated and constricted by metal rivets, bolts and
locks – all man-made items (Kirkby 71). The horrifying and brutal
notion of a mouth 'soldered' shut designates the wife as something
sub-human. At the same time, however, the apparent need to enforce
the housewife's silence suggests that she was (or perhaps still is) a
potentially dangerous informer and her evidence too damaging to be
told. Thus Dickinson captures the paradoxical position of the housewife – all-powerful and yet completely restrained.

In Poem #187 the woman is not only silenced and rendered
immobile in death, she is berated for her inadequacies after death.
The unnatural confinement imposed upon her is glossed over and
the focus is on the housewife's failings. The other connotation for
the word indolent and thus the title, 'Indolent Housewife', is tainted
with irony for it labels the housewife lazy, slovenly, listless and disobedient (Wolff 207). The task of keeping order, with which the housewife has been invested, is unattended to and chaos threatens as the
natural world begins to impinge upon and even take over the civilised
house. Dickinson has exaggerated the excessive demands made of
the housewife to the point where not even death is an acceptable
excuse for her failure to behave as a domestic woman should.

This poem presses the construction of women as docile and
pathetic to the limits. The dead or 'still' woman is actually constructed as the ideal. Loss of consciousness, invisibility and silence
are all qualities of death and, as this poem reveals, also of marriage
(Dobson, *Strategy of Reticence* 73). The very order upon which the
male subject depends suffocates female subjectivity. This presents
yet another interesting paradox, for the still housewife is at once
berated and belittled for her inadequacies but also deemed essential
in the hierarchy of patriarchal social order.

The complexity of the housewife's position in society is best
expressed in the absence of any clear distinctions between interior
and exterior spaces. In the often-quoted Poem #465 ('I heard a fly
buzz – when I died – ') the fly interferes with the clean transition from

life to death; it blurs the speaker's literal and spiritual vision. Similarly, in Poem #187 the flies confuse the conception of space and place. They buzz on the window but we do not know whether they are inside trying to get out or outside trying to get in. Are they 'dull' because they are dying inside or because the glass is muffling their noise? The flies alert us to the fact that we really do not know where the housewife or the speaker is situated. Is the speaker lamenting on behalf of the housewife from beyond the grave? Has the housewife transcended her grave and embraced her immortality as a space of possibility? Is her grave a site of escape and freedom? Are her attackers' torments and accusations falling on deaf ears or is she forced to listen to them while powerless to respond verbally? If she is suffering their taunts then this puts the housewife anywhere between death and immortality. Perhaps this poem is simply providing a critical appraisal of the social relations of the time; after all even as the boundaries between life and death, inside and outside are blurred, the speaker is still positioned *within* the house.

Despite her potent attack on the restrictive and debilitating separation of women into the domestic sphere, Dickinson also reclaims the home and makes it possible to redefine gender within that space. In Poem #617 Dickinson cleverly plays with the notion of what art and work are:

> Don't put up my Thread and Needle –
> I'll begin to Sow
> When the Birds begin to whistle –
> Better Stitches – so –
>
> These were bent – my sight got crooked –
> When my mind – is plain
> I'll do seams – a Queen's endeavor
> Would not blush to own –
>
> Hems – too fine for lady's tracing
> To the sightless Knot –
> Tucks – of dainty interspersion –
> Like a dotted Dot –
>
> Leave my Needle in the furrow –
> Where I put it down –
> I can make the zigzag stitches
> Straight – when I am strong –

Till then – dreaming I am sowing
Fetch the seam I missed –
Closer – so I – at my sleeping –
Still surmise I stitch –

The poem details three interwoven images: the farmer at work sowing in his fields, the woman at work sewing in the home and the poet at work in her mind piecing together poetry. In the nineteenth century sewing was almost exclusively women's work and confined to the interior domestic sphere. In contrast, to *sow* is traditionally the work of men, performed in the wide-open world of male activity.

Historically women's domestic work has been invisible. Women have been so self-effacing that they and their work have become a 'dotted Dot –', a double negative, a nothing (Wolff 209). However, in Poem #617 the speaker esteems women's work as being of equal importance to men's. Gilbert acknowledges that 'Dickinson knew perfectly well, it is women who perform the primary transformations of culture: raw into cooked ... fiber into thread, thread into cloth, cloth into dress, lawless baby into law-abiding child' (41). Griffin Wolff also speaks of Dickinson's recognition of women's work: 'Dickinson could turn a great many seemingly trivial routines of the home into signs of ... simple dignity' (207). Thus, although in other housewife poems by Emily Dickinson women's work is damned as numbing to the mind and the home is represented as a torturous prison, in Poem #617 the speaker redefines the home as a place of prestige and even power for women. Equating sewing with sowing this poem seems to project the breaking down of strict gender boundaries and to look forward to a time when women's and men's work might be equally valued.

The sewing/sowing metaphor extends further. Poem #617 can be read as a celebration of the female poet, and of Dickinson's poetry as both her 'handiwork and her labour' (Bode 165). The poet's work can be seen as equally skilful as the housewife's or the farmer's if we read stanza three as an example of the poet's seamless work. The hard work – the craft of poetry – is invisible. As in the finest hand-sewn garment, in poetry it is what is not seen ('the sightless knot', the 'tucks') that holds a poem together, creating such beauty and precision that 'a Queen's endeavour/Would not blush to own' it. This metaphor is particularly suggestive in relation to Dickinson's work as a poet since the needle and thread were literally the tools of her self-publication: she sewed her poems into little booklets which became the now famous fascicles (Bode 164).

There is some indication in the fifth line of the poem that there is trouble with the poet's writing ('my sight got crooked –'), be it trouble with her eyesight or the clarity of her intellect or poetic vision. However, there is a sense of assurance that although the work is not finished it can and will be 'when I am strong –'. In the final stanza the work of farmer, housewife and poet are conflated. The 'so' in the penultimate line of the poem appears to be signalling a dream combination of the activities of sewing and sowing. The merging of gendered work seems to suggest that Dickinson is arguing for a breaking down of female and male boundaries in general and in artistic life in particular (Bode 164). She appears to be speaking especially for women poets whose more subtle form of writing tended to be overshadowed by the large male epics of the nineteenth century (such as *Moby Dick* or Whitman's verse). She advocates recognition of different forms of art.

The double meaning of key words in Poem #617 enables an acceptance of several possibilities, not only in the reading of this poem but in thinking about the housewife at home. Through Dickinson's representations of domesticity and through the contradictions inherent in domestic ideology, we see that different meanings can co-exist (Foster 240). Finding herself located within the domestic sphere Dickinson draws on the images of this space to reveal and explore the condition of domesticity while offering possible resistance against it. Sometimes, as in Poem #617, a disruption of the ideology of home is written about as if it has already been achieved.

It is important to note that in Emily Dickinson's poetry there is no real escape from the home. This can be seen both in a negative light (as entrapment) and positively (as women's need for domesticity). Moreover Dickinson asserts that it is impossible to separate women from identification with the female position within the home reinforced by the ideology of separate spheres. At the same time, it is possible to see Dickinson's poems as 'continually attempt[ing] to enter a space beyond her own [domestic] life and to define the positive value and social content of such a space' (Thomas 245). For Dickinson the home need not always be a hostile place and domesticity need not even be in direct conflict with what women want. A number of Dickinson's poems, after all, were written on the backs of recipes (Gilbert 38). The housewives of Dickinson's poems and Dickinson herself, although remaining in the home, elude placement securely in the role of true domestic woman or alternatively in the role of transgressive mad woman – a concept discussed in detail in the following essay by Rosemary Moore. By focusing on the notion of a woman remaining 'homeless at home' (Poem #1573) Dickinson is able radically to explore female identity in the contexts of both submission to and resistance against domestic containment, speculating in particular on what that means for female creativity.

Works Cited

Bingham, Millicent Todd. *Emily Dickinson's Home: Letters of Edward Dickinson and His Family*. New York: Harper, 1955. New York: Dover Publications, 1967.

Bode, Rita. 'Dickinson's "Don't Put up My Thread and Needle"'. *The Explicator* 52 (1994): 161–165.

Chase, Richard. *Emily Dickinson*. London: Methuen, 1952.

Cott, Nancy. *The Bonds of Womanhood: 'Women's Sphere' in New England 1780–1835*. New Haven: Yale UP, 1977.

DeLamotte, Eugenia C. *Perils of the Night: A Feminist Study of Nineteenth-Century Gothic*. New York: Oxford UP, 1990.

Dickinson, Edward. 'Female Education'. *New England Inquire* January 5 (1827):100–101.

Dobson, Joanne. *Dickinson and the Strategies of Reticence: The Woman Writer in the Nineteenth Century*. Bloomington: Indiana UP, 1989.

——. 'Emily Dickinson and the "Prickly Art" of Housekeeping'. *Women's Studies* 16 (1989): 231–237.

Ellis, Kate Ferguson. *The Contested Castle: Gothic Novels and the Subversion of Domestic Ideology*. Urbana: University of Illinois Press, 1989.

Ferguson, N. L, ed. *The Young Ladies' Oasis: Gems of Prose and Poetry*. Philadelphia: n.p, 1849.

Foster, Thomas. 'Homelessness at Home: Placing Emily Dickinson in (Women's) History'. *Engendering Men: The Question of Male Feminist Criticism*. Eds. Joseph A. Boone and Michael Cadden. New York: Routledge, 1990.

Gilbert, Sandra. 'The Wayward Nun Beneath the Hill'. *Feminist Critics Read Emily Dickinson*. Ed. Suzanne Juhasz. Bloomington: Indiana UP, 1983.

Johnson, Thomas H., ed. *Emily Dickinson: The Complete Poems*. London: Faber and Faber, 1970.

——, ed. *The Letters of Emily Dickinson*. 3 vols. Cambridge, Massachusetts: Belknap Press of Harvard UP, 1958.

Kirkby, Joan. *Emily Dickinson*. London: Macmillan Education, 1991.

Kristeva, Julia. 'Women's Time'. Trans. Alice Jardine and Harry Blake. *Signs* 7.1 (1981): 13–35.

Paglia, Camille. *Sexual Personae: Art and Decadence From Nefertiti To Emily Dickinson*. London: Yale UP, 1990.

Ransom, John Crowe. *'A Poet Restored'*. *Emily Dickinson: A Collection of Critical Essays*. Ed. Richard B. Sewall. Englewood Cliffs, New Jersey: Prentice-Hall, 1963.

Rich, Adrienne. *On Lies, Secrets, and Silence: Selected Prose 1966–1978*. New York: W.W. Norton, 1979.

Ryan, Mary. 'The Empire of the Mother: American Writing About Domesticity 1830–1860'. *Women and History* 2/3 (1982): 1–170.

Tate, Allen. 'Emily Dickinson'. *Emily Dickinson: A Collection of Critical Essays*. Ed. Richard B. Sewall. Englewood Cliffs, New Jersey: Prentice-Hall, 1963.

Welter, Barbara. *Dimity Convictions: The American Woman in the Nineteenth Century*. Athens, Ohio: Ohio UP, 1976.

Wolff, Cynthia Griffin. *Emily Dickinson*. New York: Alfred A. Knopf, 1986.

Zeigler, Sara L. 'Marriage, Labor, and the Common Law in Nineteenth Century America'. *Social Science History* 20.1 (1996): 63–96.

Further Reading

Bianchi, Martha Dickinson. *Emily Dickinson Face To Face: Unpublished Letters With Notes and Reminiscences*. Hamden, Connecticut: Archon Books, 1970.

Green, David L. 'Emily Dickinson: The Spatial Drama of Centering'. *Essays in Literature* 7 (1980): 191–200.

Hughes, Gertrude Reif. 'Subverting the Cult of Domesticity: Emily Dickinson's Critique of Women's Work'. *Legacy: A Journal of Nineteenth Century American Women Writers* 3.1 (1986): 17–28.

Jackson, Stevi. 'Towards a Historical Sociology of Housework: A Materialist Feminist Analysis'. *Women's Studies International Forum* 15.2 (1992): 153–172.

Juhasz, Suzanne. 'Introduction'. *Feminist Critics Read Emily Dickinson*. Ed. Suzanne Juhasz. Bloomington: Indiana UP, 1983.

——. *The Undiscovered Continent: Emily Dickinson and the Space of the Mind*. Bloomington: Indiana UP, 1983.

Fiction: Gendered Readings

Jane Eyre:
Passion versus Principle

R o s e m a r y   M o o r e

J*ane Eyre* is written by a woman; its title bears a woman's name; it is about a woman's experience; and it speaks to women readers in a special way. As such it offers a challenge to the idea that writing in the nineteenth century is reserved for men. Its central protagonist is a woman of vision and imagination, whose experience of being a woman in a man's world causes her to feel split within herself – split between the good girl she is and is supposed to be and the bad girl with a propensity to passion whom she is told she is.

Jane is represented as both good and bad, and the resulting split in her characterisation is central to the unfolding of the meaning of her story. While she can justifiably regard herself as good by contrast with the Reed children, it fuels her sense of injustice that they are regarded as nice children whereas she is treated as a pariah by all. Consequently she cannot resolve the disparity between her self-estimation and the way others see her. Furthermore she fears that her detractors might be right, that she is after all the monster she is accused of being. If she proves to be merely a creature of passion she must be condemned as both mad and bad, since it is impossible to flout the ideals of femininity and gentility without being punished for it.

So, while it is natural to see from her own point of view and to believe in her own goodness, the judgments of others reveal her hidden fears about herself. Thus we look to the comments of others, not simply to Jane's account of herself, in order to understand her personality and conflicts. Her positive identifications and disidenti-fications are of great help to the reader in coming to understand deeply conflicting emotions which cannot easily be translated into rational speech. However, the division in Jane's character is not a quirk of personality, since it reveals the bifurcation of the idea of woman in traditional thought. Female characters are either the descendants of Eve or of the Virgin Mary, excessively passionate or redemptively sacrificial, and viewed correspondingly as bad or good.

The narrative is woven around Jane's conflict with the stereo-types of woman as devil or angel, witch or sprite, slave or doll. Jane reveals that she is not identical with the way she is represented, and that there is a measure of self that eludes identification with an image. Yet, if her aim is to discover who she is independently of her representation, it is impossible for her to evade a double gender identification since reason is deemed a male quality and passion is associated with the female. Christian principle must guard her against her propensity for passion. Yet her feelings lead her to seek aims which she consciously rejects as improper, and her desire for erotic love conflicts with the concept of Christian love which she believes constitutes the basis of a Christian marriage. In addition, her quest for love comes into conflict with her need to work and have a job which would give her satisfaction as well as a subsistence.

These conflicts suggest that Brontë's central themes link ques-tions of sexuality and gender with writing, and that the problem of writing about female experience is associated with the problem of women's representation in writing. It is not just the way women are represented in novels written by men that is at issue. It is the fact that the concept of woman is constructed over a wide variety of dis-courses – medical, psychological, social, moral and religious. Jane's quest for self-knowledge involves a confrontation with her represen-tation as a woman in the discourses of her time.

The fact that she rebels against the stereotypical association of women with evil, yet seeks her identity in motherhood and respectability, shows the importance of gender to identity. It also shows what a difference it makes to our understanding to have a woman's perspective on truth and reality. Brontë not only enters the field of public culture as a writer who happens to be female. She reveals more about the nature of the self than was previously known, and thus alters the way personality and identity are understood. She also gives us in Jane a female character who is endowed with psychological depth to the extent that she reveals the nature of the human mind in a new way.

Jane's feelings reach a climax when she claims in chapter twelve that women are equal to men. However, while she longs for 'a power of vision which might overpass' (140) the limit of her sequestered life, she listens at the same time to strange sounds emanating from the passage that leads to the room where the first Mrs Rochester lies hidden. As she gains relief by walking up and down listening to the movements of her own heart, she is excited by her relationship to a passionate existence of which she is as yet unaware, symbolised by Rochester's first wife. This enables her to open 'my inward ear to a tale that was never ended – a tale my imagination created, and narrated continuously; quickened with all of incident, life, fire, feeling, that I desired and had not in my actual existence' (141). This is a highly significant statement because it shows that while Jane will allow feeling and intuition to open her imagination to the depths of her own desire she remains in the grip of the unconscious. If she is on one level the author of her own fiction, she is on another a being created by the stories that construct her. She will also allow her destiny to unfold by following intuition and instinct as if she were not directly in control of her life.

Brontë anticipates modern concepts of personality which concede that the individual is not in rational control of knowledge or self, but is, alternatively, divided and at the mercy of the unconscious. Imagination, not reason, will lead Jane to self-discovery. Since her life unfolds as if it were a story about someone else, she is able to follow her desires without having to repress them because they are unacceptable. Yet, because they are unacceptable they are projected onto another who is her unconscious double. This is a protection against full awareness, yet fantasy functions precisely through the staging of desire by eliciting scenes in which others act out the various parts of an internal conflict, thus opening a path to understanding.

If Jane is formed by her contestation of the constructions of woman which circulate in her society, we cannot expect to find in her the characterisation of a unified self or a person who has mastered her world. At the same time Brontë establishes Jane's character by representing her as a child who sees through hypocrisy and who is a critic of society. As she has yet to become acculturated she is able to speak out against prejudice and injustice. The reader is witness to a process in which a self is produced by questioning the way things are rather than meekly accepting that as a poor orphan she is a woman without a place in a man's world. The fact that Jane is a woman of imagination who seeks to understand her own desires in a period in which it was supposed that respectable women were without a sexual dimension makes her a figure of transgression.

Jane Eyre is regarded as a realistic novel because it gives us the illusion of representing life as it is. But it is also a Gothic novel which draws on the fantastic and represents a woman's real experience as if it were a nightmare. The fact that Brontë draws on two genres generally regarded as being in opposition to one another indicates the difficulty of writing as a woman within genres that have been structured on the basis of masculine experience and emotional life. In this context the freedom to employ Gothic fantasy allows Brontë to suggest things which could not be stated rationally, and thus allows her to be more innovative in revisioning ideas about the nature of the self and society.

The Gothic form as established in male writing foregrounds the problem of evil and the significance of numinous experience in relation to the creation of a mythology of the mind. Although women writers are equally interested in the mind, the female Gothic has a particular relation to fantasy and to the body. Ellen Moers argues that in female Gothic fantasy dominates over reality, the strange over the commonplace, and the natural over the supernatural. She thinks its ability to scare the reader has a particular way of getting at the body, and of quickly arousing and allaying physical reactions to fear, so that there is an emphasis on the reader's physiological responses to the fiction. She claims that there is a compulsion to visualise the self in women's Gothic, which distinguishes it from male experience and forms of writing, especially as it gives visual form to the fear of the self women experience because female sexuality is seen by men to be both horrifying and monstrous.

Gothic romance, as Eugenia DeLamotte shows, has centred on the presence of a kind of architecture that is an embodiment of the past and of mystery. In this way the architecture symbolises the idea that women's bodies are a mystery to themselves and that their problems with sexuality are in some way related to the past because they inherit a physical constitution that is a precise replication of their mothers' biological make-up. Discovery of the truth involves a hidden relationship which is exteriorised as an adventure in which a questing subject sets out to solve a mystery embodied in a mansion or house. To discover the secrets it hides it is necessary to confront the mystery of the architecture itself, with its use of labyrinthine passages, locked doors, and forgotten rooms. The architecture is baffling and may hide a threatening occupant who will give evidence of a life history which is unwelcome because it corresponds to the quester's fears. The protagonist's adventures in this architectural setting symbolise the terrors of a spirit engaged with the forces of violence, which may become manifest in the figure of an arbitrary tyrant, patriarch or priest, the lust of a libertine, or the machinations of a woman scorned. *Jane Eyre* draws on the tradition of Gothic romance and develops it in an extremely original way so that the reader has a sense of entering Jane's mind and thereby coming to understand more about the nature of the human mind in general.

The function of the Gothic here is to provide a language for those ideas which cannot be given rational expression. Given that Jane is in quest of knowledge, love, identity, and self understanding in the context in which she is confronted by images of self which distort and misrepresent her as an angel or a fiend, the Gothic provides a language in which it is possible to break away from these stereotypes in order to discover the existence of a self independent of its relationships to others and to the culture. We see Jane as having a body, physical needs, and desires of her own, in addition to having a mind. She is therefore not the embodiment of womanhood as perceived by male writers. Yet she remains an innocent in a world in which a knowledge of sexuality would brand and exclude her from polite society as it does her double and opposite, Bertha Mason.

The Gothic enables Brontë to consider problems specific to women instead of merely drawing on the traditional understanding of women drawn from male literature. Here the problem of how to deal with permeable boundaries to the self is a crucial issue. To know herself Jane must learn to distinguish her self from representations of self. But being female her process of growth does not require her to separate herself from her mother in order to become an individual. In addition, there is a same sex identification between a daughter and her mother that hinders the process of separation necessary to individuation. How to tell what belongs to herself as opposed to what of herself belongs to another becomes an issue in adult life when she is faced with the prospect of becoming a love object for a man whose possession of her, legally and psychologically, threatens to subsume her. She will lose her name, her independence, and her life. Furthermore, romantic love involves a concept of complementarity which means that two separate individuals make a couple in the same way as two halves make one whole and in order to achieve this harmonious result the lesser must be absorbed into the greater half. The woman must become a wife, subsidiary to her husband.

The Gothic reminds us that the body is like the castle, the last bastion of personal integrity – the final barrier separating the self from an other. In Gothic fiction boundaries shift, identities are blurred, and it becomes difficult to distinguish reality from fantasy. Women may fear being alone and isolated as well as being intruded upon. A lover may present an illusion of service and turn out to be a tyrant. How can Jane separate the lover from the despot? However impeccable he is in relation to his own life, St John Rivers would make a tyrannical husband. Jane comes to realise she would serve God through serving him, while he would seek God's greater glory through using her as his instrument. And, though Rochester is her true lover, she is obliged to see him as a false shepherd who would deny her the right to an eternal life by putting her soul at risk. Jane seeks to be her husband's equal, not his inferior.

Jane Eyre embodies an impediment to marriage in the shape of the first Mrs Rochester, and her existence indicates that Jane is blocked off from an understanding of something to which she should have access, a knowledge of self which comes through an other. Jane can only know what Rochester chooses to tell her, but he deliberately deceives her lest he should lose her. There is an identity between the two Mrs Rochesters which Jane cannot afford to recognise consciously, but which Brontë highlights by showing the potentialities in the wild cat child to become the bestial mad woman. The existence of an impediment to marriage suggests the need to remove a barrier before the marriage can take place, but though Bertha is the external cause of the collapse of Rochester's marital plans, the real barrier to marriage is internal to Jane's psychology. Jane cannot afford to let sexual passion obliterate her love for God, nor can she marry a man capable of flouting God's law by marrying her bigamously.

Like Jane, the reader is involved in a process of interpretation which unfolds as barriers to understanding are gradually lifted, veils drawn aside, masks removed, and doors opened that no longer separate the questing self from her object – the knowledge of self that comes from love and work. Jane discovers her identity through working to support herself before she enters on a marital partnership which is conceived of as an egalitarian marriage between equals. The importance of the courtship period is that it explores the consequences of inequality in defining a sexual relation as a power relation between a master and his slave. There is no doubt that the bride who is prepared to become the ornament and the sexual slave of a husband who is her total master is on the path to madness and to Bridewell. The supposition that a man is his wife's lord and master leads to total inequality and powerlessness for the woman. When Rochester finally admits his dependence on God he is in a position to enter a Christian marriage and receive Jane as his reward. Thus Brontë keeps the concept of Christian marriage in place, while questioning the patriarchal bias of its interpreters, and in so doing she offers a reinterpretation of the nature of woman and her place in the world.

Fifty five years before the publication of *Jane Eyre* in 1847, Mary Shelley's mother, Mary Wollstonecraft, wrote *A Vindication of the Rights of Woman*. She stated that if men wish women to be more than brutes who are dependent on the reason of men they should let women 'attain conscious dignity by feeling themselves only dependent on God'. For she claims that 'God gave me strength of mind to dare to exert my own reason, till becoming dependent only on him for the support of my virtue, I view, with indignation, the mistaken notions that enslave my sex' (36–37). Jane's struggle is equally to keep the law of God as sanctioned by man, but to take her cue directly from God where His law differs from the way men interpret it.

Wollstonecraft argued that if women were to be held responsible for crimes they must have souls and that therefore they must have a capacity to think rationally. And if they were rational beings they should be accorded full human rights and thus be treated in the same way as men, instead of being regarded as little better than children. Wollstonecraft believed that women were kept in a state of childishness in consequence of their definition as sexual beings. As such they were confined to the home, 'immersed with their families and groping in the dark' (5). Women were not only left in ignorance. They were prevented from gaining strength of mind through education and the use of their mental faculties. Thus they were denied virtue. For Wollstonecraft women would never fulfil the peculiar duties of their sex until they should become enlightened citizens.

Wollstonecraft therefore argued that egalitarian marriage was the prototype of genuine democracy. Realising that men and women were equal in intelligence and sensitivity, she believed they should both participate equally in decision making and in child rearing. If their roles were those of nurturing and caregiving, this simply increased women's need for an education to fit them for their grand duties. Wollstonecraft states what *Jane Eyre* implies, that the intercourse of the sexes will never deserve the name of fellowship till women should have equality with men, which they can best establish if permitted to profit by their own industry. To earn their own subsistence would grant women independence from men. J. S. Mill noted a movement from dominance and submission to equal and free associations between men and women in this period, which confirms the possibility of egalitarian marriage.

In refusing to be an accessary to a man Jane speaks for many other women. However, Brontë understood that to achieve this aim it was necessary to revise the myth of creation which tells us that Adam was created in God's image and that Eve was produced out of Adam's rib to be his helpmeet. If all women were, metaphorically speaking, the daughters of Eve, they were burdened by being held responsible for the Fall. This was the justification of Adam's function in ruling his wife as well as husbanding the world's natural resources, and came to justify a husband's treatment of his wife in daily life. In each of the novel's five sections Jane experiences a fall from grace that requires her to confront her inheritance as a daughter of Eve and to prove her human worth in contradistinction to this founding myth. Eve is, in fact, the prototype of the feminist rebel – a woman who disobeys God's decree in the hope of becoming like a God herself. But as she brought sin and death into the world it required a second Eve to redeem mankind in the shape of the Virgin Mary. Women could thus be seen as men's saviours if, like Mary, they were prepared to obey and serve men selflessly.

Bertha Mason is an Eve figure because she is held responsible for Rochester's fall, but, unlike Jane who claims a voice and the right to tell her own story as a man might do, she is not allowed to represent her life from her own point of view. We see her only as others see her. Bertha reminds us that if women were like children they were likewise to be seen and not heard, and were thus silenced. The fact that Bertha's voice is heard before she is seen is evidence of her desire to be heard. Her laugh strikes Jane's ears because it is 'curious', 'distinct, formal, [and] mirthless'. It varies in intensity, ending 'in a clamorous peal that seemed to echo in every lonely chamber, though it originated but in one'. Subsequently the laugh is repeated in a 'low, syllabic tone' terminating 'in an odd murmur' (138). To Jane, the sound is 'as tragic, as preternatural a laugh as any I ever heard' and as such induces fear, but it also shows that a woman's speech is often unintelligible because it is not understood.

Bertha remains invisible, ghostly and mysterious, but the strangeness of the sounds she emits is compelling. Since she symbolises sexual excess we can see a link between Jane's desire for and fear of passion. If passion were allowed to dominate reason this would be tantamount to madness. Brontë endorsed the view that sin is equivalent to madness when she wrote in a letter that 'all sin is a species of insanity.'[1] Bertha therefore represents female sexuality as violent, bestial and self-destructive, as the other side of the ideal of sexual innocence enforced on women. Jane's interest in Bertha represents an unconscious interest in her own sexuality, which Bertha represents because the two women are biologically the same. However, the taboo against sexual knowledge cannot be affronted, and what Bertha stands for must be eradicated if Jane is to enjoy a respectable married life.

Bertha is a beast because sexual licentiousness turns people into beasts, but she is also a vampire. This means that she is a strong woman, for the idea that vampires require regular supplies of blood in order to live refers back to the primal notion that all life depends on the magic of menstrual blood, which in former times led people to believe that supplies of blood could recall the dead to life. As versions of the un-dead they are also associated with the moon, which was thought to be the original home of the dead and the source of rebirth. This is no doubt why Rochester plays with the idea of taking Jane to the moon during their courtship. However, with the rise of Christianity the vampire's bite was associated with sinful sex through the similarity between biting and kissing, and vampires were thought to act under the influence of Satan. Thus Bertha is represented as a beast without reason, a mad and daemonic creature, and a witch or imp possessed of an evil force. Yet she is merely a sexually virile woman. Jane describes her without the colouring of emotion as a woman, tall, large, and with thick hair hanging down her back, dressed in a gown or shroud. However, seen through the filter of gender ideology she is a monstrous creature who has shed her humanity. J. S. Mill said of women that 'no other class of dependents have their characters so entirely distorted from its natural proportions by their relations with their masters' (238). Thus distortion is essential to her representation.

For Rochester an intemperate nature renders Bertha unchaste, no better than a professed harlot, and a slave by nature. For him she is 'a woman by nature most gross, impure and depraved' (334). As a creature of giant propensities and pigmy intellect, she is the opposite of Jane. As a woman who is violent, unprincipled and possessed of a mindless will, she represents the inclinations of all who reject reason in favour of passion. Rochester holds Bertha responsible for his downfall. His wife represents a filthy burden he must bear, and a curse upon his life. He argues that hideous and degrading agonies must attend a man bound to such a wife. For him Bertha's conjugal embrace is tantamount to a homicidal assault. Under these circumstances he claims that he is free, but his reasoned defence of his right to marry a woman who will revitalise him involves an abuse of right reason which should lead him to God. The fact that he is bound to

Bertha is dramatised when he tries to rescue her from the consequences of her own violence as Thornfield burns.

Like Jane we can see Bertha as 'a creature masked in an ordinary woman's shape' (240), who, beneath the Gothic trappings that surround her, is a woman whose energy and vitality are deemed evil. But she also represents Jane's feminist tendencies writ large, since anger and outrage at the injustices meted out to her have blossomed into open rebellion. A tendency to question makes her a mocking demon and, without an outlet for her feelings, she turns to violence. In addition, she represents the plight of the wife imprisoned within the home, silenced, and forced to live a half-life, half-death, like a ghost of herself. She anticipates the view that a wife is no different from a whore insofar as marriage may be regarded as licensed prostitution, since any woman can be bought and sold on the marriage market to become the sexual slave of her possessor. Thus while Bertha is superficially abhorrent, the excessive terms in which she is portrayed mask the fact that she is a prototypical feminist protester.

She functions to warn Jane of the consequences of allowing her passion for Rochester to overcome her principles, and sets Jane on the contrary path to spiritual salvation. Such violent passion as must erupt in fire and flood inexorably leads to a violent death in which Bertha is consumed by her own fires, preparatory to her spiritual death, when as St John Rivers puts it, 'the unbelieving shall have their part in the lake which burneth fire and brimstone, which is the second death' (442). Moral insanity is ascribed to the inability to control the lower emotions, and Bertha's madness is evidence of moral madness as a medically recognised condition exemplified by a patient who demonstrates intense malevolence without ground or provocation, whose condition could lead to criminal activity and to perversions of natural inclination. Often hereditary, it might break out in insane acts which were exaggerations of propensities before the outbreak of madness itself.

Though death is Bertha's punishment for the excesses of a disobedient and violent will, it functions as a sacrifice to purge Rochester's house of the stain of sexual sin. A ritual purification of Rochester's house prepares Jane to enter marriage as a sacred institution in which the blood of generation is no longer defiled. Jane thus remains true to Miss Temple's teaching since she has kept her body as a temple in reserve for marriage as a religious way of life.

Brontë draws on imagery that connects intense sexual passion with violence and death. Rochester views Jane as a Sleeping Beauty who has yet to be violently awoken by her prince because an awakening of her sleeping soul is associated with excessive erotic pleasure or with sin. He warns Jane that she

> *will come some day to a craggy pass in the channel, where the*
> *whole of life's stream will be broken up into whirl and tumult,*
> *foam and noise; either you will be dashed to atoms on crag*
> *points, or lifted up and borne on by some master-wave into a*
> *calmer current – as I am now.' (173)*

Since love has been degrading for Rochester, 'to live ... is [for him] to stand on a crater-crust which may crack and spew fire any day' (245). Yet he hopes for an experience of elevating love with Jane, though his own passionate excess must destroy such a possibility.

Rochester courts Jane while ostensibly engaged to Blanche in order to provoke a confession of her love by inspiring her jealousy. Her awakening to love is as Rochester divines, since he succeeds in making her feel 'as if I had been wandering amongst volcanic looking hills and had suddenly found the ground quiver, and seen it gape' (217). When she discovers his attempt to marry her bigamously she is so overwhelmed by the tide of passion which threatens to destroy her that she loses consciousness for the second time. Although Jane tries to deny her physical presence when she speaks to Rochester face to face as two souls equal before God, she remains a creature with a physical life vulnerable to a cultural heritage that encourages the dichotomy between the idealised mother and the degenerate whore. Somehow she must choose gender roles without succumbing to either of these gender constructs.

It is not until Freud that we have a concept of childhood sexuality. Yet Brontë reveals Jane's potential similarity to Bertha in childhood when she is castigated as a little demon, a fury, a madcat, and a precocious actress. Mrs Reed sees her as a compound of virulent passions, mean spirit and dangerous duplicity, but she is unaware that her own children are liars and hypocrites. Because we know Jane is not guilty of being John Reed's aggressor, she appears to be punished because of her sex, since any passionate female is evil. Her imprisonment for her violent outburst against Mrs Reed foreshadows Bertha's imprisonment by her husband for intemperate behaviour. Being branded as bad and mad when she knows she is innocent alienates Jane from herself so that her image in the mirror seems to belong to someone else. This strange little figure gazing at her, with a white face and glittering eyes of fear, is a ghostly presence split off from the heated emotions of her rebellious body. If Jane is to conform to the social ideal of spirituality she must subdue the anger and outrage that belong to her physical being.

The episode in the red-room is highly symbolic. The room is dominated by a chair which resembles a stately throne and overlooks a bed like a tabernacle, a trope for the female body with its hidden niche sacred to procreation. The room is awesome because it is a memorial to the dead, but it is doubly fearful because it speaks of the secrets of sex and sin in their relation to death. There is a link between Mrs Reed's jewel case and secret drawers (symbolic of her private parts) and the representation of her marriage bed as a deathbed. The room speaks of patriarchal rule and evokes Jane's fears of the coming of a herald from another world because she supposes he will be a father of retribution, not her saviour. As yet she has no perspective on her suffering and is overcome by her fear that God wills her death in punishment for her wickedness. She therefore falls prey to a species of fit which causes her to lose consciousness. Thus, although she is later able to make a complaint to the apothecary who helps her to move from Gateshead to Lowood, she speaks initially through her suffering body like an hysterical woman.

When she arrives at Thornfield Hall upon her maturity Jane is overtly threatened by her own sexuality. The house is a fitting emblem for the body, with its upper and lower rooms, its backstairs and passages which resemble the doors in the Bluebeard story that tells how wives are murdered for disobeying their husbands' orders and for being too curious. Jane's pursuit of the secret at the heart of Thornfield turns out to reveal her potential identification with the imprisoned madwoman who indicates what Jane would become if she were to let her principles go. Yet Brontë is an heir of the Romantic movement, and she endows Jane with an intensity of feeling that feeds her imagination and provides her with visionary powers. Jane is nevertheless caught up in a conflict between regulating her language to notions of a refined propriety and resorting to language so intense that it could transform imagination into madness. The conflict between passion and propriety is carried over into the problems she faces with her two suitors. Either she gains erotic pleasure and loses her soul, or she gains service to a spiritual ideal that denies her mental and emotional being. No clear choice between passion and propriety is possible since both positions are taken to excess by her lovers who thus threaten to destroy her.

When Jane explains to Rochester why she loves Thornfield she implies that live burial, ignorance, and stasis constitute the real conditions of women's lives:

'... I love Thornfield: I love it, because I have lived a full and delightful life, momentarily at least. I have not been trampled on. I have not been petrified. I have not been buried with inferior minds and excluded from every glimpse of communion with what is bright and energetic and high. I have talked face to face with what I reverence, with what I delight in – with an original, a vigorous, an expanded mind. I have known you, Mr Rochester'. (281)

Jane assumes that Rochester's life is more expansive and stirring than her own, but the narrative itself makes clear that it is Jane's story which matters. Thus, though Brontë intervenes in the narrative to endow Jane with the means of marrying within her own class – money and family connections – she nevertheless allows Jane choice over her destiny. She does not become a slave to either man and she resists conforming to the stereotypes of woman that each holds in his mind. Jane can choose to become a wife and a mother in conditions where she can establish her identity positively by entering marriage on equal terms and thus claim the rewards of love and service. The exorcism of Bertha functions to contain and tame Jane's rebellious desires so that she might enter marriage by proving her moral worth and by proving her ability to support herself through work in the world. She therefore enters marriage on the basis of mutuality and equality in the expectation of fulfilment in fellowship with her own kind. Ferndean offers a safe haven where the wanderer can stay her 'weary little wandering feet on a friend's threshold' (273) according to Rochester's original promise.

St John Rivers is the representative of the socially prescribed norm for men, for whom the standard of propriety lay in purity and sexual continence. Incontinence was regarded as a kind of spending, wasting, and improvidence. By contrast, Rochester represents the incontinent man, who has experienced sex outside of marriage, and who seeks reform through a relationship with a pure woman who will revitalise him emotionally and spiritually. Though Rochester wishes to be saved from the consequences of lust, he must repent and humble himself before God, instead of expecting Jane to renew his spiritual life. St John Rivers is ambitious of the martyr's crown and marriage is for him merely a means to an end. He seeks Jane as a helpmeet and requires her subservience to him through her desire to serve God. Such a marriage is a repetition of Eve's relationship to Adam: he for God and she for God and him. He would be her mediator and she would be the instrument of his will, and since he could justly command her obedience, she could only be compliant to his wishes. Despite the priority given to Christian principle, St John Rivers's violent will cannot be distinguished from the excesses of Rochester's passion, and Jane's life would be similarly put at risk if she were to succumb to the torrent of his will.

The language of *Jane Eyre* draws on the European religious and philosophical tradition which sees the body as sinful, and seeks to transcend physical desire in the form of an ethereal love, exhibited primarily in the form of brotherly love or Christian charity. In consequence love becomes polarised into erotic and benevolent love with the result that concepts of love and sex remain disconnected from each other. Women, taught to distrust passion, were prompted to seek friendship in higher forms of love in marriage to men taught to practice continence in marriage, yet free to seek sexual gratification outside of marriage. As Cominos has shown, the conflict of conscience which led to this division promoted a double standard of purity and continence in marriage and a system of prostitution outside of it. Though the prostitute was an example of the supreme type of vice and bore the burden of men's sexual sins, she functioned in effect as the safeguard of the virtuous wife in the same way as Bertha's licentiousness serves to promote Jane's marriage. Thus prostitution can be seen as an integral part of the marriage system, and Jane's wedding could not take place without the prior existence of Bertha though she is a legitimate wife.

The concept of sexual purity, respectability, family, and inherited wealth go together in *Jane Eyre* and mirror a society in which the industrious, thrifty and sober individual earns a high reputation in the economic field and in moral terms. As a modest woman Jane develops a love of home and domestic duties along with her capacity to work hard in a happy domestic environment with her cousins. But the contrast between the Moor House and Thornfield episodes indicate that the sexual purity enforced on women of a respectable class served to perpetuate the opposition between ethereal and sexual love. Jane can only marry Rochester upon his reform. He must be taught to subdue his passionate nature and to develop the power to postpone the gratification of desire for a future good. It is stated in the Bible that it is better to pluck out one's right eye or cut off one's right hand in preference to committing adultery. Jane would follow this dictate herself were it necessary, but it is Rochester's sin that requires reform. Therefore in the fire in which Thornfield is burned down one of Rochester's eyes is injured and one hand is smashed, requiring amputation.

Though St John Rivers offers Jane a Christian marriage, he is so consumed by spiritual ambition that he denies the existence of human love. He seeks spiritual transcendence, while she remains mired in immanence. However, he speaks impersonally, claiming to be God's representative on earth. Thus Jane momentarily feels the power of God's voice speaking through his apostle, but she also sees that St John Rivers is only a man and, as a Protestant heroine, she must seek direct access to God without mediation. By contrast, St John's version of Christianity is Calvanistic since he relies on the concepts of election, predestination and reprobation – concepts which could exclude Jane from attaining spiritual grace. Furthermore, he would commit her to a life without human love though she is prepared to endure a life of poverty, obscurity and service. To live without love is unthinkable to Jane. Brontë nevertheless awards St John Rivers the spiritual crown in recognition of a heart undivided and unclouded by human emotion. Thus the single-mindedness of his ambition makes it evident that women's achievement is obstructed by their divided aims. Jane must choose between two vocations that are mutually exclusive in her time: work and marriage.

In fact, St John Rivers's spiritual rewards are won at the cost of what makes him human, since he has struggled with his desire to become a poet and a priest. And though he is a man of blameless habits, zealous in ministerial labours, who preaches contentment with one's individual lot, he is far from content himself. For he must renounce worldly fame and renown to seek a spiritual goal. And to achieve this he must renounce what he holds most dear – his love of Rosamond and his hopes for a literary career. He thus represents literary fame as an aim no woman writer can appropriately seek. The suppression of the desire for fame in respect of artistic endeavour must reflect Brontë's view about her own artistic ambitions as a woman writer, debarred from a world in which creativity is the preserve of men. In the context of his repressed worldly ambitions, he mirrors negatively what Jane seeks – knowledge of the world, contact with her fellows, and the achievement of personal authority through her development as an artist, teacher, and visionary soul. Their hidden comparison suggests why Jane appears to relinquish her quest for a vocation and to remain content with her achievements on a personal level as a wife and mistress of a household.

Initially, Rochester's attitude to women is traditional. They are angels or devils to be revered or distrusted. However, he learns to see Jane as a person in her own right, to take responsibility for himself instead of blaming others, and he is redeemed through an act of pure moral courage when he tries to save Bertha's life though he has nothing to gain by it. He undertakes Adele's care though he denies he is her father, and his love for Jane leads him to accept God's lawful rule. Thus his sins are expiated, his vision is partially restored, and his life becomes centred. His redemption serves to enhance his humanity, evident from the first because of his association with life enhancing qualities: with light brought to a darkened house, with the sound of water flowing, with all the movement, life and energy Jane originally lacked. However now he is not a god-like idol who would reduce her to dependency. He is a sympathetic listener prepared to allow her time and space in which to develop.

To comprehend the significance of Jane's achievement we only need to compare her with the conventional woman defined by class, status, and family: Blanche Ingram. Although a beauty, Blanche has no opinions of her own, imitates and repeats phrases from books, and is totally without tenderness, sympathy or pity. By contrast Jane is an original character with powers of mind, penetration, and intelligence combined with intensity of feeling. She is no man's inferior. Rather it is she who sets the standard of what it means to be fully human. But she is the heir of a cultural tradition in which as a woman she must confront the image of woman in order to establish her identity. She therefore discards the roles given to women of doll, slave, child and monkey, in order to become her own mistress.

The courtesy title prefixed to the Christian or surname of an unmarried woman is a title of respect applied to a teacher. For Jane to assert that 'I am my own mistress' (459) is to convey the idea that she is her own woman. A mistress in this sense is not an illicit wife. She is a woman who rules and controls, a woman who employs others in her service, a woman who has authority over others, and who has the power of control over property and possessions at her disposal. She is a woman in possession of herself. In recognising this we need also to acknowledge that it is possible for a woman writer to speak with authority in such a way as to advance the cause of women by promoting a better understanding of what women feel without being accused – as Jane is accused by St John Rivers – of using words which are violent, feminine, and untrue and which 'merit severe reproof' because they 'betray an unfortunate state of mind' (438).

Notes

1. Letter to W.S. Williams, Haworth, 4 Jan. 1848. Quoted in *Jane Eyre*.
   Ed. Richard J. Dunn. New York: W.W. Norton, 1987, 421.

Works Cited

Brontë, Charlotte. *Jane Eyre*. 1847. London: Penguin, 1966.

Cominos, Peter T. 'Late-Victorian Sexual Respectability and the Social System'. *International Review of Social History* 33 (1968): 238–240.

DeLamotte, Eugenia C. *Perils of the Night: A Feminist Study of Nineteenth Century Gothic*. Oxford: Oxford UP, 1990.

Mill, J.S. *The Subjection of Women*. London: Dent Everyman's Library, 1970.

Moers, Ellen. 'Female Gothic'. *Literary Women*. London: The Women's Press, 1978, 90–112.

Wollstonecraft, Mary. *The Rights of Woman*. [1792]. New York: Norton, 1975.

Further Reading

Adams, Marianne. '*Jane Eyre*: Woman's Estate' in *The Authority of Experience*. Eds. Arlyne Diamond and L.R. Edwards. Amherst: Massachusetts UP, 1977: 137–159.

Boumelha, Penny. *Charlotte Brontë*. London: Harvester Wheatsheaf, 1990: 58–77.

Gilbert, Sandra M. and Susan Gubar. *The Madwoman in the Attic*. New Haven: Yale UP, 1979: 336–371.

Grudin, Peter. 'Jane and the other Mrs Rochester: Excess and Restraint in *Jane Eyre*'. *Novel* 10 (1977): 145–157.

Kucich, John. 'Passionate Reserve and Reserved Passion in the works of Charlotte Brontë'. *ELH* 52 (1985): 913–937.

Rowe, Karen. '"Fairy-born and human-bred": Jane Eyre's Education in Romance' in *The Voyage In*. Ed. Elizabeth Abel. Hanover: University Press of New England, 1983: 69–89.

Elizabeth Jolley's The Well *and the Female Gothic*

Amanda Nettelbeck

Elizabeth Jolley's *The Well* is a novel that invites reading on several levels: it is about forms of and fears about sexuality, about the potential of repression and obsession, about exile and isolation: all recurring themes, of course, of Gothic fiction. Stylistically, too, *The Well* slips readily into a Gothic mode, pushing constantly as it does at the borders of realism. Although its isolated rural setting enhances its Gothic potential, *The Well* most visibly draws upon Gothic allusions in its exploration of the sinister aspects of everyday life. According to M.H. Abrams's *Glossary of Literary Terms*, the Gothic mode opens up to fiction 'the perverse impulses and the nightmarish terrors that lie beneath the orderly surface of the civilised mind', and, by extension, 'often deals with aberrant psychological states' (72).

Feminist critics have elaborated on the significance of this mode in women's writing, extending an understanding of the Gothic to include the anxieties of closure and, perhaps, repression that underlie women's everyday domestic lives. Emily Brontë's *Wuthering Heights* (1847) and Charlotte Perkins Gilman's *The Yellow Wallpaper* (1892) might be taken as particular examples of this genre of the 'female Gothic' (Fleenor). In this sense, we can regard the Gothic form as extending beyond a concern with 'aberrant psychological states' to a concern with unsettling the knowable, given social order of things, a concern with the disturbing underside of conventional domestic tranquillity. As John O'Brien writes of Jolley's novel: '[*The*

Well] is rich with images of rustic domesticity. The idyllic surface, however, betrays a complexity that deserves detailed consideration' (O'Brien in Bird and Walker 131).

The Gothic mode has another dimension in the Australian context, in which the landscape has been historically imagined as alien to a European aesthetic, and particularly alienating for women. This was, after all, not only an austere and forbidding landscape in the imagination of new colonial arrivals, lacking the contained, cultivated quality of England's rural landscapes, but was also construed in particularly masculine terms. It was a land which had to be tamed, conquered and possessed: in short, it was 'no place for a nervous lady' (Frost). In *The Well*, the traces of such colonial anxieties about the Australian landscape echo in the novel's setting, which, although beloved by Hester, is nonetheless isolated and claustrophobic. Jolley no doubt deliberately exploits the Gothic potential of such a setting, which is not innocuous and inanimate, but rather functions as an almost-animate presence in the text.

The well itself, of course, is the most potent feature of the landscape brought to life by what it keeps hidden from view. The atmosphere of brooding anxiety that infects the novel is based in the mystery of what the well contains. A creature never defined, 'it' might be a man or a fairy-tale invention: a troll, a beast, a prince charming, depending upon what Hester and Katherine choose to imagine. Both a prison and a source of potential liberation, the well is the site of fears and desires. The mystery of the well is the premise of various narrative styles enlisted by Jolley in this unsettling and playful text. Not only a narrative of Gothic horror, it is also a novel of psychological exploration, a fairy-tale, a mystery thriller. It is a 'dark and disturbing parable', the flyleaf tells us: 'a detective novel without a detective, a thriller without a conclusion'.

How, then, are we to read this strange, multi-faceted text? The central question of what lies in the well drives the narrative forward, yet of course it is a question without an answer. Because this is not a realist novel, in the sense of mimicking the real world, an answer to that question is not even important. Of importance here is not what 'really' lies in the well (if anything) but rather the possibilities that the well contains, possibilities that give rise to the characters' fears and desires, and that undermine the seeming tranquillity of domestic life in the cottage. Even before the crucial accident on the dark road, the well is associated for Hester and Katherine with pleasures to be had, and fears to forget. Above all, it is, from the very beginning, associated with mystery:

> *The well had become for Hester and Katherine a place where they*
> *liked to sit sunning themselves. On bright hot days, where they*
> *could see a little way into it, the inside of the well seemed cool*
> *and dark and tranquil. Mysterious draughts of cold air seemed to*
> *come from somewhere deep down in the earth. If they bent their*
> *heads close to the unclosed part of the cover they thought that,*
> *even though the well was dry, they could hear from its depths the*
> *slow drip drop of water ... Sometimes they threw small stones*
> *into the well and though they sometimes hit the sides of the shaft*
> *they never heard them reach the bottom.*
>
> *To amuse themselves they pretended that someone lived in*
> *the well. A troll with horrible anti-social habits had his home in*
> *the depths. They invented too an imprisoned princess, the*
> *possession and plaything of the troll. She was later changed to a*
> *prince as Katherine felt it would be more exciting and 'more*
> *trewly romantic Miss Harper dear', if a prince on a white horse*
> *came out from the well one fine day. (31–32)*

Here are some of the different versions of the well's contents:
Katherine's dreams of romance lead her to imagine the well's 'treasure' as a prince, whom she wants to release. Yet a man is exactly
what Hester wants to keep within the well. Partly this might be
because a man would figure as an intruder into her life with
Katherine. Partly, too, a man might figure as a reminder of the illicit
and frightening aspect of sexuality that she glimpsed, as a child,
when she witnessed her governess's (self-procured?) miscarriage
during the night. For Hester, the image of the beast is closely associated with the image of man. 'For that which befalleth the sons of
men', she recites to Katherine from Ecclesiastes chapter eight, 'befalleth beasts ... yea, they have all one breath; so that a man hath no
preeminence above a beast ... Who knoweth the spirit of man that
goeth upward, and the spirit of the beast that goeth downward to the
earth?' Like Dr Jekyll in Robert Louis Stevenson's classic Gothic tale,
Hester is both fascinated and horrified by the animal impulses she
imagines lying just beneath the 'civilised' surface of humanness.

Underlying the contentment and peace of Katherine's and
Hester's life in the cottage, then, are two quite different but equally
crippled visions of domesticity. Katherine's is a sanitised one based
on Hollywood movies and Walt Disney fairy-tales, in which a woman
can be swept off her feet by a prince charming and live happily ever
after. Hester's is a vision that assumes femininity to be innocent of sin
and masculinity to be sexually predatory. The existence of a sexual

economy between men and women is, in Hester's history, best forgotten or ignored. Its associations are bound together in the image of
her governess Hilde Herzfeld bleeding in the night, the brute strength
of the farmer Mr Borden, the sight of the animals in the paddocks:

> *Not all that for Katherine. None of it for Kathy. How could she,
> Hester, Miss Harper dear, have ever considered it. How could she
> have suggested to Kathy that she make herself pretty and go down
> for what was cowshed and corner-of-the-paddock business. The
> mating of cattle for stock was all right for the beasts and for some
> people but it was not for Kathy. Not for her dainty innocence.*
>> *She did not want to bring this man out of the well. She had a
> very good reason for putting him there in the first place. (150)*

The catch here is that Kathy's 'dainty innocence' is an idealisation
rather than a reality. Despite the childish frocks Hester chooses for
her, Katherine is a young woman on the threshold of adulthood who
is, the reader guesses, schooled in the ways of the world well before
her arrival on Hester's farm.

At this point it is worth considering the way in which Jolley treats
time in the novel. The story seems timeless, in the same way that
fairy-tales and myths seem to stand outside of history. This sense of
timelessness contributes to the novel's Gothic quality, suggesting
as it does a vague setting beyond any specific temporal and social
scheme. There is also a sinister dimension to this quality of timelessness, since Hester introduces an unnatural stasis into her life
with Katherine, hoping to prevent Katherine's development and, she
fears, desertion. Yet the story does have a specific history and can be
placed in time. (Think, for instance, of Kathy's references to American
popular culture; she is a fan of John Travolta in *Grease*.) Despite the
impression on the farm that time stands still – an impression Hester
encourages through the repetition of domestic routines and the rejection of change – time *is* passing; towards the end of the novel, it is
something of a shock to realise that Kathy, still dressed by Hester in
frocks with Peter Pan collars, is twenty two years old.

This is a world, then, that can be read in two ways. On one level
there is, in the community of *The Well*, a common-sense ordinariness.
This is a world occupied by characters such as the Borden family, the
storekeeper Mrs Grossman, the neighbour Mr Bird: characters who,
though somewhat eccentric, live out an everyday social existence.
On another level there is a more disturbing side to this familiar existence. This is the world that is drawn out by the Gothic narrative: a

world which seems to stand outside of time and history, one based upon mystery, manipulation and constraint. Indeed, manipulation and constraint lie at the very core of Hester and Katherine's homelife of seeming domestic contentment. On the one hand, we witness an all-embracing domesticity that is quite hedonistic in the pleasures it yields to Hester and Katherine: they wash and brush each other's hair, tend the garden, cook wonderful meals. If they don't feel like washing the dishes, they simply throw them down the well. Yet underpinning the cottage life of pampering and care is unacknowledged oppression. Each watches and manipulates the other in the hope of bringing about her own desires; Hester's primary wish to 'protect' Kathy from the outside world, we quickly come to realise, is manifested as a form of suffocation, reflecting her own emotional crippledom. Kathy's pampering of Hester, too, spills into the realm of manipulation and control. At the heart of the often silent struggle between them is the well and its hidden treasure.

Although the mystery of what the well contains is without a solution, the potential it holds structures the plot of the novel as well as the relationship between Hester and Katherine. Just as the world of *The Well* can be read in an ordinary or an extraordinary light, so it is possible to regard the 'thing' inside the well in both realist and Gothic terms. In one, literal sense, that thing might be the body of an ordinary thief, accidentally killed by Miss Hester's truck on the dark road outside the town. After all, there has been gossip in the small town of a thief in the neighbourhood, and Miss Hester's money has gone missing. It may also be the body of Joanna, whose visit to the cottage is expected, and who does in fact figure in Hester's mind as a form of thief, one who will steal away Katherine, her most precious possession. In Hester's mind Joanna also represents that unwanted and corrupted world of the outside – the world which Katherine, before her arrival at the farm, has already inhabited – which threatens Hester's ideal of Katherine's 'innocence': 'Hester was vague in her mind about the life this other girl could have had, but it was dirty and infected and should be kept away from the freshness and purity of their own lives' (45). It is significant that later, in Hester's mind, the image of Joanna becomes entangled with the image of a man in the well; both are figures of intrusion who could threaten Hester's relationship with Katherine and displace Hester's own importance:

> *Hester thought of the new pretty curtains and the bed coverlet*
> *prepared for the other unwanted guest ... Perhaps the three of*
> *them – Joanna and the man and Kathy – would want to live in the*

house. 'Miss Harper dear,' she could hear the purring voice, 'we
have found the darlingest rest-home for yew – in town – yes we'll
be able to visit you, Miss Harper dear … (152)

We know that Katherine is speaking of Joanna's visit just before
Hester notices something on the road (80); has Joanna arrived early,
to become a victim of Hester's truck?

This kind of literal reading, however, is difficult to sustain
throughout the novel as the story moves further away from realist
into internalised, psychological territory. A clue to the less realist and
more symbolic potential of the well's contents might lie with the
novel's opening paragraph, which is not actually part of the story
itself but serves as a narrative frame:

'What have you brought me Hester? What have you brought me
from the shop?'
  'I've brought Katherine, Father,' Miss Harper said.
'I've brought Katherine, but she's for me.'

The register of this conversation shifts us away from expectations of
realism, and gives the reader an indication, before the novel even
begins, of the symbolic importance of Katherine's arrival to the
Harper household. The deviations from realism that pervade the
novel from this very first page enable a reading of the thing in the
well – a thing about which the two women are collusive in identifying as a man – as not real but imagined; in other words, as a manifestation of Hester's fears (of sexual 'corruption'), of Katherine's
desires (of a life of romance, in which she would be adored and
'saved' by a man), and of the struggle between them to control the
other according to each's own wishes. The story of a man in the
well allows Katherine to elaborate upon her desires, expressing them
in 'conversations' with him; yet for Hester, the 'arrival' of a man in the
well means that the painful memories on which her fears are
founded, long hidden or deliberately forgotten, now threaten to rise
to the surface:

the well water gurgled and splashed slapping as it was forced
upwards from below. She could imagine the holes in the rocks far
down through which the water was making its way, trickling
slowly in places and then gushing to fill caverns. As more water
flowed underground and the small openings and channels became
blocked with earth and stones, more water would be forced

upwards in the wide shaft of the well ... Perhaps it would
surface ... on the desolate edges of the salt lakes, those ugly
places, unvisited, somewhere further on, far off and lower down
beyond the end of the track. Places where Hester had never
wanted to go. (151)

In fact, in a scene which is perhaps the novel's most explicitly Gothic
moment, the well will eventually yield to Hester its nightmarish contents. Like the moment in Mary Shelley's novel in which
Frankenstein's monster is 'born', this moment mingles the imagery of
birth with that of horror and death:

As her torch flashed again to the water making curious rings and
rippling patterns of light on the black surface, she was sure she
saw a hand grasping the lowest metal rung ... She thought as the
water slapped crazily against the stonework that she saw too a
man's head which, because of being drenched, was small, sleek
and rounded ... Peering, she waited for some sign. To her horror
the water seemed to be rising even more. Soon, she thought, it
would cover the next rung and then the next ... Trembling and
fearful at the thought of what was now so close to the edge of the
coping, she raised her stick and tried to lean into the hole ... Not
able to reach she struck wildly and without effect with the stick.
He must go down.
   'Down!' she said in a voice which she did not know was her
own. 'Go down!' (148–149)

Clues to Hester's sense of horror are given in bits and pieces through
the narrative. Initially, as a girl under Hilde Herzfeld's tutelage, Hester
had cherished romantic dreams not unlike Katherine's, but in which
domestic romance was chaste, untouched by the physical dimension
of sexuality and childbirth. The 'Hope Chests' filled with her embroidered household linens and the daily rituals of washing were the
outward signs of such dreams, which were encouraged and elaborated by Hilde Herzfeld:

She had in her room chests packed with household linen
embroidered during the years with Miss Herzfeld. Laughingly in
drawn-thread work and with generous smooth stitching, white
upon white, the two of them had initialled sheets, table cloths,
table napkins, little linen towels and pillow slips with an
elaborate monograph designed from a double aitch: Hilde

*Herzfeld and Hester Harper ... Miss Herzfeld, making her way
into the youthful Hester's heart, taught her to wash her neck every
day with cold water so that it would be beautiful to receive, when
the time came, the necklaces and pendants and jewels some man
would want to cherish her with. Both of them had washed their
necks religiously even on the coldest mornings with the coldest
water. (54)*

Yet the pure and idealised vision of romance that Hester develops
under the teaching of Miss Herzfeld is destroyed when she is made
aware of Miss Herzfeld's 'illicit' affair with Hester's father and wit-
nesses its outcome: a miscarriage during a night, which figures for
Hester as a scene of pain, fear and blood. The child Hester is compelled to collude in the household's treatment of the affair as a
shameful secret when Miss Herzfeld is whisked away the following
day in a conspiracy of silence.

The self-imposed absence of a sensual life for Hester before
Katherine's arrival becomes part of the novel's comic dimension.
Trying to convince Hester to sell her land to Mr Borden, the neighbouring farmer, Mr Bird tells her: "'remember, your stubble's thin ...
Your slopes," Mr Bird seemed ruthless. "Your slopes", he repeated,
"don't seem to conserve moisture as they once did"' (55). But
Katherine's arrival brings back into Hester's life a desire for sensual
pleasures, which are realised in their dancing and cooking, their
making of clothes in the softest of wools and the finest of silks. The
possibilities of indulgence and romance that she cherished in her
youth are again real for Hester, but with Katherine, rather than with
a male suitor, as their focus:

*During the night Hester, sitting in the moonlit window while
Katherine brushed her hair gently, forgave Mr Bird his insult about
her stubble. Never, she thought, while the hairbrush steadily
pressed the long sweeps of her strong hair downwards, had her
paddocks looked so beautiful. (56)*

In this sense, Hester emerges as a character whose life until
Kathy's arrival has been blunted by the forces of social taboos and,
we are led to understand, the restricting hand of a powerful patriarch. Yet in other ways she is a much more ambiguous figure than
this. She has the appearances of both power and powerlessness, in
different ways. A woman of property, having inherited her father's
wealth, she is given a form of respect in the small rural community

that is usually the privilege of men. However, although capable of running her own farm, she often gives the *appearance* of being helpless or vulnerable in the face of men, particularly Mr Borden, whom she despises but whose physical potency is comically rendered in the powerful thighs with which he leaps over fences and the throbbing tractor on which he surveys his land. She is made vulnerable, too, by her lack of status as an unmarried woman, a woman living alone in a community whose respectability is monitored according to women's activities as wives and mothers.

Yet the constraints that mark Hester's behaviour may in fact mark out her control over events; for example, when she chooses which version of the story to give the Borden children, she 'draws her lips together in one of her half smiles, the smallest smile a person can give' (175); when she requests Mr Borden to cover over the well (and its contents), she 'gave a small wave, the smallest wave one person can give to another' (153). Is the vulnerability Hester displays in the 'smallness' of her gestures a sign of her lack of power, or does it rather disguise her power? We already know that she is capable of great determination and even cruelty: when a crowing rooster disturbs her, Hester wrings its neck (50); when a lonely young wife visits with her baby, Hester dismisses her (29); when she thinks the starving child from the third world whom she supports is old enough to earn his own keep, she severs his funds. Hester, then, is perfectly capable of manipulating events to suit herself. But what of Katherine's own powers to control? From Hester, Katherine has much to gain. Who is manipulating whom? Clearly, the well gives to each woman a purpose that she has to protect from the other: for Katherine the something in the well represents a promise, whose rise to the surface would realise her dreams of romance and escape; for Hester it is a threat, which must be kept from surfacing if her ideal world is to be sustained.

Here it is important to recognise the significance of storytelling in the novel, because storytelling is the means by which Katherine and Hester assert their desired realities, as well as the means by which they form their relationship to one another. Remember that Hester tells Katherine stories of her past in ways that enable her to repress unwanted memories: the tales she tells of her childhood with Hilde Herzfeld exclude feelings of pain and instead are 'happy little stories ... [told] as if bestowing charming little gifts, with nods and smiles and certain embellishments till there was an ever increasing merging of fact and desired fiction' (121). Similarly Katherine's anecdotes about her past are shaded, told not for their truth value but for their effect. Other forms of storytelling surround the well. Even before it is filled with the 'body' of the intruder, the well is the focus of the stories they tell to one another of trolls and princes, the characters from fairy-tales who, they imagine, might dwell there. Later, Katherine regards her conversations with a longed-for man in the well as part of a larger movie plot, in which she stars as the heroine and he is the hero. Later again, Hester retells the events surrounding the well as a horror story to amuse the Borden children. Each woman, then, has different tales to tell of the well's significance. In this sense the novel is not just about the power of the well itself but also about the power of interpretation. Who, ultimately, controls the story of the well? In order to answer this question one must look not at what might 'really' lie in the well (since that is impossible to say) but at the *stories* of what lies in the well.

During the course of the novel, there is more than one version of the accident leading to the dumping of the thing in the well. One version is told in the novel's first chapter (5–6), a version which is repeated slightly differently later (80–81); another is about to be told in the novel's last pages, in the story Hester invents for the Borden children (175–176). These two parts of the novel – the very first and the very last chapters – are the only parts of the novel narrated in the present tense; everything in between is narrated in the past tense. What effect does this have on the chronology of the story, on our sense of its order: how can we tell where the story begins and where it ends? It may be, for instance, that the story Hester is about to invent for the Borden children in the last chapter is actually the starting point for the rest of the narrative. Is, then, the whole story an invention by Hester? Or, alternately, is Hester's telling of the story to the Borden children (a story that will unfold out of the reader's sight after the final sentence) a way of gaining control over events that have occurred without her will, a way of making her version dominant? Does she hope, perhaps, to regain control over Katherine by determining the story of the well to suit herself? She is, after all, a person capable of manipulation: 'Hester draws her lips together in one of her half smiles, the smallest smile a person can give' (175).

On the other hand, perhaps Hester's telling of the story works at the novel's end not as a form of control over the events but as a means of release from them. In turning the events into a simple horror story for the Borden children ('Miss Harper, real scarey! Make it real scarey!' [175]) might she and Katherine be freed from the past to begin life afresh? If we choose to follow this second line of argument, we might regard the well not just as the source of Hester's darkest fears and memories but as the source of her freedom, as the means by which she can come to grips with the long-hidden past. There is also another way of reading this multi-threaded tale: remember that Hester speaks to a woman in Grossman's store who is writing a story about an intruder who comes to an isolated farming community. Is the story of *The Well* the very story by the woman in Grossman's store?

In the end, of course, the novel itself withholds any kind of certainty about how it might be read. It is a novel whose narrative is deliberately entangled. Not only is it composed of a series of stories within other stories, but it also stitches together several variations of genres (Gothic horror, black comedy, psychological thriller, fairytale parable). We are left not with a sense of closure but with a series of tantalising and not-quite-knowable possibilities. This, too, is what makes *The Well* so characteristic of the Gothic mode: the reader is not allowed easy resolutions, only the awareness that some things are beyond reasonable understanding.

Works Cited

Abrams, M.H.*Glossary of Literary Terms*. Fourth Ed. New York: CBS Publishing, 1981.

Brontë, Emily. *Wuthering Heights*. 1847; rpt.Oxford: Oxford UP, 1976.

Fleenor, Juliann. Ed. *The Female Gothic*. Montreal: Eden Press, 1983.

Frost, Lucy, ed. *No Place for a Nervous Lady: Voices from the Australian Bush*. Melbourne: McPhee Gribble, 1984.

Jolley, Elizabeth. *The Well*. Ringwood: Penguin, 1987.

O'Brien, John. 'Myths of Domesticity in the Novels of Elizabeth Jolley' in *Elizabeth Jolley: New Critical Essays*. Eds. Delys Bird and Brenda Walker. North Ryde, NSW: Angus and Robertson, 1991.

Perkins Gilman, Charlotte. *The Yellow Wallpaper*. 1892; rpt. London: Virago, 1985.

Further Reading

Bird, Delys and Brenda Walker, eds. *Elizabeth Jolley: New Critical Essays*. North Ryde, NSW: Angus and Robertson, 1991.

Gelder, Ken and Paul Salzman. *The New Diversity: Australian Fiction 1970–1988*. Melbourne: McPhee Gribble, 1989.

Interview with Elizabeth Jolley in Candida Baker, *Yacker: Australian Writers Talk About Their Work*. Sydney: Pan, 1986: 210–233.

Jolley, Elizabeth. 'Cloisters of Memory'. *Meanjin* 3 (1989): 531–539.

What it Means to be a Man: Reading the Masculine

Philip Butterss

The idea of masculinity – what it means to be a man – is currently undergoing considerable change. Over the last few decades Australia has seen the widespread movement of women into the workplace and, to a lesser extent, into positions of power; it has also seen the increasing public prominence of gay men, indigenous men and men from non-English speaking backgrounds. Such changes have resulted in substantial renegotiations of men's roles and redefinitions of what is permissible behaviour for men. Adolescent males today are confronted with a complex mixture of conflicting messages about what adult masculinity means, while older men are often undergoing major readjustments in their attitudes and their domestic and public activities. The changes have also resulted in an understanding that the idea of masculinity as a single, 'natural' or 'true' entity does not fit the world as we know it. There are clearly differences between men arising from many factors including class, race, and age, so that it is probably better to talk about the existence of a variety of 'masculinities' rather than a single 'masculinity'.

Certainly there is some evidence to suggest that biological differences between men and women can influence behaviour but, as the redefinitions just mentioned indicate, much of what it means to be a man is culturally determined. In spite of the current popularity of books like Anne Moir and David Jessel's *Brain Sex*, there is good evidence to question conclusions that over-emphasise biological factors at the expense of cultural factors (Segal xv-xvii). Indeed some commentators would argue that the former are of little consequence. For example, Don Edgar suggests that the current research on gender difference can find 'virtually no differences between men and women on any psychological trait, mental ability, physical capacity or attitude at all. The differences between individual men and individual women (within-group differences) are greater than any differences between the two groups' (29).

In a period of profound change, it is not surprising that the study of masculinity is an area currently receiving a deal of attention in the humanities and social sciences. Some feminists have wondered whether this is going to allow male academics and students to revert to what they have traditionally done – talked and written about themselves to the exclusion of women; for example, the study of masculinity might really be an excuse to return to History as the history of great men, or English as the study of great male writers. Much of the academic work on masculinity, however, has complemented feminist research. In the first place, there has often been a focus on gender relations, so that the study of masculinity has involved the critical analysis of the distribution of power between men and women, and the ways in which particular masculinities have been, and still are, implicated in the distribution of power. Secondly, much contemporary work on masculinity has had an eye towards the possibility of change. An important consequence of seeing masculinity not as pre-determined by biology but as culturally constructed is that it opens up new options, freeing men to behave outside the bounds of what in the past has been regarded as the 'truly masculine'. It thus allows the chance to develop non-hierarchical masculinities – masculinities that are not predicated on dominance over women, or dominance over other masculinities.

In the same way that much feminist literary analysis has involved examining what a text states explicitly about women, what it implies about women, and what gaps or silences it might contain in relation to women, reading for masculinity can look for statements, implications and silences about masculinity. Bob Connell has identified four main relations among masculinities in the current Western gender order, and these can form useful categories for examining the way that masculinities are represented within cultural texts. His relational categories are hegemony, subordination, complicity and marginalisation.

Connell derives the term 'hegemonic masculinity' from Antonio

Gramsci's work on class relations. For Gramsci, hegemony is achieved when ideas that support a group or class's dominance permeate the whole culture, making its position appear natural and legitimate. Connell adapts the term for use in the area of gender relations, so that 'hegemonic masculinity' is the kind of masculinity which suggests that men deserve their position in the system of patriarchy – dominant masculinity that suggests men are naturally powerful, and deserve to hold power (77).

Within the overall framework of a patriarchal society there are also, as Connell points out, 'specific gender relations of dominance and subordination *between* groups of men'. He suggests that in contemporary Western cultures 'the most important example' of this power differential between different groups is 'the dominance of heterosexual men and the subordination of homosexual men' (78). While gay men may be the most obvious example of 'subordinated masculinity', Connell points out that 'some heterosexual men and boys ... are expelled from the circle of legitimacy', and he lists a range of derogatory terms used to describe those males, the most printable of which are 'wimp', 'sissy', and 'mother's boy' (79).

Connell notes that most men do not 'rigorously practis[e] the hegemonic pattern in its entirety'. But he suggests that in spite of this, 'the majority of men gain from its hegemony, since they benefit from the patriarchal dividend, the advantage men in general gain from the overall subordination of women' (79). Such men, then, are complicit with the operation of hegemonic masculinity, even if they do not consistently embody it.

The fourth relation among masculinities outlined by Connell is that of 'marginalisation'. He uses the term to take account of 'the interplay of gender with other structures such as class and race' (80). Some men are marginalised through their class position and/or through their race or ethnicity. Marginalised masculinities can have a certain power in particular contexts, for example the gang violence of working class youths, often directed at other men. Certainly men marginalised through class position or race can still exercise power in relation to many women (83). But the masculinities of those in marginalised classes or ethnic groups are usually outside the mainstream of power.

Given the importance of cultural factors in the construction of masculinity, one would expect that the specifics of what constitutes different masculinities would vary substantially over time and between cultures, and a survey of historical or anthropological research bears out that expectation. However, one might also expect certain similarities in the relations between masculinities in cultures that shared some features. For example, two cultures that were patriarchal and homophobic might both be expected to have relations of hegemony and subordination, although the specific forms that those relations took might be very different in each case.

In the limited space available here, it is probably most useful to give some suggestions about the directions that readings might take if a number of specific literary texts – *Things Fall Apart*, *The Tempest*, *Heart of Darkness* and *An Imaginary Life* – were to be examined for what they say about being a man. Although all tell different narratives about masculinity, one factor that links them is their concern with the processes of colonisation, and it has often been noted that imperialism, itself, has had some significant influences on contemporary models of masculinity.

In *Masculinities*, Connell points to the importance of the creation of global empires in the construction of masculinity as we know it, arguing that 'the men who applied force at the colonial frontier ... were perhaps the first group to become defined as a masculine cultural type in the modern sense' (187). Secondly, he suggests that as religious legitimations for men's dominant position in Western culture have declined, there has been a rise in the importance of exemplary masculinities – high profile individual examples of masculinity as can be found in 'the pulp Western, the thriller, the sports broadcast ... and the Hollywood movie' (214). Exemplars of masculinity, whether legendary or real, have often been men of the frontier – Davy Crockett and John Wayne in North America, for instance. In Australia, of course, the bush has been particularly prominent as a source for models of masculinity that privilege male power.

One of the ways in which *The Tempest* has been read in the latter part of the twentieth century is as a play about the complex interactions of colonisation, as Stephen Orgel demonstrates (Shakespeare 23–28). Certainly it would be easy to argue that, at times, the play contains representations of the masculinity associated with the colonial frontier – for example, Prospero's harsh treatment of Caliban. More generally, *The Tempest* could be read as a tale concerning the proper performance of masculinity. In the history we are able to reconstruct from the play's events, Prospero has lost his kingdom to his brother, in part, through not conforming to the practices of hegemonic masculinity. By focusing on his books, and failing to exercise the power and authority vested in his position, he moved outside that type of masculinity. Although the play does not approve of

Antonio's actions, it is probably true that he policed the culture's norms, removing this unacceptable model of a ruler from the kingdom.

On the island Prospero starts afresh, returning to a form of masculinity that Connell would label hegemonic. In his shifting roles he sometimes behaves according to the accepted bounds of dominant models of masculinity, and sometimes exceeds them, so that he can be seen, as he has been in recent years, as 'a noble ruler and mage, a tyrant and megalomaniac . . . a colonial imperialist, a civiliser' (Orgel in Shakespeare 11). For much of the play Prospero operates as an exemplar of hegemonic masculinity, but the play is also wary of his excesses, and in the end he promises that he will become a more stable exponent of hegemonic masculinity, disposing of his staff – that signifier of excessive masculinity – and returning to the mainland to take up his rightful position as ruler. Caliban, too, could easily be fitted into Connell's categories, as an example of marginalised masculinity – powerful in some contexts, but outside the mainstream of power. In terms of Connell's categories, Caliban is a version of masculinity marginalised through race or class position.

Heart of Darkness is also a text that explores the nature of imperialism, and one that can be read as being, to some extent, 'about' masculinity. The novel opens with Marlowe sitting on a boat on the Thames, preparing to tell a story, and making reference to a vast horde of tales of men in the service of empire:

> *The tidal current runs to and fro in its unceasing service, crowded with memories of men and ships it had borne to the rest of home or to the battles of the sea. It had known and served all the men of whom the nation is proud, from Sir Francis Drake to Sir John Franklin, knights all, titled and untitled – the great knights-errant of the sea. It had borne all the ships whose names are like jewels flashing in the night of time, from the* Golden Hind *returning with her round flanks full of treasure, to be visited by the Queen's Highness and thus pass out of the gigantic tale, to the* Erebus *and* Terror, *bound on other conquests – and never returned. It had known the ships and the men. They had sailed from Deptford, from Greenwich, from Erith – the adventurers and the settlers; king's ships and the ships of men on 'Change; captains, admirals, the dark 'interlopers' of the Eastern trade, and the commissioned 'generals' of East India fleets. Hunters for gold or pursuers of fame, they all had gone out on that stream, bearing the sword, and often the torch, messengers of the might within the land, bearers of a*

spark from the sacred fire. What greatness had not floated on the
ebb of that river into the mystery of an unknown earth! ... The
dreams of men, the seed of commonwealths, the germs of
empires. (29)

But instead of being a celebration of heroic deeds of frontier masculinity, the text operates largely as a critique of the operation of
empires, and of the different forms of masculinity that were necessary to uphold them. The reader is provided with damning portraits
of both those who exert brutal force at the frontier, and those who
exercise power more sedately in the administration of the empire.
Heart of Darkness can be read as having a dialogic relationship to the
ripping yarns that were being produced during the same period by
Rudyard Kipling and others, and it offers another perspective on
those tales of the nobility of empire. Kurtz is, in many ways, the
antithesis of the heroic image of frontier masculinity.

David Buchbinder has identified two somewhat paradoxical features
of masculinity under patriarchy, features that are prominent in our
own culture, in Chinua Achebe's *Things Fall Apart*, and also in *The
Tempest*. Buchbinder argues that in patriarchal societies men are
encouraged to compete with one another, while at the same time also
carefully supervising one another (*Masculinities* 35). He goes on to
point out that 'the individual man feels that he is constantly being
watched by other men and that any slips or falterings in the patterns
of behaviour broadly labelled "masculine" are noted' (36).
Buchbinder observes that as a response to these feelings of surveillance, some men in contemporary western culture

will strive for a hypermasculinity, that is, an excessive
masculinity, whether signified by a huge, muscular body, an
impressive sexual scorecard (which may not bear any relation to
reality – here, as in other aspects of masculine behaviour, it is the
reputation which is important, not the actuality), a powerful car or
a high-flying job. (36)

Although it depicts a profoundly different culture from our own,
Things Fall Apart signals its interest in the competitiveness of masculinity from the outset, opening with a description of Okonkwo's
prowess as a wrestler, defeating a great opponent who had not been
beaten for seven years. The book makes it clear that hegemonic
masculinity for Ibo culture has prowess in tests of physical strength

as an important component, and we learn immediately that Okonkwo excels in this area. Also relevant is providing food for one's family, but yams are particularly important in themselves as signifiers of hegemonic masculinity. 'Yam stood for manliness' (23), we are told. When he has eventually demonstrated his capacity to produce this food source, Okonkwo is living out the kind of masculinity that, within the terms of Ibo culture, suggests that men deserve their position of power.

Alongside the competitiveness associated both with physical prowess and the production of yams is a strong sense that masculinity is under surveillance. In *Things Fall Apart* Okwonko's father occupies a position of subordinated masculinity – poor, lazy, a debtor, barely able to provide enough food for his family and 'a coward' who 'could not stand the sight of blood' (5). As a young boy Okonkwo experiences the surveillance of others, and he comes to internalise the values of the culture, policing his own masculinity, and deliberately defining himself against his father. His greatest fear was that he might be seen to resemble his father. Indeed his

> *whole life was dominated by fear, the fear of failure and*
> *weakness ... Even as a little boy he had resented his father's*
> *failure and weakness, and even now he still remembered how*
> *he had suffered when a playmate told him that his father was*
> agbala. *That was how Okonkwo first came to know that* agbala
> *was not only another name for a woman, it could also mean*
> *a man who had taken no title. And so Okonkwo was ruled*
> *by one passion – to hate everything that his father Unoka had*
> *loved. One of those things was gentleness and another was*
> *idleness. (9–10)*

Okwonkwo's response to Ibo culture's surveillance of masculinity is, in Buchbinder's words, 'to strive for a hypermasculinity'. The fact that he was 'ruled by one passion' indicates the excessive nature of his quest for a particular form of masculinity, and the novel is sprinkled with instances of his excesses – incidents such as beating a wife during the week of peace, and killing Ikemefuna for fear of being thought weak. In exile he undergoes a kind of rehabilitation in which his mother's family attempts to teach him the value, and the power, of the traits regarded by Ibo culture as feminine. But it seems that Okonkwo is not able to shift to a less excessive, and therefore less socially destructive version of masculinity, and this inability is evidenced by his rejection of his son, Nwoye, whom Okwonkwo feels has abandoned Ibo ways to 'go about with a lot of effeminate men clucking like old hens' (108).

Okonkwo's final killing of the messenger is portrayed as an excessively violent act: one which the rest of the Ibo do not support. Certainly the novel is saying that Okonkwo's masculinity is too extreme, but it is also asking questions about the dominant version of masculinity in the culture as a whole. Christianity is able to gain a foothold in Ibo society precisely because of its ability to fulfil a nurturing role, alien to that culture. According to *Things Fall Apart* the dominant masculinity associated with Christianity has a certain strength – both Mr Brown and Reverend Smith are 'firm' in their dealings with the Ibo – but Christianity is also able to care for twins, outcasts and the 'worthless or empty men'. In the new colonial society which disrupts the traditional Ibo lifestyle, the exertion of physical force is compartmentalised – delegated to specific representatives of the State – so that the Christians like Mr Brown and Reverend Smith are able to occupy positions of power, without themselves resorting to physical coercion.

Although David Malouf's *An Imaginary Life* is set about 2000 years ago, it can be read as a fictional examination of several issues that are relevant to contemporary masculinity. Perhaps the most important underpinning of hegemonic masculinity in recent Western cultures has been the way that physical power and rationality have both been coded as masculine. Connell identifies a tension within contemporary hegemonic masculinity that may have its ultimate roots in these two supposedly gendered features. He suggests that 'historically there has been an important division between forms of masculinity organised around direct domination (e.g., corporate management, military command) and forms organised around technical knowledge (e.g., professions, science)' (165). *An Imaginary Life* examines and rejects two cultures whose dominant masculinities give different prominences to rationality and physical power, before going on to propose its own utopian model of masculinity.

The form of dominant masculinity identified in Roman society closely parallels the form of language used in Rome. In Ovid's words, Latin is 'a language for distinctions, every ending defines and divides' (98). Its complex grammatical inflexions that mark the different declensions, conjugations, moods and tenses make it the perfect language for expressing abstractions. Latin is the language of reason, and the Augustan age privileges a form of masculinity at whose centre is rationality, order, clarity, definition, and distinction. Ovid comes to realise, however, that Latin is a language of alienation, a force that alienates the self from the natural world. Malouf's interest in such features of Roman culture is also an interest in a form of hegemonic masculinity that claims to embody the power of reason.

Ovid finds that Getic, the language he gradually learns during the course of the novel, is better able to represent 'the raw life and unity of things' (65). The scene at the burial ground where Ovid imitates the old man's bloodcurdling cry is a rite of passage for him, allowing him to enter a new masculinity, and a new language. Ovid is not taught to speak words, at this point, but he learns to make sounds that belong to the culture of Tomis. His shout is at once a signifier of a new, more aggressive masculinity than the one he had exhibited in Rome, and it is his first attempt at communication from within Getic culture. Getic may represent 'the unity of things', but the masculinity of the Getae is also predicated, at least to some extent, on a struggle to survive against the forces of nature.

Ivor Indyk has suggested in his book on Malouf that Ovid and the Child set off into the wild in the final section of *An Imaginary Life* in 'heroic masculine terms' (16). It is true that the pair leave Tomis to face a harsh landscape with no food and meagre clothing, and Ovid's words as they set out into that landscape are drawn, in part, from tales of heroic adventure, or perhaps from explorer narratives:

> I am going out now into the unknown, the real unknown,
> compared with which Tomis was but a degenerate outpost of
> Rome ... What else should our lives be but a continual series of
> beginnings, of painful settings out into the unknown, pushing off
> from the edges of consciousness into the mystery of what we have
> not yet become, except in dreams that blow in from out there
> bearing the fragrance of islands we have not yet sighted in our
> waking hours, as in voyaging sometimes the first blossoming
> branches of our next landfall come bumping against the keel,
> even in the dark, whole days before the real land rises to meet us.
> (135–136)

However, the journey into the landscape in this final section is far from an expression of heroic, frontier masculinity. In fact Ovid and the Child are setting out to try to make peace with the landscape, and to become one with it. This is no heroic journey where men pit themselves against the natural world and attempt to defeat its obstacles. It is a mission to produce a different kind of masculinity, a masculinity that is not marked by reason, or by physical strength and opposition to the natural world. Ovid is trying to become one with the natural world, and to collapse the divide between reason and nature.

Although what constitutes masculinity has often been regarded as 'common sense' and 'natural', it can be seen from even a cursory examination of a handful of literary texts that masculinity should not be seen as a fixed and obvious category. Literature, film and television are sites where ideas concerning masculinity are constantly examined – if not always explicitly – and they are fruitful places to examine how societal tensions over the meanings attached to 'the masculine' are played out. *The Tempest* works, ultimately, to uphold the dominant values relating to masculinity in the culture that produced and consumed the play. In *Things Fall Apart*, Chinua Achebe looks back at his ancestors, criticising some aspects of what were dominant ideas about being a man in Ibo culture. *Heart of Darkness* is also critical of an important exemplar of masculinity, providing another aspect to the ripping yarns about heroes at the imperial frontier. And *An Imaginary Life* looks at a society that privileges rationality and a society that privileges physical strength, before turning its back on both of them, and proposing a utopian way of being in the world – a masculinity not concerned with direct domination or with technical knowledge, but with living peacefully and in harmony with the world. Reading for masculinity opens up cultural texts to interpretations such as these and, in doing so, underlines the fragility of hegemonic masculinity in our own culture, making it evident that change is not only possible – it is already under way.

Works Cited

Achebe, Chinua. *Things Fall Apart*. London: Heinemann, 1962.

Buchbinder, David. *Masculinities and Identities*. Carlton, Vic: Melbourne UP, 1994.

Connell, R.W. *Masculinities*. St Leonards, NSW: Allen and Unwin, 1995.

Conrad, Joseph. *Heart of Darkness*. Harmondsworth: Penguin, 1985.

Edgar, Don. *Men, Mateship, Marriage: Exploring Macho Myths and the Way Forward*. Pymble, NSW: Harper Collins, 1997.

Indyk, Ivor. *David Malouf*. Melbourne: Oxford UP, 1993.

Malouf, David. *An Imaginary Life*. Woollahra, NSW: Picador, 1980.

Moir, Anne and David Jessel. *Brainsex: The Real Difference between Men and Women*. London: Mandarin, 1991.

Segal, Lynne. *Slow Motion: Changing Men, Changing Masculinities*. London: Virago, 1997.

Shakespeare, William. *The Tempest*. Ed. Stephen Orgel. Oxford and New York: Oxford UP, 1987.

Further Reading

Buchbinder, David. *Performance Anxieties: Re-producing masculinity*. St Leonards, NSW: Allen and Unwin, 1998.

Kaufman, Michael, ed. *Beyond Patriarchy: Essays by Men on Pleasure, Power, and Change*. Toronto and New York: Oxford UP, 1987.

Morton, Tom. *Altered Mates: The Man Question*. St Leonards, NSW: Allen and Unwin, 1997.

Nettelbeck, Amanda. *Reading David Malouf*. Sydney: Sydney UP, 1995.

Re-Writings

Interpretation and Intertextuality: Conrad's Heart of Darkness *and Charlotte Jay's* Beat Not the Bones

Marc Vickers

[F]or any reader a text functions within a maze of other texts, some closely related, some more distantly so, but all of which bear on its reading. There is no transcendental law that draws a line between the class of genuinely relevant texts and the inappropriate ones (although, of course, there have been plenty of attempts to fashion one). Texts exist within a cluttered landscape, so to speak, and it is our contingent view of the landscape, as much as the text, that determines how it looks . . . (Ian Saunders)

Joseph Conrad's turn-of-the-century novel, *Heart of Darkness*, has influenced a wide variety of twentieth-century works of fiction. The nature and extent of this influence is as varied as the works influenced are diverse. T.S. Eliot, for example, originally planned for the epigraph to his poem *The Waste Land* (1922), a well-known landmark of modernism, to be the passage from *Heart of Darkness* that concludes with Kurtz's words, 'the horror, the horror!' And Eliot's later poem, *The Hollow Men* (1925), takes as its epigraph the memorable announcement of Kurtz's demise in *Heart of Darkness*: 'Mistah Kurtz–he dead'. Eliot's choice of epigraphs reflects the fact that both poems clearly echo the modernist theme that is presented so dramatically in *Heart of Darkness*: the theme of the hollowness of Western civilisation.

In other works the influence of *Heart of Darkness* is particularly pervasive. Francis Ford Coppola's film *Apocalypse Now* (1979) shares with Conrad's novel the view of civilisation as a thin veneer: Western man, removed from the restraining gaze of society, quickly reverts to a barbarous state. *Apocalypse Now*, like *Heart of Darkness*, uses as a structuring motif a journey up a river (the main character's journey of self-discovery). Smaller incidents and other characters familiar from Conrad's novel also appear in the film. From one perspective, then, *Apocalypse Now* re-writes *Heart of Darkness*, shifting the narrative in time and space from the Congo in the 1860s to Vietnam in the 1960s and 70s.

The influence of *Heart of Darkness* on other works, such as Chinua Achebe's *Things Fall Apart* (1958), discussed in the following essay by Dianne Schwerdt, and Charlotte Jay's *Beat Not the Bones* (1952), discussed towards the end of this essay, is less obvious. But what is it about Conrad's text that invites re-writing or writing back? *Heart of Darkness* demands the active participation of its readers in the construction of its meaning: in one sense, all readers of Conrad's novel are forced, in their minds at least, to write, or re-write, the novel. While it can be argued that all texts do this to some degree, there are certain features of *Heart of Darkness* that demand more participation than usual in the construction of meaning.

Heart of Darkness is a difficult and complex novel. Part of its complexity arises from the number of ways it can be read. In some respects the work is a traditional nineteenth-century adventure tale, like those of Rudyard Kipling, or Rider Haggard, the author of *King Solomon's Mines* (1885). These traditional nineteenth-century adventure tales see a European main character, or protagonist, set out into the unknown, often into 'darkest Africa', in search of someone or something (usually wealth). Read like this, *Heart of Darkness* is the story of Marlow's journey from Europe into the unknown heart of 'the dark continent' where he must battle against natives and rescue the European Kurtz who, contaminated by Africa's unfathomable mysteriousness, has gone mad. (By simply replacing Europe with America and Africa with Asia, this crude summary of *Heart of Darkness* serves equally well as the basic plot outline of *Apocalypse Now*.)

In another way, *Heart of Darkness* presents Marlow's psychological journey of self-discovery. Read like this, *Heart of Darkness* can be seen as a long prose poem similar to *A Season in Hell* (1873) by the French Symbolist poet Arthur Rimbaud. Kurtz is the mad, creative genius within the writer that Marlow, as the more rational part of the writer's psyche, must control, and whose discoveries he must turn into a readable report. Marlow, we are told, struggles with Kurtz's soul, before returning to tell his tale 'in the pose of a meditating Buddha' (162), implying perhaps that he has reached some sort of spiritual enlightenment somewhere along his journey. As the title of the novel suggests, this enlightenment may well be a particularly dark one.

Reading *Heart of Darkness* as a prose poem of self-discovery complements reading it as oblique autobiography. Conrad, like Marlow, 'did once turn fresh-water sailor for a bit' (51) and through his aunt secured a position as the captain of a river steamer in the Belgian Congo. Like Marlow, Conrad was nearly killed by the experience but returned the wiser, reportedly telling a friend that before he went to the Congo he 'was a mere animal' (Jean-Aubry 175).

While *Heart of Darkness* can be read as the discovery of self-knowledge, it is clear that Marlow learns about more than just himself and Kurtz. He also learns about the horrors of colonialism. From the pointless shelling of the African continent by the French warship, to the grove of death where African slaves, mistreated by Europeans, retire to die, the impression we get of colonialism is unflattering. Marlow's discovery is not merely personal, therefore, but political as well. Conrad himself discovered the horrors of colonialism when he went to the Congo. In his *Last Essays* he describes Belgian colonialism as 'the vilest scramble for loot that ever disfigured the history of human conscience' (17). *Heart of Darkness*, then, can be read as a critique of colonialism and Western 'civilisation'.

Reading *Heart of Darkness* as a political critique of Western colonialism does not exclude reading it simultaneously as an adventure tale and as a journey of self-discovery. Much of the novel's complexity, it can be argued, arises from Conrad's skilful interweaving of these themes. Colonialism and civilisation are shown to be based on lies that mask European greed and African suffering. Kurtz abandons civilisation and its hypocritical moral codes and turns to his own soul for guidance. However, as Marlow discovers, this is no better, and the reader is left to decide which is the lesser of the two evils: the self or civilisation. Conrad's views in letters written at the same time as his novel demonstrate how intertwined his views on man and civilisation are:

Man is a vicious animal. His viciousness must be organised.
Crime is a necessary condition of organised existence.
Society is fundamentally criminal – or it would not exist.
(Collected Letters Vol. 2, 160)

Kurtz chooses to abandon the restraint of a criminal society, giving in to his viciousness, his 'various lusts' (131), 'monstrous passions' (144), 'sombre pride' and 'ruthless power' (149). Marlow appears to choose to keep working within this criminal society's rules – despite seeing his fellow workers as 'sordid buccaneers', and describing their mission as one designed 'to tear treasure out of the bowels of the land ... with no more moral purpose at the back of it than there is in burglars breaking into a safe' (87).

While the reader shares Marlow's discovery of the complexity of the problem, he or she is not forced to share Marlow's response to it. This is due, in part at least, to what the anonymous listener on the *Nellie* calls the 'inconclusive' nature of Marlow's tales. This inconclusiveness forces readers to draw their own conclusions and participate in the construction of the text's meaning. While not as difficult to read as James Joyce's *Ulysses* (1922), for example, Conrad's novel exhibits the modernist tendency to match the style of the telling with the tale itself. It is hardly surprising then, that in a tale that deals with Marlow's bewilderment and his moral and spiritual disorientation, the prose style should, in places, confuse and bewilder the reader. This feature of Conrad's writing manifests itself most obviously in what the critic F.R. Leavis terms Conrad's 'adjectival insistence upon inexpressible and incomprehensible mystery' (173–183). Often in *Heart of Darkness*, where we think we are being given description, we are in fact receiving the opposite, with adjectives such as 'unearthly', 'impenetrable', 'unspeakable', 'inscrutable' and the like. Such adjectives, as Leavis notes, 'muffle rather than magnify' meaning (177). *Heart of Darkness,* according to Leavis, demands that the reader construct meaning from phrases such as, 'it was the stillness of an implacable force brooding over an inscrutable intention' (177). Leavis both protests against the reader being forced to share Marlow's incomprehension and sense of bewilderment and sees the demand that the reader share Marlow's struggle to construct meaning as a weakness of *Heart of Darkness*. In my view this is a poor criticism to make of a novel that often dramatises the processes by which we make sense of the incomprehensible.

Many of the incidents Marlow recounts were strange and incomprehensible to him when they happened and have only shown their meaning, or become understood by Marlow, with time. Looking closely at *Heart of Darkness* we find that Conrad often uses a narrative technique that the critic Ian Watt has termed 'delayed decoding' to dramatise Marlow's gradual comprehension of the meaning of an episode (174–179). On board the river steamer, for example, when they are attacked and his helmsman is killed by a spear, Marlow's description of the episode demonstrates his only gradual comprehension of what has happened:

> *Something big appeared in the air before the shutter, the rifle went overboard, and the man stepped back swiftly, looked at me over his shoulder in an extraordinary, profound, familiar manner, and fell upon my feet. The side of his head hit the wheel twice, and the end of what appeared a long cane clattered round and knocked over a little camp-stool. It looked as though after wrenching that thing from somebody ashore he had lost his balance in the effort. The thin smoke had blown away, we were clear of the snag, and looking ahead I could see that in another hundred yards or so I would be free to sheer off, away from the bank; but my feet felt so warm and wet that I had to look down. The man had rolled on his back and stared straight up at me; both his hands clutched that cane. It was the shaft of a spear. (111–112)*

Along with Marlow, the reader only understands a few moments later that Marlow's feet are warm and wet because his shoes are filling with his helmsman's blood. This 'delayed decoding' contributes to the drama of comprehension that we get in *Heart of Darkness*. As readers we come to see and, in a sense, are forced to participate in, the processes by which Marlow makes sense of, or finds meaning in, the unknown of Africa, the horror of colonialism and the enigma of Kurtz. But we also see Marlow try to communicate the meaning thus discovered to others. For Marlow's narrative is framed by the story of his telling his tale to the listeners on the boat. Strictly speaking, the novel is not set on a boat in Africa but on a boat on the River Thames in England. *Heart of Darkness* can thus be read as the story of Marlow's telling of his tale. Certainly, the problem of communicating the meaning of what happened to him in Africa appears to concern Marlow a great deal over the course of his narration. In fact, he interrupts his tale proper a few times to ask his listeners on the boat: 'Do you see the story? Do you see anything?' complaining on one occasion:

No, it is impossible; it is impossible to convey the life sensation of any given epoch of one's existence – that which makes its truth, its meaning – its subtle and penetrating essence. It is impossible. We live, as we dream – alone ... (82)

Marlow continually stresses the importance of telling the truth. As we have seen, however, the nature of the truth in *Heart of Darkness* is often unclear to Marlow and sometimes only emerges with time. As Marlow says to his audience on the boat, 'of course, in this you fellows see more than I could then. You see me, whom you know' (83). Certainly, the narrator who introduces us to the scene on the small boat does appear to know Marlow well, as he makes a very important point about his tales:

The yarns of seamen have a direct simplicity, the whole meaning of which lies within the shell of a cracked nut. But Marlow was not typical (if his propensity to spin yarns be excepted), and to him the meaning of an episode was not inside like a kernel but outside, enveloping the tale which brought it out only as a glow brings out a haze, in the likeness of one of these misty halos that sometimes are made visible by the spectral illumination of moonshine. (48)

This complex metaphor can be taken to mean a number of things. The above passage suggests that the meaning of *Heart of Darkness* lies in the remarks made by Marlow and the narrator who intro- duces us to him before Marlow begins his tale proper. The meaning is not inside the tale like a kernel in a nut, but rather envelops the tale. This suggests that the comments made by Marlow and the narrator who introduces us to the scene of Marlow's telling of his adventure on the *Nellie* are of particular importance. For while Marlow tells a tale about a journey into the heart of Africa, the framing commentary suggests that the darkness is in Britain itself. Marlow, for example, speaking of the Thames and London, prefaces his tale by saying: 'And this also ... has been one of the dark places of the earth' (48). After Marlow has told his tale, at the very end of the novel, the frame narrator notes that:

The offing was barred by a black bank of clouds, and the tranquil waterway leading to the uttermost ends of the earth flowed sombre under an overcast sky – seemed to lead into the heart of an immense darkness. (162)

This suggests that *Heart of Darkness* is about the West and not Africa, as Marlow's tale itself might imply. At the very least, the reader of *Heart of Darkness* is being asked to make connections between England and Africa.

Another productive interpretation of the complex metaphor of the 'kernel' passage above suggests that the ultimate meaning of Marlow's tale lies not purely with Marlow but with his listeners on the boat. And if the meaning of Marlow's tale lies with his listeners, then the meaning of *Heart of Darkness* can likewise be seen to reside with its readers. According to Conrad, 'a work of art is seldom limited to one exclusive meaning and not necessarily tending towards a definite conclusion'. He suggests that the reason for this lies in part with the role of the reader in constructing meaning:

> *I have given all the truth that is in me; and all the critics may say can make my honesty neither more nor less. But as to final effect my conscience has nothing to do with that. It is the critics' affair.* (Conrad in Jean-Aubry, 275)

These, then, are the features of *Heart of Darkness* that demand the active participation of its readers in the construction of its meaning. Its generic ambiguity, its adjectival insistence on unknowability, its modernist prose style that bewilders, its delayed decoding and its narrative framing all contribute to the work the reader must do to convert this text into a readable report. This suggests that the novel invites re-writing. More than that, though, there are features of this novel that demand writing back to, not just re-writing.

From a feminist perspective, the feature of *Heart of Darkness* that stands out most starkly and demands writing back to is that of Marlow's attitude towards women. Firstly, there is Marlow's claim that women have nothing to do with his tale. In the middle of the narrative, Marlow accidentally mentions Kurtz's fiancée ('the girl') back in Europe, and consequently has to explain himself to his audience:

> *Oh, she is out of it – completely. They – the women I mean – are out of it – should be out of it. We must help them stay in that beautiful world of their own, lest ours gets worse.* (115)

While Marlow sees women as having nothing to do with his tale, readers of *Heart of Darkness* might disagree. Firstly, Marlow secures his job in Africa through his aunt. As Marlow puts it so indelicately, the men in his family fail to find him a job: 'Then – would you believe it? – I tried the women. I, Charlie Marlow, set the women to work – to get a job' (53). On being offered a job, Marlow presents himself to his employers in 'the city that always makes [him] think of a whited sepulchre' (55). At the company's offices in this sepulchral city (a city that can readily be identified as Brussels since that is where the colonial administration of the Congo River was based in Conrad's time), Marlow is met first by two women dressed in black and knitting black wool. Marlow describes these women later as seeming 'uncanny and fateful' as if they were 'guarding the door of Darkness' (57). This suggests that women for Marlow, at some level at least, *are* important. If the whole story is about the heart of darkness then what guards the entrance to this 'horror' should be important. Within the adventure tale itself, Kurtz's African mistress also appears to be an important figure. She is described as 'a wild and gorgeous appari- tion of a woman' (135), as 'savage, wild-eyed and magnificent' and as walking with 'measured steps', 'proud', 'stately and deliberate' (135–136). Finally, it is the concluding episode in which Marlow meets Kurtz's 'Intended' in the sepulchral city, Brussels, that highlights the importance of women in *Heart of Darkness* and proves that Marlow's claim that 'they are out of it' is wrong.

The final episode suggests why Marlow might insist that women are 'out of it' and how he keeps them out. It also illustrates what it is about Marlow's attitude towards women that demands writing back to. Early in the tale Marlow makes much of trying to convey the truth and tells his listeners how much he hates a lie: 'You know I hate, detest, and can't bear a lie, not because I am straighter than the rest of us, but simply because it appals me' (82). Yet, in the final interview with Kurtz's 'Intended' Marlow lies to her about Kurtz's last words 'the horror, the horror', telling her instead that Kurtz's last word was her name (161). As Marlow puts it, he lays 'the ghost of [Kurtz's] gifts at last with a lie' (115), claiming that the truth 'would have been too dark – too dark altogether' (162) for women.

This has led critics such as Nina Pelikan Straus to complain that:

> 'Truth' in Heart of Darkness *is directed at and intended for men only ... Marlow speaks ... to other men, and although he speaks about* women, there is no indication that women might be included among his hearers, nor that his existence depends upon his 'hanging together' with a 'humanity' that includes the second sex. (124)

Straus's criticism of the novel draws our attention to the fact that Marlow is telling his tale to a group of men on board the *Nellie*. While the listener on the *Nellie* who tells us about Marlow and his tale (the frame narrator) makes no such assertion, it is worth noting that *Heart of Darkness* was first published in serial form in *Blackwood's Magazine*, a publication that was read mainly by men. So it can be argued that as Marlow's tale is for men's ears only, Conrad's novel was, in its initial serial form at least, directed mainly to men.

Before we condemn Conrad along with Marlow for his sexist views it must be pointed out that Conrad's letters indicate that he recognised the importance of the final scene and the lie to the Intended. In a letter to his publisher he argues that

> *in the light of the final incident, the whole story in all its descriptive detail shall fall into place – acquire its value and its significance. This is my method . . . I call on your own kind self to witness . . . the last pages of* Heart of Darkness *where the interview of the man and the girl locks in – as it were – the whole 30,000 words of narrative description into one suggestive view of a whole phase of life and makes of that story something quite on another plane than an anecdote of a man who went mad in the Centre of Africa. (*Collected Letters *Vol. 2, 417)*

This suggests that we must read *Heart of Darkness* carefully for Conrad's ironic treatment of Marlow. It is clear from the letter above that we should not simply take Marlow's views on women for Conrad's. The irony in Marlow's statement that 'the girl is out of it' is that for Conrad, she is clearly *not* out of it. Despite Marlow's attempts to exclude them, women appear throughout the tale, and in particular in very important parts of the story – at the beginning, and at the end.

Whatever Conrad's views about women are, Marlow's are a problem and they need answering back to. While the reader has witnessed and in a way been involved in constructing the tale's meaning, he or she may not agree with the version Marlow tells. Arguably, a strength (and possibly also a weakness) of *Heart of Darkness* is that the reader is unsure just how much Marlow's voice is Conrad's and therefore who needs to be addressed in any writing back to the novel.

Beat Not the Bones both re-writes and writes back to *Heart of Darkness*. This novel is set, for the most part, in Papua New Guinea in the late forties or early fifties. Papua at that time was an Australian colony, and as such was considered the last frontier of Western cultural contact. Starting out from Sydney, Stella, the heroine of the story, sets off to find out the truth about her husband Warwick, a Kurtz-like figure who has died working in Papua New Guinea. She goes on a Marlovian journey, starting from the cosmopolitan centre, in this case Australia, to the Europeanised outpost on the coast of Papua New Guinea (Marapai in the book, Port Moresby in real life) and then finally up a river into the heart of the jungle. Here she confronts horror in the form of, 'murder, murder' (65) – words echoing Kurtz's last utterance to Marlow: 'the horror, the horror' (149). Like *Heart of Darkness*, Jay's book can be read as an adventure tale set in the exotic unknown in which the 'European' protagonist discovers a terrible truth.

Likewise, the book can be read as a journey of self-discovery for its protagonist. In *Beat Not the Bones* Stella starts out as a very naive young woman. We are told that when she hears of her husband's death, she is barely out of the convent where she has been educated and that 'She had had no time or opportunity to formulate notions of wickedness' (40). However, in her search for the truth Stella learns a great deal about evil and lies. Also, like Marlow, she finds it necessary to lie herself. Moreover, over the course of Jay's tale Stella develops a much more sophisticated understanding of people. Compare her first view of Trevor Nyall with her last words on him. At their first meeting his superficial kindness fills her eyes with tears, and we are told that 'She was happy. She had found a friend. He would look after her, tell her what to do and how to do it', and she 'fixed on him the wide, dependent, childlike gaze that had so endeared her to her father and her husband' (61). By the end of the book, however, she sees him quite differently: 'He's a monster ... He doesn't know what it's like out there. He didn't even see his own victims. He spills blood by remote control' (213).

Like *Heart of Darkness* Jay's book has an autobiographical element to it. Just as Conrad spent some time in Africa working for a Belgian company, Charlotte Jay, or Geraldine Halls to give the author her real name, spent some time in Papua New Guinea working for the Australian administration there.

Jay's book re-writes the attitudes towards colonialism that we see in *Heart of Darkness*. *Beat Not the Bones* paints a damning picture of Australia's colonial behaviour in Papua New Guinea. The reality of colonialism there is just as horrible as that in *Heart of Darkness*. Both works depict whites exploiting and killing native people out of greed for material wealth. Both Stella and Marlow, however, offer a defence of the idea behind colonialism. In *Heart of Darkness* Marlow says of colonialism that 'it is not a pretty thing when you look into it too much' but that 'what redeems it is the idea only' (51). After a long tirade against colonialism by another character in *Beat Not the Bones* Stella argues: 'that's half the picture ... Good comes out of it ... or will one day' (195). Just as Conrad's view on colonialism appears ambivalent in *Heart of Darkness*, Jay's view on colonialism is far from certain. Stella, after all, chooses to stay in Papua New Guinea at the end of the narrative. So, in a number of ways *Beat Not the Bones* rewrites *Heart of Darkness*. Like Conrad's novel, Jay's work can be read as an adventure tale, a journey of the protagonist's self-discovery, a semi-auto-biographical tale and a slightly ambivalent, political critique of colonialism.

Jay's work, however, also writes back to Conrad's novel. Parallels exist between Stella and Marlow, suggesting that Stella takes a Marlovian journey. But it is not just Marlow that Stella reminds us of; she also reminds us of Kurtz's fiancée, his Intended. Stella is only just 'un-Intended', so to speak, since she has only been married to her husband Warwick for four months. Marlow's view of women is restricted and restricting; he actively seeks to keep them ignorant. In Jay's book too, men try to keep Stella innocent. For example, although she is not a Catholic, 'her father had believed a convent training suited a child he hoped would turn out gracious, submissive and "womanly"'(40). Like the Intended, Stella is shielded from the truth about her husband's behaviour and death. In a mirroring of *Heart of Darkness* Stella is told a lie about her husband's death. In fact she is told a number of lies by men throughout the book. Her father starts by hiding the truth of her husband's behaviour by throwing his letter into the fire before (somewhat melodramatically) dying, uttering the words 'murder, murder'. More blatant lies are told to her once she seeks to find out what these words mean. In a figurative slap in the face to Marlow, Stella rejects the lies and points out to one of the men who lie to her: 'The truth is too much trouble for you' (116). Unlike *Heart of Darkness*, *Beat Not the Bones* starts, more or less, with lies, rather than ending with one.

Heart of Darkness can be described as blaming women for colonialism. For Marlow at least, not only do women guard the door to darkness, but his aunt procures work for him in Africa in the first place and talks enthusiastically of 'weaning those ignorant millions from their horrid ways' (59). If we look closely at Kurtz, we can see that even his aberrant behaviour is blamed on women in one respect. Like Marlow, he would not be in Africa if it were not for women. Kurtz goes out to Africa, Marlow suggests, because his engagement with the Intended 'had been disapproved by her people. He wasn't rich enough or something' (159). This blaming of women is addressed in Jay's book. Stella demands to know the truth, confronting Marlow's implicit blame head-on. At one point she is told 'the painful truth' that she never loved her husband:

> *'Everyone loved him!' she replied.*
> *'Some did,' he said, 'but you aren't among them.'*
> *She floundered in the very heart of rage and pain. She could not speak. His face broke and blurred in the tears that started to well in her eyes.*
> *His quiet, ruthless voice went on. 'You expect the best of him. If you loved him you would expect the worst. You never knew him – how could you? He had no choice to hide from you what he was.' (78–79)*

Later, Stella appears to have understood the blame in this charge when she asks of another character: 'Was it my fault or would it have happened anyway?' (207).

Rather than finding the necessity of Marlow's lie in *Heart of Darkness* an insurmountable problem, Jay's work dramatises the only way beyond it – for women to seek out the truth themselves. In places, *Beat Not the Bones* echoes the comments on the evasiveness of the truth that we find in *Heart of Darkness*. In the first chapter we learn that the

> *people down south when they heard the truth – or that part of the truth that was made known – were incredulous. They could not accept such events. They were partly right. What happened could not have happened anywhere else. (2)*

Jay's work suggests that the only way for these people, women included, to discover the truth, is to go and see for themselves.

Jay's response is to have her heroine discover the truth, and handle it better, for that matter, than the men represented in her narrative. In this way, *Beat Not the Bones* writes back to *Heart of Darkness* from a feminist perspective. It claims the right of women to know the truth, and their ability to discover and handle that truth. While Marlow would keep women ignorant, Jay's Stella develops, and learns. In fact, in some ways she goes beyond Marlow. Throughout *Heart of Darkness* Marlow sees the jungle and Africa as unknowable. Stella's views, however, change as she becomes more familiar with her new environment. When she arrives in Marapai she observes that 'The garden was not behaving according to laws known to her.' Furthermore:

> It struck her that this country had passed the limits of beauty and richness and dived off into some sort of inferno. She ... decided, as so many who feared their own passions had decided before her, that the country was evil. (37)

However, later on in the narrative, she thinks differently:

> Her gaze moved around the walls and came to rest in the flame trees outside the window. Morning sunlight bathed the floor and the faded cover of the bed. The trees were breaking daily into more and more scarlet blossom. She had ceased to think them overdone and come to regard them as miraculously beautiful. She found herself thinking now ... I like this place, I should like to live here. (150)

Initially Stella projects her fears on to the place where something bad has happened. Confronting her fears, her perceptions change. Conrad's Marlow, by way of contrast, describes his journey into Africa, even a long time after the event, as a journey into hell that is too dark for him let alone women.

Beat Not the Bones both re-writes and writes back to *Heart of Darkness*. However, while points of interconnection (intertextuality) between the works are numerous, these interconnections do not define the works themselves. While Jay's work addresses some of the issues raised by *Heart of Darkness* as well as sharing some of its themes, there is much more to both *Heart of Darkness* and *Beat Not the Bones* than just these issues and themes. If we were to represent the two works diagrammatically as two overlapping circles on a piece of paper, what this essay has done is explore only the area of overlap; there remains much outside this area to reward other ways of looking at both works.

Notes

1. Charlotte Jay was born Geraldine Mary Jay in 1919 in Adelaide, where, until recently, she lived and worked under her married name, Geraldine Halls, as a writer and oriental art dealer. She grew up in Adelaide, and worked as a secretary in Australia and London during the 1940s and as a court stenographer for the (Australian) Court of Papua New Guinea

during 1949. She then travelled extensively before returning home. Charlotte Jay was the name Geraldine Halls used to publish most of her mystery novels, which first appeared between 1951 and 1964. They reflect a life spent travelling and her fascination with local cultures and ethnological questions, as do her seven 'straight' novels published under the name Geraldine Halls. Only her first and last novels, *The Knife is Feminine* (1951) and *This is My Friend's Chair* (1995) are set in Australia. Geraldine Halls died in Adelaide in 1997.

Works Cited

Conrad, Joseph. *Heart of Darkness*. 1902. London: Dent Collected Edition, 1946.

——. *Last Essays*. 1926. London: Dent Collected Edition, 1946.

——. *The Collected Letters of Joseph Conrad: Volume 2 (1898–1902)*. Eds Frederick R. Karl and Laurence Davies. Cambridge: Cambridge UP, 1986.

Jay, Charlotte. *Beat Not the Bones: A Tale of Terror in the Tropics*. 1951. Kent Town, South Australia: Wakefield Press, 1992.

Jean-Aubry, Gérard. *The Sea Dreamer: A Definitive Biography of Joseph Conrad*. Translated by Helen Sebba. London: Allen and Unwin, 1957.

Leavis, F.R. *The Great Tradition*. London: Chatto and Windus, 1948.

Sauders, Ian. *Open Texts, Partial Maps: A Literary Theory Handbook*. Centre for Studies in Australian Literature. Nedlands, Western Australia: University of Western Australia, 1998.

Straus, Nina Pelikan. 'The Exclusion of the Intended from Secret Sharing in Conrad's *Heart of Darkness*.' *Novel* 20.2 (Winter 1987): 123–137.

Watt, Ian. *Conrad in the Nineteenth Century*. London: Chatto and Windus, 1980.

Further Reading

Smith, David. '*Beat Not the Bones – Heart of Darkness* Re-visited' in *Southwords: Essays on South Australian Writing*. Ed. Philip Butterss. Adelaide: Wakefield Press, 1995.

Dancing Masks: Narrating the Colonial Experience in Achebe's Things Fall Apart

Dianne Schwerdt

Chinua Achebe's *Things Fall Apart* challenges the way in which narratives of empire tend to portray the colonial experience in Africa. The novel persuades us that there can be different ways of viewing the same moment in history and that we should be wary of privileging one version over another. Achebe's portrayal of first contact in nineteenth century Nigeria, read against prevailing colonial discourses, reminds us that narrative 'truth' is not absolute but relative, that perspective is always a defining factor in any narrative process. This is of particular interest when we read postcolonial texts as works that 'write back to the centre' for in a very real sense these texts argue the centrality of alternative views. They are a means by which the once-colonised world can powerfully reconstruct itself, making manifest what has been repressed, consciously or unconsciously, in western versions of the colonial experience.

Achebe himself has consistently espoused an inclusive view of history. Such inclusiveness is well-expressed in the frequently-quoted Ibo proverb – 'Where one thing stands another will stand beside it' – and in *Arrow of God* where we learn that the 'world is like a Mask dancing. If you want to see it well, you do not stand in the same place' (46). If we bring these ideas to bear on *Things Fall Apart*, for instance, on our reading of the conversation between Ibo elders that takes place while Okonkwo is in exile, this idea of multiple perspectives is again reinforced. When the elders visit Okonkwo bringing news of European activities in Africa, the talk centres on the reported British massacre of the neighbouring Abame clan. Obierika, Okonkwo's friend and a man of wisdom, speaks for his generation when he says 'I am greatly afraid. We have heard stories about white men who made the powerful guns and the strong drinks and took slaves away across the seas, but no one thought the stories were true.' Uchendu, a man of great age and equal wisdom, replies 'There is no story that is not true ... The world has no end, and what is good among one people is an abomination with others' (101). The response, among other things, is a warning against adopting too narrow a view of events and an acknowledgment that difference has always prevailed.

Acknowledging otherness is one thing. Tolerance of it, however, has not been a strong characteristic of western colonial narratives. Achebe's response to Conrad's *Heart of Darkness* in his controversial essay, 'An Image of Africa', was that it was a novel 'in which the very humanity of black people is called in question' (10). To Achebe, Conrad was 'a thoroughgoing racist' (8). When we look at *Things Fall Apart* after reading *Heart of Darkness* we become aware of another point of view – one which may never have occurred to us as readers shaped by Western literary traditions. In fact it is not a point of view that was immediately apparent to Achebe who was himself educated in the Western literary tradition. In an interview that reflects back on Conrad's novel Achebe comments:

> *I went to the first university that was built in Nigeria, and I took a course in English. We were taught the same kind of literature that British people were taught in their own university. But then I began to look at these books in a different light. When I had been younger, I had read these adventure books about the good white man, you know, wandering into the jungle or into danger, and the savages were after him. And I would instinctively be on the side of the white man. You see what fiction can do, it can put you on the wrong side if you are not developed enough. In the university I suddenly saw that these books had to be read in a different light. Reading* Heart of Darkness, *for instance, which was a very, very highly praised book and which is still highly praised, I realised that I was one of those savages jumping up and down on the beach. Once that kind of Enlightenment comes to you, you realise that someone has to write a different story. And since I was in any case inclined that way, why not me? (Moyers 343)*

Heart of Darkness has always been regarded as one of the great books of English literature, and it probably still is. But Achebe's objection to the status this book enjoys in European culture and the novel Achebe himself produced encourages us to read *Heart of Darkness* differently. Achebe's novel explores issues that are both relevant and to the point in a world that has come to question the right of nations to build empires, claim racial superiority and dispossess indigenous people. While we may not necessarily agree with Achebe in his dismissal of *Heart of Darkness*, we are inclined to listen when he says:

> *I have no doubt that the reason for the high rating of this novel in Europe and America is simply that it fortifies fears and prejudices and is clever enough to protect itself, should the need arise, with the excuse that it is not really about Africa at all. And yet it is set in Africa and teems with Africans whose humanity is admitted in theory but totally undermined by the mindlessness of its context and the pretty explicit animal imagery surrounding it. In the entire novel Conrad allows two sentences in broken English to Africans: the cannibal who says 'Catch 'im, eat 'im', and the half-caste who announces 'Mistah Kurtz – he dead'.*

When Western critics applaud *Heart of Darkness* as a masterpiece, they are thinking about culture as, for example, something represented in the review pages of the Saturday newspapers, or the *Sunday Review* on television. But this is not what culture means to Chinua Achebe and writers like him. For writers from the once-colonised world, culture is vitally bound up with notions of national identity, and therefore, in countries like Africa, inextricably bound to political struggle. The 'culture' of the Saturday and Sunday arts programmes and newspapers of the Western world is, moreover, an imperial culture. If, like Chinua Achebe, you happen to be on the receiving end of imperialism, what imperialism means is 'not only the exploitation of cheap labour-power, raw materials and easy markets but the uprooting of languages and customs – not just the imposition of foreign armies, but alien ways of experiencing' (Eagleton 215).

In *Heart of Darkness*, Conrad paints a grim picture of European profit-mongering in Africa. For the time, his was a liberal view, critical of the Belgians but not the British as brutally barbaric in their exploitation of Africans. However, Conrad also portrayed Africans as less than civilised: creatures of the landscape, primitive, without language and culture. Here was a race dangerously capable of subverting civilised values as we see in the ultimate degradation of

Kurtz. In countering this view of Africa Achebe seeks to redress an imbalance made popular in nineteenth and early twentieth century representations of Europeans in Africa. *Things Fall Apart* seeks to amend and revise the view of Africa as Europe's Other portrayed in *Heart of Darkness* and similar texts of the period. It writes back to the centre, reconstructs history from an indigenous point of view, asserts the centrality of Africa and Africans to African history and rewrites the narrative of empire. And if we have forgotten what this means by the end of the novel, Achebe reminds us by juxtaposing his own lengthy narrative with the District Commissioner's planned paragraph – an ironically placed contrapuntal reading of the events of the novel. At the end of *Things Fall Apart*, when we have seen the complex and paradoxical way in which Okonkwo and his people have both accommodated and resented the colonial presence, we feel sympathy for the tragedy of Okonkwo, a great man among his people, and appalled at the arrogance of the British District Commissioner whose ignorance is encapsulated in his decision to reduce Okonkwo's life to a mere paragraph in his proposed history of the conquest of a people.

When Chinua Achebe writes, then, he writes as an African responding to pressure to use his talents in the service of reasserting cultural and political autonomy. He writes to re-educate his readers – African and non-African. He writes to proclaim the importance of a culture that has been at best ignored and at worst denigrated by others. In an essay entitled 'The Novelist as Teacher' – and teacher is the role he thinks is most important for the African novelist – Achebe writes:

> we [Africans] do have our sins and blasphemies recorded against
> our name. If I were God I would regard as the very worst our
> acceptance – for whatever reason – of racial inferiority. It is too
> late in the day to get worked up about it or to blame others, much
> as they may deserve such blame and condemnation. What we
> need to do is look back and try and find out where we went
> wrong, where the rain began to beat us. (29)

Elsewhere, just a few years after Nigerian independence, in 'The Role of the Writer in a New Nation', Achebe argues strongly that the most fundamental theme for an African writer must be the assertion that

> African people did not hear of culture for the first time from
> Europeans; that their societies were not mindless but frequently

> *had a philosophy of great depth and value and beauty, that they*
> *had poetry and, above all, they had dignity. It is this dignity that*
> *many African people all but lost during the colonial period and it*
> *is this that they must now regain. The worst thing that can happen*
> *to any people is the loss of their dignity and self-respect. The*
> *writer's duty is to help them regain it by showing them in human*
> *terms what happened to them, what they lost ... In Africa he*
> *cannot perform this task unless he has a proper sense of history.*
> *(157)*

And this belief, of course, is fundamental to *Things Fall Apart*. Achebe is a writer with a mission – to show his readers that Africa's past, as he says, 'was not one long night of savagery from which the first Europeans acting on God's behalf delivered them' ('The Novelist as Teacher' 30). This strong commitment, in turn, affects his reading of works like *Heart of Darkness*. Conrad's novel presents Africans as silent, inarticulate, mysterious, savage and essentially all the same. Whether this makes him a 'racist' or not is arguable, but certainly the absence of African culture, the absence of the African voice, is something Achebe sets out to correct in his portrayal of the order, rationality, social structure, political organisation and religious beliefs of one African clan.

Things Fall Apart, set roughly between 1850 and 1900, recreates the Ibo land of Achebe's grandfather, a period in Nigeria when the influence of the Europeans was only just beginning to have an impact on some of the villages and rumours were spreading that the newcomers were a force to be reckoned with. Achebe describes the social and political structures of a society that had maintained itself for centuries through the agency of religious ceremonies and rituals, and good democratic government. Tradition and custom facilitated decision-making and regulated action both within and between groups. Faced with the intrusion of a new group – the Europeans – a group that exhibited aggressive and assertive tendencies, the Ibo people found themselves having to deal with different kinds of conflicts without recourse to precedents. Despite Okonkwo's memorialising of the old ways, the past provided them with no solution to their current problem.

The conflict between two seemingly unyielding cultures – the Ibo, championed by Okonkwo, and the European in the form of the local colonial administrative authority – drives the narrative. Each side wants supremacy, but there can be just one victor. It is only when we are made aware of the nature of the African culture that is to be eclipsed that we are able to see, in the passing of African autonomy, a loss that is tragic. The inclusion of culturally defining details alerts us to what is under threat and the weaving of this information through the narrative becomes crucial to its success. What we learn is that Achebe's representation of the Nigerian past bears no resemblance at all to Conrad's representation of an indigenous African population in the Congo.

However, Achebe is not creating an idealised version of Ibo history and culture in his text. Nor is he writing a plea for preserving the African past intact. Rather, the novel suggests that cultural hybridisation (the combining of elements from different cultures to produce new cultural forms) is a foreseeable outcome of any colonial intrusion into Africa. Further, Achebe exposes the brittleness inherent in a traditional way of life rigidly maintained in the face of potential disruption. *Things Fall Apart* suggests strongly that cultural transformation is a natural state of human becoming. The novel endorses a view of society as organic, subject to a process of change and alteration that is as desirable as it is inevitable. To resist change, to demand stasis, as Okonkwo does, is to go against what is natural, posing too great a risk to survival. In both the preface to the novel and more overtly in its title Achebe refers us to Yeats's poem 'The Second Coming' and his notion of the passage of history as a continuum in which seemingly stable civilisations are relentlessly succeeded by others, collapsing from within even as the replacement civilisation threatens it from without:

> *Turning and turning in the widening gyre*
> *The falcon cannot hear the falconer;*
> *Things fall apart; the centre cannot hold;*
> *Mere anarchy is loosed upon the world;*
> *The blood-dimmed tide is loosed and everywhere*
> *The ceremony of innocence is drowned.*

Achebe uses this intertextual link to reflect on the passing of Ibo cultural integrity in the context of Europe's colonial eclipsing of a society already in the process of foundering. Without unity Ibo society is in danger of unravelling itself not solely because of outside pressures but equally because of its own internal inadequacies, and its inability to adapt quickly enough to changing circumstances. Obierika makes us palpably aware of these flaws when he ruminates on the harshness of some of the Ibo customs, as does Nwoye, whose defection to Christianity signals the discontent he feels about his role in Ibo society and in his father's household, neither of which adequately accommodate his needs as an individual. What attracts Nwoye is not 'the mad logic of the Trinity' but

> *the poetry of the new religion, something felt in the marrow. The hymn about brothers who sat in darkness and in fear seemed to answer a vague and persistent question that haunted his young soul – the question of the twins crying in the bush and the question of Ikemefuna who was killed. He felt relief within as the hymn poured into his parched soul. (106)*

This passage, like others in *Things Fall Apart*, suggests that the discontent prompted by such criticisms of tradition, unheeded, serves to widen the fissures increasingly evident in the fabric of Ibo society, giving entry to outside forces for change and, as a result, 'things fall apart'.

In one sense the text is clearly elegiac. Two tragedies unfold: the tragedy that befalls Okonkwo, a Umuofian 'clearly cut out for great things' (6), and the wider tragedy that threatens Umuofia itself, site of one of the greatest of Ibo clans. Okonkwo and Umuofia are thus inextricably linked: both are internally flawed. At the end of the novel we come to see that the death of Okonkwo prefigures the imminent destruction of the old way of life in Umuofia. The once ordered, integrated society is in disarray, its gods sinned against, its customs ignored. Umuofian autonomy is not only under threat, it has ceased to exist.

If we look more closely at Okonkwo we recognise that he is representative of all the qualities traditional Umuofian society reveres. Thoroughly the product of that society, he is the epitome of masculinity, or, more accurately, hypermasculinity (discussed previously in this volume by Philip Butterss), since Okonkwo takes everything to extremes. And this is an important point to remember when we look at the way in which Achebe constructs Ibo masculinity. Okonkwo has all the attributes of a hero: the strength and agility of a wrestling champion (an accomplishment that has won him an extra wife) and proven courage in battle. He is also a significant landholder, a successful farmer, respected by his peers, a titled member of the governing council of elders and, as well, a member of the elite secret society of the egwugwu. Umuofia, an aggressively materialistic society, values highly its most productive members. With two barns full of yams, three wives, numerous children, and two of the society's three possible titles Okonkwo is a rising star in a community that demands a great deal from its men.

Nevertheless we would be wrong to read Okonkwo as entirely emblematic of Umuofian society. Although ambitious by nature, Okonkwo is, in fact, driven to the point of obsession in his desire to succeed. What drives him is an exaggerated fear of failure, a paranoia that eventually destroys him. Afraid of being thought weak like his father, Okonkwo is hypersensitive about how his masculinity is perceived by his peers: this fear of failure, Achebe tells us

> *was deeper and more intimate than the fear of evil or capricious gods of magic, the fear of the forest, and of the forces of nature, malevolent, red in tooth and claw. Okonkwo's fear was greater than these. It was not external but lay deep within himself. It was the fear of himself, lest he should be found to resemble his father. (9–10)*

Deeply shamed by his father's failure to live up to Umuofian standards of masculinity – failure to farm his land successfully, failure to provide adequately for his family – Okonkwo comes to despise everything his father stood for, hating idleness and gentleness in particular (10). When he believes he sees traits in his son, Nwoye, that remind him of his father Unoka he is moved to declare: 'I will not have a son who cannot hold up his head in the gathering of the clan. I would sooner strangle him with my own hands' (24).

Okonkwo's quick temper as well as his fear of disapproval leads him to acts of violence that go beyond the firmness that Umuofian society expects of its men and earn him the criticism of his peers. Harsh and unforgiving, he beats his youngest wife in the Week of Peace (a sin – not the act of beating his wife but doing it in the Week of Peace) and his second wife for taking three leaves from his banana tree. He tries to shoot her when she makes a snide remark about his gun. He kills his friend's son accidentally. These acts mark him as a man who shoots first and asks questions later, solving problems with violence rather than negotiation, impetuous action rather than reflection and compromise. If he seems without feeling, however, we have only to look at his love for his daughter Ezinma, expressed well out of the public eye, his compassion for his wife Ekwefi (who has lost so many children), his fatherly pride in Ikemefuna and his deep respect for his friend Obierika. While keeping this part of his nature carefully reined in, he presents himself in public as a man who adheres rigidly to traditional guidelines with regard to male behaviour and honour.

While it is important to see Okonkwo as very much a product of nineteenth century Ibo society, he is, nevertheless, only one example of what it means to be an Ibo male. Obierika, in his rational approach to the continuing relevance of certain Ibo customs, however appropriate they may have seemed in the past, helps to balance the text's construction of Ibo masculinity. Where Okonkwo takes things to violent extremes, we come to rely on Obierika for the more thoughtful perspective. Through Obierika both Okonkwo and Ibo society are shown to err on the side of austerity and inflexibility in their beliefs and practices and this, not simply a disruptive colonial presence, helps to erode Ibo stability. In an interview published in 1981 Achebe makes the point that 'Igbo culture lays a great deal of emphasis on differences, on dualities, on otherness' and that he regards being 'fanatically singleminded' as indeed Okonkwo was, as quite problematic (Ogbaa interview 2). It is therefore important to recognise that Achebe draws a distinction between Okonkwo's fate and that of Umuofia. Okonkwo cannot change; nor can he accept change among his people. His death demonstrates this. Umuofia, on the other hand, shows itself open to change and therefore it survives, though not in its original form. Something is lost along the way.

Through the division of the narrative into three parts Achebe maps the slow but insidious intrusion of missions and western administration into traditional African life. In Part One Ibo life is portrayed as stable, ordered and still isolated from European influence. Here in the most substantial part of the novel, Achebe establishes Ibo society as one governed by ancient laws, highly organised and culturally rich. Careful not to portray the traditional past as an idyllic interlude from which Africans were 'rudely awakened' by the arrival of Europeans in Africa, Achebe, here and in Part Two, pin-points the weaknesses that made colonisation possible – the harshness of customary laws and the unmitigated cruelty involved in killing twins, rejecting outcasts and slaughtering humans as sacrifices. Europeans, mentioned indirectly and referred to as 'lepers' on account of their white skin, are not seen, at this stage, as a threat to a society that maintains its strength by casting out the weak and the sick.

Part Two hints more broadly at an impending clash between culturally opposed groups. The talk of white men changes from rumour to first-hand accounts. The whites, now seen as rapacious 'locusts', come to 'eat up all the land'. As invaders they show scant respect for indigenous gods and customs. Chielo, the priestess of Agbala, pronounces the converts to Christianity 'the excrement of the clan' and the new religion 'a mad dog that had come to eat it up' (130).

Undeterred, the new church was content to attract 'efulefu, worthless, empty men' into its steadily swelling numbers, and those rejected by Ibo society found ready acceptance at the mission. For the first time, perhaps, individual Ibos had a choice: of gods, lifestyle and community. Despite being associated with disease and aggression the interlopers, by agreement with the Ibo people, insinuated themselves into parasitic proximity and fed off the clan's rejects to the point that it became strategically difficult to dislodge them. On Okonkwo's return from exile Obierika cautions him against trying to drive out the white man:

> It is already too late ... Our men and our sons have joined the ranks of the stranger. They have joined his religion and they help to uphold his government. If we should try to drive out the white men in Umuofia we should find it easy. There are only two of them. But what of our own people who are following their way and have been given power? They would go to Umuru and bring the soldiers, and we would be like Abame ... The white man is very clever. He came quietly and peaceably with his religion. We were amused at his foolishness and allowed him to stay. Now he has won our brothers, and our clan can no longer act like one. He has put a knife on the things that held us together and we have fallen apart. (126–127)

By encouraging defection from traditional religion the Christian missions struck at the very roots that gave Umuofian society its cohesion and durability. As an Ibo elder puts it on the eve of Okonkwo's return from exile:

> I fear for you young people because you do not understand how strong is the bond of kinship. You do not know what it is to speak with one voice. And what is the result? An abominable religion has settled among you. A man can now leave his father and his brother. He can curse the gods of his father and his ancestors, like a hunter's dog that suddenly goes mad and turns on his master. I fear for you; I fear for the clan. (120)

Carroll notes that converts 'were not simply substituting a Christian for a tribal god; they were exchanging a religion through which they were identified with the tribe for a religion without any such affiliations' (8). Moreover, this led to a situation in which the converts, having 'jettisoned the rationale of traditional African life ... were to be given a vital role in the new forms of society which the missionaries were creating out of the destruction of the old' (9). Part Three describes the collapse of traditional life, from the erosion of the elders' authority through their poor treatment by British authorities, to the death of tradition's champion, Okonkwo.

Throughout the novel we do not lose sight of its protagonist and his relationship with Umuofia. It is not only his long exile at a crucial moment in colonial history that queers Okonkwo's pitch. His own propensity for impulsive and ill-advised action, culminating in the moment of Ikemefuna's ritual slaughter, is the critical factor. The moment he raises his machete against the boy, Okonkwo's successful life sours. Carroll argues convincingly that this is the turning point of the novel (44) and certainly the economy of the description, Okonkwo's panic, his frantic response to the boy's cry for help marks this as a decisive moment in the text. From this moment on he finds himself increasingly marginalised, both spatially and attitudinally, from the rest of his people. Indeed, he is ultimately so distanced from them that he transgresses Ibo religious codes and takes his own life, becoming, in death, an unsettled ancestral spirit capable of endangering the continued well-being of his people.

The whole tragedy of Okonkwo's life and death only becomes fully revealed in the final pages of the novel, when, unsupported by the other members of the group, he behaves in his usual courageous warrior-like way, violently beheading the court messenger. In the past such an action would have been appropriate. In the changed circumstances, however, the uncomprehending crowd asks 'Why did he do it?' (147). The same could be asked of Okonkwo's suicide, for in taking his own life he negates all that his life as an Ibo male has stood for. The tragedy lies in the fact that a man of such strength of will and such material success in the eyes of his community could despair so much as to believe that his life is no longer worth living, either in the present world or in the next.

Okonkwo is portrayed as a typical tragic hero with a particular flaw that seals his unhappy end. But is this novel suggesting that the society that produced Okonkwo is similarly fated? Despite the fact that there are close connections between the flaws in Okonkwo's character and the flaws in the traditional Ibo prescriptions for living, I doubt that Achebe is seriously suggesting there is no hope for Africans who want to continue to know themselves as Africans. On the contrary. The narrative establishes Africanness by giving back a lost past – by telling African history from an African point of view – one quite different from the history colonisers published in their books. Furthermore the novel contains some advice – some warnings – that are clearly to do with survival. The emphasis is on the importance of adaptation (not assimilation, which is something entirely different). Mr Brown, the missionary, is not wrong when he predicts that those who learn the English language and accept an English education will be future leaders. The message is to be flexible, to make judgments and act according to circumstances. And to do this it is necessary to think carefully, to reflect, to consider what actions might be appropriate in different sets of circumstances. This is Okonkwo's problem. He relies doggedly on the precepts of the past, deaf to the nuances of change, an advocate of violence over mediation. Nor does he listen to the advice of his elders when they caution him, most significantly when he is told it is not necessary to take part in the killing of his adopted son. The elder Ezeudo stresses that it is unnatural for a man to kill a boy who calls him father, even if the council of elders has decreed that the boy must die anyway: 'They will take him outside Umuofia as is the custom, and kill him there. But I want you to have nothing to do with it. He calls you father' (40). But obsessive fear – of his own feelings, which he interprets as weakness – drives Okonkwo on, and in his usual way he overcompensates for those moments of perceived weakness by doing far more than is required by his community or his gods.

By way of contrast, the wiser elders of Umuofia think about, and even begin to question prescribed customs, taking note of alternatives. They recognise that the way things are done in Umuofia is not the way things are done everywhere. In chapter eight, for example, where Obierika waits to meet the family of the boy who wishes to marry his daughter, the men are sitting drinking palm-wine and talking about the customs of their neighbours:

> *'It was only this morning,'* said Obierika, *'that Okonkwo and I were talking about Abame and Aninta, where titled men climb trees and pound foo-foo for their wives.'* [Needless to say, Okonkwo had found this idea preposterous.]
>
> *'All their customs are upside-down. They do not decide brideprice as we do, with sticks. They haggle and bargain as if they were buying a goat or a cow in the market.'*
>
> *'That is very bad,'* said Obierika's eldest brother. *'But what is good in one place is bad in another place.'* (52)

These are wise words: an acknowledgment that rules, laws and customs are neither universal nor absolute.

When Okonkwo is banished from Umuofia for seven years for accidentally killing a boy at a funeral ceremony, Obierika questions the harshness of the punishment – just as he questions other kinds of suffering that result from the inflexibility of Umuofian laws:

> *Obierika was a man who thought about things. When the will of the goddess had been done, he sat down in his obi and mourned his friend's calamity. Why should a man suffer so grievously for an offence he committed inadvertently? But although he thought for a long time he found no answer. He was merely led into greater complexities. He remembered his wife's twin children, whom he had thrown away. What crime had they committed? (89)*

If, as an elder, Obierika questions decrees to exact punishments to appease the earth goddess, then the strength and coherence of traditional life is already breaking down. Victims of the most rigid of Umuofian customs and values are choosing to leave their clan for protection in the Christian mission. And others, under the benign influence of Mr Brown, who treads 'softly' on the religious beliefs of the clan and believes in compromise and accommodation, begin to see some advantages in the white man's presence. As well, trade in palm oil and kernel increases profits and a different future seems possible for some. In the time that Okonkwo is away in exile profound changes have occurred in Umuofia, suggesting that potential for change does exist within Ibo society. Though traditional ways are under threat and the changes are not all for the better, extinction does not seem likely. In one way Okonkwo's stand against the changes that result from white contact is an heroic resistance; but in another, his rigidity and impatience are as damaging as that of The Reverend James Smith who sees no shades of grey, only black and white. Smith sees the world as a battlefield 'in which the children of light were locked in mortal conflict with the sons of darkness' (132). Of course, given that The Reverend James Smith has the might of empire behind him, he is a much more dangerous man than Okonkwo, who, in the end, can only destroy himself.

In any contact zone where people from different cultures interact, there will be conflict. This is particularly so when an imperial culture seeks to impose itself on an indigenous one, for the power structures are unequal and the consequences of contact for African society were gross misunderstanding, damage, corruption and bloodshed. Expansion of empire, tempered by philanthropy but propelled by the promise of economic advantage was never a matter of tidy, business-like contracts and backing missionary activity with military support was necessary if self-serving.

But the point of Achebe's narrative is that although traditional Ibo culture disintegrated under the impact of the white man, some of the values of that culture, such as kinship, survived and have the potential to become rejuvenating forces in an independent and resilient Nigerian identity. This is a story about the history of Nigeria. It is a history that is absent in Conrad's *Heart of Darkness*. It is fitting that at the end of this story, Achebe reduces to a footnote the white man's history of Nigeria, underscoring the District Commissioner's standard colonial view of Africa. As we have seen, this is an ironic twist. The District Commissioner thinks he might be able to write an interesting paragraph on the story that has occupied us for one hundred and fifty pages. And we know that the District Commissioner's paragraph will be a different story from the one we have read. We know that Achebe's story is much more than a narrative about a man who killed a messenger then hanged himself. 'One must be firm in cutting out the details' thinks the District Commissioner as he contemplates his book—after all *The Pacification of the Primitive Tribes of the Lower Niger*, which is what he proposes to call his book (and of course Achebe is being ironic here too) is a big project: 'cutting out the details' is precisely what makes it possible to reject the full humanity of the indigenous people. So the novel ends on an ironic note that highlights the tragedy of Okonkwo and a clan in the process of profound social and economic upheaval. The lack of understanding of the culture that white fictions (like *Heart of Darkness*) and white histories eclipsed is very clearly conveyed as Achebe's narrative ends. Finally we must acknowledge the absurdity and inappropriateness of the European chronicler who thinks he can reduce the events of *Things Fall Apart*, events that represent the passing of an era, to a mere paragraph. We have to acknowledge, that when the West produces a narrative about colonisation, it is only one version of the story. There are other stories which, until recently, were suppressed or erased and Achebe's *Things Fall Apart* is one of those stories.

Works Cited

Achebe, Chinua. *Arrow of God*. Rev. ed. African Writers Series. 1964: London: Heinemann, 1974.

——. 'An Image of Africa: Racism in Conrad's *Heart of Darkness*'. *Hopes and Impediments: Selected Essays 1965–1987*. London: Heinemann, 1988.

——. 'The Novelist as Teacher'. *Hopes and Impediments: Selected Essays 1965–87*. London: Heinemann, 1988.

——. 'The Role of the Writer in a New Nation'. *Nigeria Magazine* 81
(1964):157–60.

——. *Things Fall Apart.* African Writers Series. 1958. Oxford; Portsmouth
N.H.; Ibadan: Heinemann, 1986.

Carroll, David. *Chinua Achebe: Novelist, Poet, Critic.* 1980. London:
Macmillan Press, 1990.

Conrad, Joseph. *Heart of Darkness.* 1902. London: Dent Collected Edition,
1946.

Eagleton, Terry. *Literary Theory: An Introduction.* Oxford: Blackwell, 1985.

Moyers, Bill. 'Interview with Chinua Achebe'. *A World of Ideas.* Ed. Betty
Sue Flowers. New York: Doubleday, 1989.

Ogbaa, Kalu. 'A Cultural Note on Okonkwo's Suicide'. *Kunapipi* 3.2 (1981):
126–134.

Further Reading

Achebe, Chinua. 'Viewpoint'. *Times Literary Supplement*, February 1 (1980):
113.

Ezenwa-Ohaeto. *Chinua Achebe: A Biography.* Oxford: James Currey;
Bloomington and Indianapolis: Indiana UP, 1997.

Gikandi, Simon. *Reading Chinua Achebe: Language and Ideology in Fiction.*
London: James Currey, 1991.

Iyasere, S.O., ed. *Understanding* Things Fall Apart*: Selected Essays and
Criticism.* New York: Whitston Publishing, 1998.

Muoneke, Romanus Okey. *Art, Rebellion and Redemption: A Reading of the
Novels of Chinua Achebe.* American University Studies. New York: Peter
Lang, 1994.

Ogbaa, Kalu. 'An Interview with Chinua Achebe'. *Research in African
Literatures* 12.1 (1981): 1–13.

Searle, Chris. 'Achebe and the Bruised Heart of Africa'. *Wasafiri* 14 (Autumn
1991): 12–16.

Aboriginalities: Jack Davis and Archie Weller

Sue Hosking

I am an Aboriginal
I am a city dweller
Jack Davis (Black Life *21)*

'Aboriginal writing' is a label applied by mainstream critics to a range of texts originating in the cultures and life experiences of people from different Aboriginal groups. In Australia some Aboriginal authors are able to identify themselves as Murris, Nungas, Nyoongahs, Kooris, Kaurna – to name a few groups. Others, although they are sure of their Aboriginality, are no longer sure of their precise ancestry. This is the consequence of colonial history and government policies that shunted Aboriginal people from one place to another, mixing and separating them without respect for their cultural ties and groupings.

Aboriginal writers like Ruby Langford dispute the idea that 'real Aborigines are the tribal ones out in the desert sitting on a rock'. For Ruby, 'real Aborigines' is a much more inclusive category extending to all 'the descendants of the indigenous people of this country' (6). Many of these descendants are urban Aboriginal people who have varied experiences and distinctive stories to tell. In order for their stories to become books, Aboriginal authors, like all authors, must negotiate with (largely non-Aboriginal) editors and publishers who select and shape their work to produce books that will sell in the marketplace, where (largely non-Aboriginal) readers will buy them. 'Aboriginality', then, becomes a complex concept. It is more appropriate to think in terms of 'Aboriginalities', and the ways in which we think about 'Aboriginalities' are determined by processes of constant renegotiation between Aboriginal and non-Aboriginal Australians.

'Aboriginal writing' belongs neither wholly to traditional Aboriginal culture nor wholly to European culture. Not uncommonly, it fails to satisfy completely either of the cultures that contribute to its making. Archie Weller's short stories, for example, are largely ignored by those who have been brought up to read the 'greats' of English literature. Neither do they necessarily conform to expectations of what is or should be 'Aboriginal'. In recent years there have been discussions in the media concentrating on issues of Aboriginal identity and 'authenticity'. Archie Weller is one of several writers who has been subjected to scrutiny in the context of these discussions. As yet, Archie Weller has not been able to prove his genealogy, although he has always claimed that his grandmother was an Aboriginal woman from around Port Augusta in South Australia. Does this mean that Archie Weller's work is 'inauthentic' and therefore not worth studying?

One way of thinking about accusations of 'inauthenticity' is to place them in the context of prejudices that were formulated as 'scientific' theories in the nineteenth century. Robert Young has written extensively about these theories, and what they signify, in his book *Colonial Desire* (1995). Essentially, the theories were a justification for racism. They suggested that if black and white blood mixed (and this would involve, horror of horrors, sex) the products of such unions would be inferior. Black blood, it was argued, contaminated white blood. The children of mixed unions would be physically and mentally deficient – quite useless for populating an expanding empire.

Of course such ideas were ridiculous, and tell us as much about sexual repression and sexual fantasies as about anything else. The evidence that white men found black women sexually attractive was abundant, and the offspring of these unions were embarrassingly fit. Although racist theories are no longer recognised as having any scientific credibility, a fear of 'contamination' still survives in some ways of thinking about cultural issues. There persists a desire to keep the cultural traditions of different races quite separate from each other. There is an underlying assumption that Aboriginal culture is acceptable when it can be clearly and safely labelled as such, like the objects in museums that represent past 'primitive' cultures and are perceived as having little or nothing to do with us today. But there *is* a living contemporary Aboriginal culture, manifesting itself in different forms, bridging the past and the present, touching non-Aboriginal lives and heading into a future where racial boundaries are blurred.

There is some resistance to the hybrid forms of contemporary Aboriginal culture – just as there has been some reluctance to accept the hybridised people that Archie Weller has chosen to write about – people who are neither wholly (traditionally) Aboriginal nor wholly European. Any piece of Aboriginal writing is 'impure', in a sense, because it represents the grafting of one culture, that is predominantly oral, communal, and inseparable from survival in and with the natural environment, on to another, that depends on written forms and literary genres highly valued for their artifice and judged according to the traditions and dictates of literary criticism and theory. The products of cross-cultural grafting, or hybridity, are often strikingly original – like Archie Weller's stories, or Jack Davis's plays, or, in the visual arts, Sally Morgan's paintings and prints. Drawing upon two very different cultures, they offer us new perspectives and open up new ways of thinking: this surely is worthy of celebration.

This essay examines two kinds of 'Aboriginality' that exist in a spectrum of possibilities. It examines a play by Jack Davis, *No Sugar*, which has an obvious and positive pro-Aboriginal political agenda, negotiated with subtlety and sensitivity that make the play much more than political harangue. On the other hand, the essay looks at short fiction by Archie Weller – a writer who identifies as Aboriginal but whose concern is with representing what life is like for a significant group of young Aboriginal people growing up in recent years in an urban environment, having lost ties with their traditional lands and consequently experiencing a fragmented, confused or contradictory identification with their traditional culture. Weller's work could (but need not necessarily) be read as representing Aboriginality in a negative sense. What these works demonstrate in common, however, is that hybridity opens up new possibilities for thinking about what Aboriginality might mean in contemporary Australia.

It is most common for Aboriginal writers, like Jack Davis, to see themselves as re-writing history, filling in gaps in the official records of the past, arguing with the official stories that exclude Aboriginal people or portray their helplessness. Davis was compelled to dramatise Aboriginal history when it became apparent that the Western Australian government was planning to celebrate in 1979 one hundred and fifty years of white settlement in that state, without any acknowledgement of previous occupation of the land by Aboriginal people. *No Sugar* is Davis's representation of the Moore River settlement, which he has described as 'a clearing house for Aboriginal people' (Davis in Bunbury 61). Others have called it a 'concentration camp without the barb [sic] wire' and an 'all purpose settlement for unmarried mothers, delinquent children and people who were not wanted' (Bunbury 59). Davis himself spent time there as a boy.

Set in the 1930s, *No Sugar* exposes the hidden agenda behind the removal of unwanted Aboriginal families from the Government Well Aboriginal Reserve at Northam in Western Australia to the distant Moore River, where they would be 'out of sight and out of mind'. The exodus was organised by Sir James Mitchell's government just prior to the 1933 election, in the hope (mistaken as it turned out) that this would please the people of Northam and secure their votes. The Government Well was by no means an ideal Reserve, but those who lived there were at least living in their own country. They were told that the shift to Moore River was a temporary move, for health reasons, and that any property they left behind would be looked after until they returned. This was a lie, emphasised in *No Sugar* in the very powerful first scene of Act III where Joe takes Mary back to his country and discovers that everything in the Reserve has been burnt. 'Bastards!' says Joe. 'They reckon they was gunna look after everything we left behind' (79).

Despite his political agenda in *No Sugar*, Davis skilfully manages to avoid setting up a crude opposition of 'black goodies' versus 'white baddies'. The white man Frank, who first appears in Act I, scene two, is a displaced person; he hasn't seen his family for six months and does not have the train fare back to Perth to visit them. In this scene Frank, the poor whitefella, is totally dependent upon the Millimurra family to feed him; this is a reversal of the usual stereotypes. Nor is Sister Eileen a stereotype: although she represents white man's religion, she expresses her incredulity at the 'unofficial directive' to discourage the natives from reading. Furthermore, in Act IV, scene four, she criticises the use of violence to enforce attendance at her religious instruction classes, sticking her neck out so far that Superintendent Neal threatens to send her to another settlement on the edge of the Gibson Desert.

On the other hand, the Aboriginal characters are not uniformly 'good'. At the Moore River settlement, Billy Kimberley, blacktracker turned 'politjman', struts about with his whip, keeping the natives in order to please his white boss. When they first meet him in Act II, scene one the Millimurra family laugh at Billy who is even blacker ('purple') than they are. Gran refuses to acknowledge him as an authority figure: 'You ain't politjman, you just black tracker' (55). But there's more to Billy's story than the Millimurras know to begin with. In Act II, scene six Davis brings his audience back to the circumstances that have deprived Billy of his cultural ties – back to the Oombulgarrie massacre which 'finished' Billy's mob and filled his country with crying ghosts. Davis, then, does more in his play than simply reverse stereotypes: he begins to dismantle them in the process of representing Aboriginality.

The breaking down of crude oppositions (Aboriginal versus non-Aboriginal) is crucial in the production of Davis's play. *No Sugar* came about through a process of collaboration – not only initially between Jack Davis and a white director, Andrew Ross, but also with the Aboriginal actors who at different times have rehearsed and performed in the play. This means that the message of the play is presented through a collective voice, but that voice is adjusted, or moderated, by a director trained in the conventions of Western theatre. This is a straightforward example of Marcia Langton's idea that ways in which we might think about the concept of Aboriginality or Aboriginalities are determined by on-going negotiations between Aboriginal and non-Aboriginal Australians (32–36). One of the consequences of this interaction is that we can find in *No Sugar* complex ways of thinking about what it might mean to be Aboriginal. We can also find subversive elements. The play affirms Aboriginality in subtle and sometimes secret ways, which may not immediately be apparent to non-Aboriginal audiences: through stage design, through the juxtaposition of historical documents with representations of Aboriginal lived experience (telling a different story), through humour, and through the incorporation of Aboriginal (Nyoongah) language.

The play is designed for what is described as a dispersed setting on an open stage. The central space is occupied by Aboriginal performers. White actors, mostly representing authority figures, are confined in cramped square and rectangular spaces – on the outer stage. On one side is the Northam police station with its two cells and the Office of the Chief Protector, with separate entrances for blacks and whites. On the other side is the Superintendent's Office at the Moore River settlement. The effect of this is that whitefellas are seen to be boxed in and constrained on the edge of the performance space, while the Aboriginal performers have freedom of movement. This is a visual reversal of the historical situation, where Aboriginal people were captured and shunted around like cattle in trucks.

No Sugar begins with the Northam Centenary Celebrations in 1929 and ends with a celebration of Australia Day at the Moore River settlement, five years later. The structure of *No Sugar*, then, reflects an orthodox linear version of Australian history, but the dialogue clearly shows the difference between how non-Aboriginal and Aboriginal Australians think of belonging to their country. One hundred, one hundred and fifty, two hundred years: these are milestones of possession for white Australians, but they are nothing for Aboriginal people. Australia Day commemorates a beginning for white Australians; Aboriginal people have no need of such celebrations, for their long past is always present, in their Dreaming. At the beginning of the play the contrast between the centenary story represented by the newspaper report, haltingly read by Joe Millimurra, and the scene before the eyes of the audience is strikingly ironic. Here, simultaneously, we are presented with different versions of history.

Negotiations between those who have made official history (the winners) and those who are absent in the history books (the losers) are presented in the play in a pattern of repression, exercised by authority figures (the Sergeant, Superintendent Neal and Mr Neville), and resistance (Aboriginal people answering back). The text of the play is the space in which possibilities for re-negotiations are made available for contemporary readers and viewers.

We see Gran, in particular, refusing to be silenced. Her humour is both a significant means of expressing resistance and a survival mechanism: to laugh is not to go under. Other serious forms of resistance include young Mary's refusal to work in the hospital where Superintendent Neal can abuse her, as he does the other girls who have been specially chosen because he finds them sexually attractive. So defiant is Mary that she submits to a whipping with the cat o' nine tails, with Billy holding her stretched out over a pile of flour bags. She prefers this punishment to the attentions of Mr Neal, even though she is then seven months pregnant (IV,ii). This scene is based on documentation contained in the Moseley Royal Commission of 1934, where Annie Morrison describes how trackers would hold girls over a sack of flour while Mr Neal beat them until they wet themselves. The flour would then be given to Aboriginal people on the settlement to eat.

The supreme example of defiance and assertion of Aboriginal identity occurs in Act IV, scene five, when the assembled inmates of the Moore River Native Settlement join voices to resist the lies in Neville's Australia Day speech:

> *It doesn't hurt to remind yourselves that you are preparing*
> *yourselves here to take your place in Australian society, to live as*
> *other Australians live, and to live alongside other Australians; to*
> *learn to enjoy the privileges and to shoulder the responsibilities of*
> *living like the white man, to be treated equally, not worse, not*
> *better, under the law. (97)*

The resistance begins as silence. Invited whitefellas clap as Neville rises; the 'natives' remain silent until Jimmy is heard muttering about weevily flour – Neville's idea of adequate food. It is expected that the assembly will sing the hymn that Sister Eileen has taught her charges.

> *There is a happy land,*
> *Far, far away,*
> *Where saints in glory stand,*
> *Bright, bright as day:*
> *Oh, how they sweetly sing,*
> *'Worthy is our Saviour King!'*
> *Loud let His praises ring,*
> *Praise, praise for aye! (98)*

Whitefellas continue singing the familiar orthodox version, but the inmates of the settlement raise their voices and break into a well practised parody which contradicts and finally drowns the hymn.

> *There is a happy land,*
> *Far, far away.*
> *Where we get bread and scrape,*
> *Three times a day.*
> *No sugar in our tea,*
> *Bread and butter we never see.*
> *That's why we're gradually*
> *Fading away. (98)*

The Aboriginal singers turn the language that has been foisted on them to their own use, expressing the realities of their lived experiences. Singing out about 'fading away', they both make their presence felt and contest official history in the making.

Just on the level of what happens in the scenes of the play, there is clearly a positive message for Aboriginal audiences. This play, while it presents the facts of a dreadful immediate past, affirms Aboriginality and denies the assumptions of white history. These people are not a vanquished or beaten race; they have retained an identity. *No Sugar*, then, projects a message of hope.

This affirmation of Aboriginality also operates on the level of language. *No Sugar* is written in English, but it incorporates a significant number of Nyoongah words and traditional songs, especially in Act II, scene six, the corroboree scene. The play is published with translations of songs sung by Jimmy and Gran and a glossary of Nyoongah words. But in order to interpret what Aboriginal characters are saying, those of us who do not speak the language must constantly be turning to the back of the book, when we are reading the play. If we get sick of this, or are watching the play in performance, in the dark, then we cannot help but become aware that we are outsiders – the speakers have some secrets from us. The authority that goes with command of language is undermined for English speakers; this is another way in which the play reverses the historical balance of power.

No Sugar encourages us to re-examine ideas we might have about the dominant Australian culture in relation to the 'first born' Australians we meet in Davis's play. The Millimurra family do not emerge as model citizens but we do respond to them as warm, generous, hospitable, spirited, passionate, resilient human beings. The physical closeness of the Aboriginal performers (most of whom to date have not been professional actors but Aboriginal people reliving their experiences and being themselves) in the centre space, particularly around the camp fire, highlights the strength of Aboriginal kinship. By way of contrast, professional actors play the roles of white authorities who constantly struggle with bureaucracy and technology to communicate and be heard – often across long distances by telephone.

Davis manages to impart a great deal of information about what it was really like for Aboriginal people in the thirties in Western Australia, and by implication, what on-going interactions between Aboriginal and non-Aboriginal people in Australia have been like since settlement. It is important that this information should be palatable to non-Aboriginal audiences or readers, and Davis achieves this largely through humour. '[S]ugar catches more flies than vinegar', says Neville to Jimmy Munday in Act I, scene seven (39). It is, perhaps, one of the many ironies in the play that Neville should express part of the Aboriginal wisdom that informs the play. Although *No Sugar* functions to educate non-Aboriginal Australians, it is quite clear that Jack Davis is equally concerned with restoring identity, dignity, authority and a future to Aboriginal people. This is the extended political framework within which Davis works and it is enabled by hybridity that makes available a space for different cultural perspectives to operate simultaneously, contributing to the processes of reconstructing identities.

Archie Weller is different in his approach to writing. He is one of the first contemporary Aboriginal writers to favour fiction over autobiography or history. He is one of the first Aboriginal writers to play with the English language, using poetic imagery in his representations of people in the space or 'contact zone' (Pratt, Introduction) between Aboriginal and non-Aboriginal cultures. Many of Weller's written descriptions rely heavily on dramatic visual contrasts, particularly contrasts between light and dark/black and white. In 'Going Home', for example, there is a strong image of the black footballer, who stands out, but who also stands alone in the team because of his colour:

> *Black hands grab the ball. Black feet kick the ball. Black hopes go soaring with the ball to the pasty white sky.*
> *No one can stop him now. He forgets about the river of his Dreaming and the people of his blood and the girl in his heart. (2)*

Forgetting about his people, his ambition soars; as an outstanding individual he aspires to what the whitefellas' world has to offer. But the story demonstrates the impossibility of remaining suspended high in the white sky. He must drop back to the earth – back, in the end, to 'his dark, silent staring people, his rowdy, brawling, drunk people' (2).

In 'Saturday Night and Sunday Morning' there is a recognition of the beauty and potential of a world unrestricted by racial taboos when Perry Dogler and Melanie make love before dawn in the indeterminate time between night and day.

> *To the girl, it is as though she is floating down a calm brown river. To the boy, it is like drinking sweet love milk, white and cool. (64)*

Without love, however, this state of indeterminacy, where there is no clear boundary between black and white/night and day, cannot work its magic. Elvis Pinnell, the third party present in the 'almost dark', remains aware of Melanie's difference. He feels only 'anguish and renewed resentment' towards the white girl whom he perceives as an 'alien influence' (65). For Perry and Melanie the dream state is shattered and events end abruptly in violence, gunshot, and blood – red, red blood. Even so, Perry's death is represented in terms of contradiction. The printed image of the death's head on his shirt bleeds, as if it were alive. Perry's blood is both a sign of his life and his death. Death ends laughter and love, but it also ends hate and sorrow. In a life that is no life, death is nothing (65). Weller's 'message', then, is ambiguous. Certainly the lives he represents in his stories are desolate, but at the same time it is suggested that there are alternatives to alienation, violence and racial discrimination.

Weller's use of poetic imagery has been criticised as detracting from the politics that are crucial for most contemporary Aboriginal people – the insistence that they are survivors, despite a history of oppression. Some postcolonial critics, like Benita Parry, would support this view, arguing that if ever situations of oppression are to change in the real world, then literary representations of interactions between colonisers (for example white men from Britain or Europe) and those they colonise (for example indigenous people in Australia or Africa) must be formulated clearly in literature in terms of power struggles, where winners and losers/whites and blacks are presented as opposites and the sources and consequences of oppression are obvious. Weller does not do this. His characters do not appear to be 'fighting back'. His stories convey the way of life of a sector of urban Aboriginal youth who have known little other than city or suburban life. The Nyoongah voice is authentic enough, coming through dialogue between Aboriginal characters, but there is little sense of a future, let alone celebration of survival. Weller's characters are usually losers, and in the political context of establishing Aboriginal identities, this is, of course, a problem. However, we could approach Weller's stories in another way.

Not all postcolonial literary critics believe that representations of oppressed peoples should reproduce the conditions of, in effect, a war. Rather than thinking in terms of opposites – the oppressed and the oppressor/black people and white people – some postcolonial critics and theorists (Homi Bhabha foremost among them) would prefer to see writers and thinkers explore the complexities that exist between the extreme positions of losers and winners. The space between what is recognisably Aboriginal and recognisably European is a very interesting one, offering writers, dramatists and artists of all kinds the potential to generate new ways of thinking and new kinds of creativity. This might be another way of moving forward towards something like reconciliation: an alternative to taking sides and fighting out differences. We should not forget, however that this kind of approach is more likely to appeal in an intellectual sense to those who have had no direct experience of racial intolerance or oppression.

Archie Weller is usually perceived as setting out in his short stories and in his novel, *Day of the Dog* (1981), on which the film *Blackfellas* (1993) was based, to tell it 'like it is' – to paint pictures of a contemporary Aboriginal urban underclass – and he has been criticised for the bleakness of his representation, which might seem to equate Aboriginality with hopelessness (Narogin [Mudrooroo] 115–116). However, Marcia Langton has argued against an underlying assumption, in some criticism of Aboriginal writing, that 'all Aborigines are alike and equally understand each other, without regard to cultural variation, history, gender, sexual preference and so on' (27). She challenges the implication that there is a 'right way to be Aboriginal'. To accept such assumptions would be to apply a kind of censorship. Why should each piece of Aboriginal writing be taken as representative of a whole culture? Who is to say what that 'whole culture' is, anyway?

In *Going Home* and *The Day of the Dog* Archie Weller offers his readers a version of urban Aboriginal life as he knows it. In these fictions he writes from the position of an urban Aboriginal youth who is removed from traditional culture, yet still feels the pull of that culture. He is neither categorically white nor black and chooses to write about 'ordinary city people who just happen to be Aboriginal', insisting

> *I write emphatically about people with red hair and green eyes, blonde hair and olive eyes, grey eyes and roan chestnut hair, etc., as well as black hair and black-eyed brethren. They have as much right to be considered Aboriginal too. It is the way of the European to divide and conquer. (Little 205)*

Archie Weller is concerned with the problems of part-Aboriginal characters, even though part-Aboriginality is a concept that most Aboriginal writers reject. For Weller's characters, the condition of part-Aboriginality produces a sense of alienation and detachment and results in entrapment in cycles of poverty and crime. In the short story 'Going Home', Billy has 'the features of his white grandfather and the quietness of his Aboriginal forbears' (3). But he belongs nowhere. When he goes in search of his Aboriginality he realises that the consequences of choosing to belong to one group are painful rather than exhilarating. A great deal of Weller's imagery is imagery of pain and discomfort. When Billy arrives home he feels the rain 'prick' him all over (7) as he steps out of his car. His story doesn't end where most stories about the Aboriginal journey home would – at the waterhole where we would expect Billy to be reconnected with his father. Rather, 'Going Home' ends with an arrest, and 'home', ironically, becomes a police van taking Billy to prison.

Billy Woodward, city-educated artist and football player, cannot return home, cannot rediscover and reaffirm his Aboriginality without also discovering the prejudice of the police who label all blacks 'mongrel bastards', and 'all the same, thieving boongs' (11). Billy's choice is no choice – to live a solitary existence as a white man among people who will never accept him on equal terms, or to belong to a people who in his heart he believes can never achieve the kind of life he wants. Weller's characters, it seems, cannot win. Prejudice and government systems (the education system, the housing system, the health system, the employment system) beat them, regardless of their individual qualities, their determination and ambition. They cannot fight oppression. Nor can they join the systems which oppress them. If they do nothing they are still beaten.

Weller's stories, over and over again, reveal the dilemma of characters like Billy Woodward who want to realise their potential but who find that part-Aboriginality renders them invisible, or brands them as 'people who [don't] mind living in [a] nothing town as nothings' ('Cooley' 213).

It is understandable why some critics (Mudrooroo, for example) have condemned Weller's stories, which can be read as having nothing positive to offer Aboriginal communities. We could, however, read the stories differently – as evidence and a critique of the destructiveness of our tendency in the Western world to define ourselves in relation to our opposites, or what we are not. (If I am white then I may define myself as not black; if I am female then I may define myself as not male.) Weller's stories could be read as an argument for transcending those kinds of categories (binaries, polarities or opposites), or at least blurring or extending them. As long as binaries, such as black/white, are our means of defining who we are, those who do not fit the existing categories will have no identity or 'no tribe' (Weller, 'Cooley' 179), no potential, no future. In effect, according to this prescription, such individuals cannot exist, and in

Weller's stories, over and over again, those who define themselves as 'not black and not white' disappear or are killed off. Cooley, from Weller's long story or novella at the end of the collection, admits that 'White man had defeated *him* on the day he was born' (179). Cooley, expressing the view that people like him, products of two races, belong nowhere, looks at the hybrid faces of his half-brothers and asks himself:

> *What were these people? Were they Aboriginals? With clothes and boots, cigarettes and cars, radios and money? Greed and hate and jealousy? And a strange mongrel language, product of their mongrel breeding? (196)*

Cooley cuts himself off from his Aboriginality: as far as he is concerned there is nothing left to rediscover. Paradoxically, though, in thinking about the past, he articulates the value of his ancestry and the magnitude of crimes committed against his ancestors (196). If he fails to survive, it is because he refuses one label, 'Aboriginal', but cannot refuse or transcend another label, 'half-caste', to realise the possibilities of a new identity.

> *'Here's a question, Reg. What would you rather be? A white man or an Aboriginal?'*
> *Cooley smiled at her. 'What would you like me to be?'*
> *'What would you like to be!' returned the girl, then they both laughed.*
> *'I dunno,' muttered Cooley, suddenly serious. (198–199)*

Why *should* Cooley have to choose? Why *should* he accept the nowhere label that becomes his epitaph: 'Only half-caste Cooley'? It is because he cannot reinvent himself that he dies 'eaten out by white man's ways, but ... killed by a black man' (213).

While the stories in *Going Home* deal with themes of loss of identity and the disintegration of Aboriginal kinship, they nevertheless perpetuate something of the special qualities of Aboriginality. This occurs when characters' memories of a better way erupt into the present. It is through communal memory (even though this is vaguely expressed at times) that Aboriginal characters are connected to their past, to their dreaming, to their tribal lands. In 'Saturday Night and Sunday Morning', for example, Perry thinks about what he would like to say to the white girl, Melanie:

He would like to tell her how once everyone shared everything
and no one was poor. How could anyone be poor with the silver
songs of birds raining down from the cool leaves, and honeyed
flowers for jewels, and diamond-eyed children with hearts of gold?
(60)

More consistently, though, Weller's stories establish a sense of Aboriginality in their emphasis on the very strong relationship between the (part-)Aboriginal characters and the natural environment. In the story 'Herbie', white children recognise Herbie's special knowledge of the land (94). Elsewhere, the pull of the land is felt in dreams, and whenever characters leave the built-up environment. The stories suggest that a connection with the land exists even when the characters themselves are unaware of it. In 'Saturday Night and Sunday Morning' Perry Dogler and Elvis Pinnell, although they wear white men's clothing, use white men's weapons and dream white men's dreams, are nevertheless described as part of Aboriginal Dreaming:

Outside in the night, trees, ghostly white or shadowy dark, stamp
out a wild dance, throwing their heavy bodies into strange and
beautiful shapes. Perhaps imprisoned in each one is an
Aboriginal soul, moaning to be let out to float up to the sky. Every
one of them is an ancestor of cruel Perry Dogler and laughing
Elvis Pinnell. But they do not know, these two ... (48)

The violence of Perry Dogler, known as the Wolf, is attributed to white society, which will not accept him, and which provides the means for him to destroy and be destroyed. But there is another part of him, waiting to be (re-)discovered. The fact that he is unable to find inner peace and recognise the value of his Aboriginality is also attributable to white society:

And when white society finishes throwing spiteful stones into the
pond, when he can get away for a little while and let the pool
become still, there is a reflection that is a most precious thing.
(59)

The necessary condition to dispel Perry's anger is 'friendship. Then perhaps love' (62). And for the briefest moment, he does find love, in a relationship with a white girl (64). Such 'love', however, is transgressive of established 'norms', and inevitably results in Perry's death.

Despite the fact that most of Weller's stories deal with the absences of friendship and love there are moments (dreams, day-dreams, special states of consciousness) when Aboriginal characters are able to transcend the harsh realities of the present and imagine a future in which, reconnected to the land, they know their special identity. One example occurs in 'Cooley', when Reg briefly acknowl-edges the spiritual aspect of his being and reclaims the land and the sunset as his. He thinks:

> when all the white men were dead and mouldering, his spirit would live on. All the other dark, silent spirits that mingled with the mists or smoke from campfires, and whose voices echoed with the wind or didgeridoo – they would return and it would be their land again. (176)

Perhaps the tragedy of Weller's characters is not so much their loss of Aboriginal identity but rather the fact that their Aboriginality lies mostly (though not always) dormant. Weller's characters may describe themselves as 'nothings'. Nevertheless, it is clear from the context of the stories that the failure of Weller's characters to belong or to materialise as proud and surviving identities is not a failure of Aboriginality, but of systems of classification, imposed and main-tained by whitefellas and fuelled by racism. Those defined as '[H]alf-brothers and cousins' (180) have always been inconvenient reminders of 'the white man's lust that had spawned this tribe' (179). Defined as incomplete, or as shameful mistakes, they are banished to somewhere (nowhere) 'out of sight and out of mind'. As long as we continue to think categorically in terms of black or white, we can render the 'not-black/not-white' invisible. But that is exactly what Weller's writing refuses to allow. Weller's stories position the 'nowhere' people where, as readers, we can no longer ignore them. They *are* his stories. They fill the pages of his books. They are in our faces. This confrontation is crucial to on-going negotiations which in the future will determine how all Australians think about themselves.

Works Cited

Bhabha, Homi. 'The Commitment to Theory'. *New Formations* 5 (1988): 5–23.

Bowden, Ros and Bill Bunbury, eds. *Being Aboriginal*. Sydney: ABC, 1990.

Davis, Jack. *Black Life: Poems*. St Lucia: University of Queensland Press, 1992.

Davis, Jack. *No Sugar*. Sydney: Currency Press, 1986.

Langford Ginibi, Ruby. *The Australian* Weekend Review May 2–3 (1992): 6.

Langton, Marcia. *'Well I heard it on the radio, saw it on the television – ': an essay for the Australian Film Corporation on the politics and aesthetics of filmmaking by and about Aboriginal people and things*. North Sydney: The Commission, c. 1993.

Little, Janine. 'An Interview with Archie Weller'. *Australian Literary Studies* 16. 2 (1993): 200–207.

Narogin, Mudrooroo [also known as Mudrooroo and Colin Johnson]. *Writing from the Fringe: A Study of Modern Aboriginal Literature*. Melbourne: Hyland House, 1990.

Parry, Benita. 'Problems in Current Theories of Colonial Discourse'. *Oxford Literary Review* 9 (1987): 27–57.

Pratt, Mary Louise. *Imperial Eyes: Travel Writing and Transculturation*. London; New York: Routledge, 1992.

Weller, Archie. *Going Home*. Sydney: Allen and Unwin, 1986.

Weller, Archie. *Day of the Dog*. Sydney: Allen and Unwin, 1981.

Young, Robert. *Colonial Desire: Hybridity in Theory, Culture and Race*. London; New York: Routledge, 1995.

Further Reading/Viewing

Aboriginal Film Institute. *First Born: The Life and Times of Jack Davis*. 1987.

Biskup, Peter. *Not Slaves, Not Citizens: The Aboriginal Problem in Western Australia 1898–1954*. St Lucia: Queensland UP, 1973.

Chesson, Keith. *Jack Davis: A Life Story*. Melbourne: Dent, 1988.

Dibble, Brian and Margaret MacIntyre. 'Hybridity in Jack Davis' *No Sugar*'. *Westerley* 4 (1992): 93–98.

Elder, Arlene. 'Self, Other and Post-Historical Identity in Three Plays by Jack Davis', *Journal of Commonwealth Literature* 30. 1 (1990): 204–215.

Hodge, Bob and Vijay Mishra. *Dark Side of the Dream: Australian Literature and the Postcolonial Mind*. Sydney: Allen & Unwin, 1991.

Little, Janine. 'Deadly Work: Reading the Short Fiction of Archie Weller'. *Australian Literary Studies* 16.2 (1993): 190–199.

Maxwell, Anne, 'The Debate on Current Theories of Colonial Discourse'. *Kunapipi* 13. 3 (1991): 70–84.

Shoemaker, Adam. 'An Interview with Jack Davis', *Westerley* 4 (1982): 111–116.

Tiffin, Chris. 'Relentless Realism: Archie Weller's *Going Home*' in *Aboriginal Culture Today*. Ed. Anna Rutherford. Sydney: Dangaroo Press, 1988 (special double issue of *Kunapipi* 10 1–2) 222–235.

Turcotte, Gerry, ed. *Jack Davis: The Maker of History*. Sydney: Angus and Robertson, 1994.

Reading Film and Popular Culture

Representation, Power and Genre in The Piano

Philip Butterss

Since the earliest feature films at the beginning of the twentieth century there have been many approaches to the study of film. Initially the new narrative form was looked down on as popular, as a form of 'mass entertainment', but from about 1915, there were those who recognised and promoted the potential of the medium for producing 'high art'. This interest in the aesthetics of film was to dominate discussion for many decades, splitting the output of the industry into art films, which were regarded favourably, and popular films, which were not. *Auteur* theory was an influential development in this way of viewing film, involving the privileging of the director as the 'author' of an art work that derived from his or her personal vision, at the expense of the rest of the large team who actually had creative input. Since perhaps the 1970s there has been a pronounced shift away from limiting the focus of film study to 'art', and a consequent broadening of the kinds of films that are appropriate for analysis (Turner 27–43). Many of the recent books on film have examined horror films, action films, teen films, and romantic comedies – the kind of material unlikely to have received much critical attention in the past.

This broadening of the kind of films available for serious analysis has coincided with the application of a diverse set of methodologies which are able to ask a much wider range of questions. Since the 1970s the analysis of film has drawn on methodologies employed by a variety of disciplines and theoretical standpoints including anthropology, history, linguistics, literary studies, Marxism, politics, psychoanalysis, semiotics, and women's studies. One of the most important approaches in recent years has been that of cultural studies. What constitutes cultural studies is a widely debated topic, and the work that goes on under the banner of cultural studies is constantly breaking boundaries. However, many would agree with Tony Bennett when he argues that what is distinctive about the approaches used in cultural studies is that they are readily applicable to the exploration of power of various kinds (Bennett 23). Cultural studies has been particularly interested in questions about power in relation to race, class, gender, and, more recently, postcoloniality and sexuality.

This essay gives examples of three different ways that contemporary film studies might approach a film. In the first section it looks at one of *The Piano*'s departures from previous conventions of cinematic representation. The second section offers a reading of some significant issues addressed in the film. And the third examines the way that *The Piano* employs some specific genres. What links these three diverse areas of film study – history, textual analysis, and genre study – as they are briefly demonstrated here, is the focus on issues of gender, sexuality and postcoloniality.

One of the things that often comes up in conversations about *The Piano* is Baines's body – the body of the character played by Harvey Keitel. It is a striking body: powerful, muscular, but also partly gone to seed; a body that is made up of many interesting lines which the camera is able slowly to trace. For a while the film is tauntingly coy about how much of Baines's body will be revealed, but finally, in soft lighting, we see the lot. It is not the *sort* of body, nor *parts* of the body, that we are used to seeing presented for our gaze.

The notion of 'the gaze' has been influential in film study since the publication in 1975 of Laura Mulvey's article called 'Visual Pleasure and Narrative Cinema'. Mulvey sets out a complex argument which is worth reading in full, but two of her most fundamental points are useful in an introductory examination of *The Piano*. First she draws interesting parallels between watching film and acting as a voyeur, suggesting that the conventions of film portray 'a hermetically sealed world which unwinds magically' before the audience, producing a sense of separation, of voyeurism. Mulvey points to the darkness of the auditorium and the brilliance of the patterns of light and shade on the screen as helping 'to promote the illusion of voyeuristic separation'. The spectator has an illusion of looking in on a private world (9). *The Piano* very deliberately draws attention to the audience's and the characters' roles as voyeurs.

Secondly, Mulvey has important things to say about gender in relation to the watching of film. For subsequent film studies Mulvey's most influential suggestion is that in representation the gaze is male, and that women, therefore, have been styled 'to-be-looked-at':

> *In a world ordered by sexual imbalance, pleasure in looking has been split between active/male and passive/female. The determining male gaze projects its phantasy on to the female figure which is styled accordingly. In their traditional exhibitionist role women are simultaneously looked at and displayed, with their appearance coded for strong visual and erotic impact so that they can be said to connote to-be-looked-at-ness. (11)*

In 1975 Mulvey argued that, in mainstream Hollywood cinema, men were not the object of the gaze, and that film audiences identified with, rather than gazed at, the male lead actor. She suggested that the audience identified, among other things, with his gazing at the women in the film (12).

In *The Piano*, we do see at least one of the male lead actors gazing, quite explicitly as a voyeur – one critic has likened Ada's husband, Stewart, to 'a furtive frustrated gentleman at a peep show'. We see Stewart observing Ada through the camera eyepiece as she poses in her wedding dress, and, more pointedly, we see him perving on Ada and Baines as they have sex instead of a piano lesson (Bruzzi 10). One might understand his looking through cracks in a wall to find out what is going on, but his deliberately crawling in under the house – with its connotations as a childhood space – is a striking sign of his stunted sexual growth. 'Stunted' is an adjective Stewart applies to Ada, but it is he who is stunted in a variety of ways.

At those moments, our viewpoint is linked to that of Stewart; we see what he sees. But at many points in the film, Campion is deliberately *drawing into question* the maleness of the gaze. Flora also peeps through the cracks. Ada herself peeks behind the curtain at Baines, who, she discovers, is undressed. More importantly the audience is positioned to see Baines as the object of *its* gaze; his body is displayed at length and sensuously as to-be-looked-at. This shift to having men displayed as the object of the gaze is a feature of contemporary popular culture. (Another striking example is the way that Brad Pitt's body is presented for the audience's delectation in the similarly feminist film, *Thelma and Louise*.) As Stella Bruzzi has commented of *The Piano*, 'in this formal Victorian world, Harvey Keitel's proud nakedness is both shocking and liberating. Convention is inverted as the man is constructed as a sexual being before the woman'. In keeping with the film's interest in altering the traditional codes of representation to a more equal version, when they finally do have sex, Baines and Ada get undressed together (10).

At the same time as deliberately challenging what has been a dominant representational practice in the twentieth century in the way it depicts and employs the gaze, *The Piano* also focuses on the issue of breaking free of restrictive social practices in its narrative. The film depicts a Victorian society that is repressive in a range of ways, particularly for women. It establishes this focus at the outset when one of the first pieces of information we learn is that Ada has been married by her father to someone she has never met. Once in New Zealand, Stewart tries to continue with this process of controlling Ada, keeping her within the bounds of convention. One of the interesting ways that the repression is represented is through Flora, who, because of her jealousy of her mother's relationship with Baines, assists in the policing of Ada's behaviour.

In *The Piano* we see that although there are many restrictions placed on Ada by her culture, these can sometimes have a liberating aspect, or else can be turned to her advantage through her own efforts. Throughout the film there is a focus on the extraordinary encumbrances which are her clothes. As Raymond Younis has pointed out, 'she constantly walks through this wilderness covered in layer upon layer – itself an interesting strategy on a symbolic level – with corset, petticoat, chemise, skirt, pantaloons, etc., and not surprisingly does experience some difficulty' (50). An example of the way clothing operates as restriction is the awkwardness with which Morag relieves herself when she has been 'caught short', as Victorians might say. One of the first images of Ada is of her being carried off the boat in full crinoline, unable to manoeuvre herself, and cumbersome for her bearers. But we soon see that she is able to use this encumbrance as a tent for herself and Flora to shelter in on the beach. Similarly her clothes are important in allowing her to avoid being raped by Stewart. The intricacies of the layers are beyond him (Bruzzi 10).

Humphrey McQueen has a chapter in his book, *A New Britannia*, discussing the considerable popularity of pianos in nineteenth-century Australia. McQueen suggests that they operated as a marker of social respectability – something particularly important for a settler society in the New World (117–119). In polite, nineteenth-century society playing the piano is a proper, ladylike pastime, but Ada transforms the practice, using the instrument as a powerful means of expression. In this she is contrasted with Morag and Nessie. While she is relieving herself, Morag talks to Nessie about how unre-strained – how unladylike – Ada's piano playing is: 'She does not play the piano as we do ... Your playing [Nessie's] is plain and true and that is what I like. To have a sound creep inside you is not all pleasant'. Interestingly, Morag, in registering her disapproval, is also inadvertently revealing that she, too, has a passionate side. She can feel the power of the music, but finds that feeling disturbing, and wishes to repress it.

Ada's decision not to speak, at the age of six, was one of the first ways that her opposition to the dominant values of the world she lived in was exhibited. In her refusal to speak, she is representative of what the medical profession would have branded an 'hysterical' woman (Bruzzi 8). But in a world which placed severe limitations on what it was possible for a woman to do and say, choosing not to speak is a decisive way to refuse to participate, and, through that, to regain a certain degree of power. One of the first examples we see of Ada's almost eerily powerful will is the image of her and Flora waiting outside Baines's house expectantly until he does what he has refused several times – take them to the beach.

Jane Campion has spoken of Ada's silence in the film:

> She chose not to speak. It's never quite made clear why, and it appears even she can't remember the reason.
>
> There is no sense of her as a handicapped person, however. It's almost as though she treats the world as if it were handicapped. At the same time, there is a great deal of suffering from this position. It is a retreat from a lot of what the world offers, which I imagine for women at that time would have been very mundane and boring – insufferable, in fact. There is advantage in her retreat, but there's a great disadvantage in it as well. (Quoted in Bilbrough 7)

Without the language of speech, Ada finds an array of different methods of communication. Campion mentions Holly Hunter's 'elo-quent eyes' as one of the ways in which Ada communicates from deep within herself, but, of course, what she really needs to say, she says with her piano. At times she uses it as one uses a voice in daily conversation to communicate simple information: when Baines first tells her that he just wants to listen, she chooses to play scales, belligerently registering that she's not particularly happy with giving him lessons. Later she interrupts his advances by shifting from sensuous music to something comical, employing music to tell him to get his hands off her. The instrument becomes a metaphor for Ada's deepest self, so that when she removes a key, it is like removing a part of herself, and, sure enough one of her own fingers is lopped off as a result. Later, when she tries to destroy the piano, she is trying to destroy herself, and the shot of the piano plunging into the sea, dragging Ada down into the depths, inseparable from her, is one of the film's most powerful images.

As Lizzie Francke suggests, much of the communication between Ada and Baines is 'based on a sensuous play of touch, smell and sound. Bodies become instruments of expression, while the piano smelling of scent and salt becomes corporeal' (11). Ada strokes its keys erotically; Baines takes off his shirt to clean the instrument, but this develops into a sensuous caressing – as if it were an extension of Ada's body. Baines massages Ada's leg through the hole in her black stocking. After such erotic and extra-verbal exchange, it is significant that Ada's use of the written word to convey her feelings to Baines brings catastrophe (11).

The central constraint that the film shows Ada overcoming is, of course, sexual repression. Perhaps the most vivid depiction of the absurdity of Victorian attitudes to sex is Flora whitewashing trees because Stewart has been so disgusted at seeing her embrace them as part of the game she has been playing with the Maori kids. He feels that she has shamed the trees, although the logic of this view is not entirely clear. Stewart is emblematic of repressed Victorian respectability, set against the relaxed sexual attitudes of the Maoris, but contrasted in more detail with the increasing sensuality and sexuality of Ada, slowly awakening through her contact with Baines. Right from the start Stewart is shown as embarrassed and puzzled to discover Ada and Flora sheltering under the hoops of her skirt. He awkwardly begins his rehearsed greeting, clearly uncomfortable in the close proximity of women's undergarments (Bruzzi 10). As Bruzzi points out:

> *Stewart . . . is frustrated by how far he is from unlocking the 'mystery' of sexuality and remains unable to break free of his social and gender stereotype. He is left stranded, yearning but unable to deal with the reality of closeness. (9)*

Perhaps surprisingly, given the way he acts on many occasions, there is a considerable degree of sympathy for Stewart and the confusion he faces as he is tormented by urges that conflict with his severe ideas about proper behaviour. In the second of those two surprising scenes when Ada, having slept with Baines, begins a kind of sexual experimentation with her husband by stroking his bare back and moving her fingers down to his buttocks, Stewart pulls his own trousers back up, in spite of the fact that he is also evidently desperate for sexual contact. He wants to touch her, but not have her touch him. He wants to fulfil *his own* desires, but a woman initiating sexual activity is too confronting for him.

Through the film we gradually see the awakening in Ada of the female desire whose existence the Victorian age was famous for denying. Perhaps the most striking image of the freedom she feels from discovering and fulfilling sexual desires is in the scene back in Stewart's house which follows her first experience of sex with Baines. One of the ways the film achieves a convincing nineteenth-century feel is with the look of the women's hair. Campion has commented on the fact that in nineteenth-century photographs the women's hair is so often greasy (Campion 139). Ada's prim Victorian sternness is well-captured in her braided, greasy hair, tightly bound around her head. But immediately after the sex scene we see that she and Flora have washed their hair and are dancing wildly around their bedroom with their hair down, swirling it about, in a way that over-excited children sometimes do.

This liberatory version of the relationship between Ada and Baines is the one that the film endorses, but it is not all there is. Baines has quite deliberately traded land with Stewart so that he can obtain the piano, an item he knows will give him an extremely powerful hold over Ada. And the deal they strike – using it to buy sexual favours of varying degrees – is clearly, at root, a version of prostitution. At one point Baines acknowledges this, telling Ada that the arrangement is 'making you a whore and me wretched'. For a number of viewers the implication that prostitution is liberating for women is one of the film's prominent, and unacceptable, meanings.

Running parallel to *The Piano*'s concerns with repressions of various sorts within the coloniser's society is an interest in colonisation itself. Our first view of the New World is of the broad expanse of the beach – it is an image, in part, of the possibility of openness, of freedom – and the pounding surf of the waves perhaps hints at the kind of passions that might be able to be revealed here. When Ada plays the instrument there seems to be a connection between the strange, wild landscape and the strange wild music she produces. It may be that in this new world there is the possibility of a new, vigorous, previously unimagined future (Younis 50). But *The Piano* contains a sustained, if low-level, criticism of the way that colonisation is operating.

Campion uses a familiar metaphor from feminism in the 1970s and 1980s to draw parallels between colonisation of the land, and male colonisation of women. Stewart is both husband, and coloniser, deeply interested in acquiring land, marking it out, holding on to it. The central act of handing the piano to Baines is, of course to gain more land, and, according to one critic Stewart 'attempts to shape it and control it, as he will attempt to control Ada and shape her life' (Younis 50).

The relationship with the Maoris is another area where Stewart is depicted as cold and hard, and unable to comprehend the world other than in material and commercial terms. He tries to buy land with buttons, blankets, and finally guns, but can have no understanding of the Maoris' relationship with the land. 'What do they want it for? They don't cultivate it, burn it back, anything. How do they even know it's theirs . . .?', he asks. Baines, in contrast, is able to see more deeply, and has a strong affinity with the Maoris. Campion uses representatives of the colonised people to offer a commentary on the colonising society from a vantage point largely outside it, with their sexual openness operating as a critique of Pakeha repressiveness.

Certainly there was some Maori input into the film, with Campion going so far as to refer to the writer, Waihoroi Shortland, as her 'collaborator' (Bilbrough 11), but several commentators have been critical of the representation of Maoris. One view is that they are, 'as a group, too homogenous in the film' (Younis 51). Stronger criticisms are expressed by Leonie Pihama:

> *What we have in* The Piano *is a series of constructions of Maori people which are located firmly in a colonial gaze, which range from the 'happy go lucky native' to the sexualised Maori woman available at all times to service Pakeha men. The perception of Maori people given in* The Piano *is that our* tipuna *were naive, simple-minded, lacked reason, acted impulsively and spoke only in terms of sexual innuendo, with a particular obsession with male genitalia. For Maori people* The Piano *is dangerous.* (240)

In exploring the position of women in a repressive society *The Piano* draws, in particular, on Gothic and Romance, two genres which were often used by women to construct narratives about women, and for women, in the nineteenth century, and whose use, in modified ways, has continued to the present. Campion talks about her debt to the work of two nineteenth-century women writers, both of whom had an interest in the Gothic: Emily Brontë, whose *Wuthering Heights*, Campion suggests, is important to the genesis of the film, and Emily Dickinson. She says: 'in a way, Dickinson led such a secret life, and my main character, Ada, does as well. She is secretive not because she closeted herself in a room, but because she won't speak'. Campion goes on to say that she admires Dickinson and Brontë and the sensibility they brought to their work: 'both were recluses and they held their sensibility at some cost to themselves'. Campion points to a poem of Dickinson's from which she draws particular inspiration – a poem that has some connections with the film:

> *Much Madness is divinest Sense –,*
> *To a discerning Eye –*
> *Much Sense – the starkest Madness –*
> *Tis the majority*
> *In this, as All, prevail –*
> *Assert you are sane –*
> *Demur – you're straightway dangerous –*
> *And handled with a Chain – (Quoted in Bilbrough 6–7)*

These lines, of course, have resonances with a number of aspects of the way Ada and others in *The Piano* are depicted. Ada is regarded as mad by Stewart and Aunt Morag; she is understood by Baines's 'discerning eye'; we know that Ada's *own* 'discerning eye' regards most of what the majority says as nonsense; and we see that at times – particularly in the Gothic section – she is, effectively, handled with a chain.

It is difficult to provide a full and clear definition of the Gothic, but it is possible to point to some of the general ways in which *The Piano* draws on its features. The Gothic story is sometimes said to have a great deal of trouble getting itself told – through mysteries at the plot level, through the failure of language, or because the horrors that are alluded to are too terrible, or, in some way, 'unspeakable'. In *The Piano* there is a powerful aura of mystery, people's motivations are difficult to discern, and the film is significantly concerned with the difficulties of language. Another important part of the Gothic is its focus on confinement – in the tomb, in the grave, and in the house. Indeed, a number of critics have argued that the medieval castle that featured in many of the earliest Gothic novels could be interpreted by readers of those novels, at some level, as a displaced version of the home – a site that could offer protection, but which also could signify entrapment and imprisonment.

As we have already seen, *The Piano* often considers the double aspect of items such as the crinoline, which is shown to be constricting, but also as offering comfort. An example more closely linked to the traditions of the Gothic is the way that Stewart boards up the house, literally turning a Victorian home into a prison, although its smallness and darkness, and perhaps its markers of suitable women's activity such as sewing, had always seemed to constrain Ada. On the other hand, enclosure is shown to have alternative possibilities, with Ada finding the enclosed space of Baines's house liberating. The film draws an explicit contrast between her refusing to obey Baines's repeated orders to get out of his house, and Stewart trapping her in his. Another staple element from the Gothic is the nightmarish feeling of being rooted to the spot, used in the film when Ada is paralysed with fear after Stewart bursts into the house with the axe. Her sleepwalking, too, has connections with some earlier instances of the Gothic, such as the Madwoman-in-the-attic section of *Jane Eyre*.

A device more specific to the medium of film is the bluish tone employed in *The Piano* to convey a dreamlike quality to its most Gothic sequences. When he knows what Ada and Baines are up to, Stewart waits for her on her way to Baines's house, jumps out from behind a tree, looking wild, and tries to rape her. The shot of his terrifying, bluish face cuts to one of her terrified expression. Perhaps not very subtly, Stewart here becomes Bluebeard, taking the audience back to the play that Campion has used earlier to provide another layer of symbols. In this well-known story, Bluebeard's last wife is given a key to a secret room, but told by her husband not to open it. When she does, she finds her husband's previous wives, dead. In most versions the key is covered in blood, and this gives her away. In the play shown in *The Piano*, the husband attacks her with an axe, and instead of her brothers coming to save her, some of the Maoris from the audience rush to her rescue. The Bluebeard story is often interpreted in sexual terms, as a coded tale: the secret room is seen as a symbol of female sexuality or female desire to be kept locked up, with strict punishments for transgression. Campion is clearly playing with these associations in the film. Stewart is Bluebeard, attempting to control his wife, but the piano key she sends to Baines reveals that her desire is not controlled, so he comes with the axe to punish her.

Finally, the landscape itself is carefully used to convey a Gothic air. Campion says that she wanted to capture 'the vivid, subconscious imagery of the bush, its dark, inner world' (Campion 139). At a number of points the bare branches of the trees appear like prison bars, and one critic has said that the landscape is 'so vividly captured that it becomes, almost, a character in the film, and its wild beauty and its desolate aspects add immeasurably to the sense of a melodrama of repression, suppression, dark passion and the consequent violence unfolding on the screen' (Younis 51). Andrew McAlpine, the production designer for the film has discussed the use of landscape for particular, often very specific, effects:

> *It's a classical pictorial depiction of silhouetted objects against the sky, with nature – through the branches of the large pohutakawa trees – like tentacles reaching out to grab the women, continuing the idea of entrapment. We often altered the landscape to heighten the feeling of a particular scene, as in the scene where Stewart attacks Ada, where the setting was too open so we gave it a web of supplejack, an anarchical tough black-branched creeper which we devised into a web, a huge net, like a tentacled nightmare in which Ada and Stewart struggle. (Colbert 8)*

The links between the Romance and the Gothic are such that the literary critic, Northrop Frye, refers to Gothic as 'dark romance'. One interpretation of the relationship between the two genres is concerned with whether or not the hero undergoes a transformation. It is suggested that in romance narrative the male hero is softened – turned from a tyrant into a more domesticated romance hero. In line with this structure, in *Jane Eyre* Rochester turns from overbearing tyrant to a softer, more loving romance hero. In Gothic narratives, however, it is suggested that the male hero remains a tyrant. In *The Piano* there is no substantial transformation of a hero; instead, it is as if Stewart and Baines already occupy the two different hero positions. Stewart begins the film cold and distant, noticing that Ada seems small. Baines begins the film as a more sympathetic character, noticing her tiredness. Their respective roles as Gothic hero and Romance hero gradually become more defined, as time passes.

It has often been noted that in nineteenth-century narratives, the kind of models that Campion was, in some ways, deliberately rewriting, there are two basic endings for the female heroes – death or marriage. *The Piano* effectively provides its audience with both those endings. The potential drowning when Ada is dragged into the water by the piano is a kind of Gothic ending, with drowning operating as a version of the stock Gothic trope of being buried alive. This possible conclusion to the film is then followed by the romance ending, where she settles down with Baines in a little house of their own.

A number of viewers of the film feel that the second ending is disappointing – that the film should have finished with Ada choosing to die with the piano, and a very powerful conclusion that would have been. People have wondered whether the more positive – and more sentimental – ending was to some extent forced on Campion. This is a common enough phenomenon – evidently Gillian Armstrong had to fight very hard not to have *My Brilliant Career* finishing with Sybylla and Harry together, which was the ending favoured by those who financed that film. Campion has not said that there was any pressure on her; rather she says that there was always going to be an epilogue, and that during the process of making the film she decided to make it 'more romantic' (Bilbrough 8).

Some readings of the film's conclusion focus on its positive aspects. For example Raymond Younis suggests that once Ada is freed from the patriarchal ethic 'which determines whom she will marry and where, she may ... learn to speak again' (51). Ada's murmurs during sex with Baines are probably the first operations of her vocal chords, the first step towards speech. Bruzzi points out that

> *through* The Piano *Ada discovers the means to articulate what she wants – ... through choosing Baines over Stewart, choosing not to be drowned by her sinking piano, and finally choosing to learn to speak when she and Baines have started a new life together in Nelson. (10)*

According to this positive interpretation of the film, the descent into the water that looked as if it was going to be Ada's death becomes a kind of birth. Ada is clearly enticed by death, but chooses to reject it.

But how uplifting is this rejection of death? Commentaries on nineteenth-century narratives have often pointed out that marriage is, in fact, a kind of textual death for the heroine. It is the point at which her life stops having narrative interest; it is the point where the novel stops. In *The Piano* the ending that involves a literal death might be rejected, but there are many ways in which life with Baines is, or will be, a kind of death for Ada. The scenes in Nelson with

Baines are brighter than the rest of the film, but it is a light that is more of a sickly brightness than a positive, sunny future. Ada is seen in mourning clothes, her head covered in a black veil. She taps out notes with the artificial finger providing a grating beat that distracts from the playing – she *teaches* the piano, a respectable occupation for a lady. Her silver finger marks her as the town freak, and this gives her a certain, limited satisfaction, as it would.

But at night she lulls herself to sleep by thinking of herself attached to the piano, skirts billowing out like a balloon, drifting in the silence beneath the sea. It is this final image, and the words spoken by the voice-over from Thomas Hood's sonnet, titled 'Silence', that we take with us:

There is a silence where hath been no sound
There is a silence where no sound may be
In the cold grave, under the deep, deep sea.

The sound of Ada's vocal chords has replaced the sound of the piano, but it is clear which of the two was the more expressive – and now it is silent.

What the double ending of *The Piano* does is to make a twentieth-century comment on the plots that were available for women in nineteenth-century fiction, and, to an extent, in nineteenth-century life. The film's contemporary feminist perspective demonstrates what was not made explicit to nineteenth-century readers – that there was a deep similarity between the two potential endings for heroines of death or marriage.

The more positive moments occur in the body of the narrative. In depicting the successful, if brief, fulfilment of female sexual desire, *The Piano* can go much further than the nineteenth-century novels whose stories the film is re-working. Similarly, the film focuses much more than nineteenth-century narratives on how a woman can resist the repressions of Victorian society in tactical ways – finding a power in silence, refusing to move from outside Baines's house until he agrees to take her to the piano, finding a haven in the crinoline, transforming the 'lady-like' activity of playing the piano into a powerful means of expression.

In doing these things in its narrative, *The Piano* is making a contribution to current debates about the power relations between men and women, both historical and contemporary, and, to a lesser extent, and perhaps more ambivalently, it is making a contribution to debates about the rights of indigenous people. And in the way that it treats the idea of the gaze, and in its representation of male and female bodies, *The Piano* is also making a positive intervention into a late twentieth-century struggle over filmic and other representation.

Works Cited

Bennett, Tony. 'Putting Policy into Cultural Studies' in *Cultural Studies*. Eds. Lawrence Grossberg *et al.* New York and London: Routledge, 1992.

Bilbrough, Miro. '*The Piano*: Jane Campion interviewed by Miro Bilbrough'. *Cinema Papers* 93 (May 1993): 5–11.

Bruzzi, Stella. 'Bodyscape'. *Sight and Sound* 5. 10 (1993): 7–10.

Campion, Jane. *The Piano* [script]. London: Bloomsbury, 1993.

Colbert, Mary. '*The Piano*'. *Sight and Sound* 5. 10 (1993): 8–9.

Francke, Lizzie. '*The Piano*'. *Sight and Sound* 5.11 (1993): 50–51.

McQueen, Humphrey. *A New Britannia*. Harmondsworth: Penguin, 1970.

Mulvey, Laura. 'Visual Pleasure and Narrative Cinema'. *Screen* 16.3 (1975): 6–18.

Pihama, Leonie. 'Are Films Dangerous? A Maori Woman's Perspective on *The Piano*'. *Hecate* 20.2 (1994): 239–242.

Turner, Graeme. *Film as Social Practice*. London and New York: Routledge, 1993.

Younis, Raymond. '*The Piano*'. *Cinema Papers* 95 (October 1993): 50–51.

Further Reading

Bruzzi, Stella. 'Tempestuous Petticoats: Costume and Desire in *The Piano*'. *Screen* 36.3 (1995): 257–266.

Dyson, Lynda. 'The Return of the Repressed? Whiteness, Femininity and Colonialism in *The Piano*'. *Screen* 36.3 (1995): 267–276.

Gillett, Sue. 'Lips and Fingers: Jane Campion's *The Piano*'. *Screen* 36.3 (1995): 277–287.

Gordon, Suzy. ''I Clipped Your Wing, That's All': Auto-Eroticism and The Female Spectator in *The Piano* Debate'. *Screen* 37.2 (1996): 193–205.

'Did he smile his work to see?' The Compelling Aesthetics of Murder in The Silence of the Lambs

Joy McEntee

When approaching film with critical intent, it is tempting to use the reading habits developed in relation to literature – particularly plays and novels. These are often useful reading strategies, but by no means do they provide a complete set of tools for analysing film. Part of the problem is that both the novel and the stage play privilege the word over the image. In film, by contrast, the image is infinitely more powerful than the word. A related complication is that the relationship between the cinematic image and that to which it refers is vastly different from the relationship between the word and that which it signifies. Monaco gives a succinct account of the philosophical problem involved:

> For semiologists, a sign must consist of two parts: the signifier and the signified. The word 'word,' for example ... is a signifier; what it represents is something else again – the 'signified.' In literature, the [flexible or 'slippery'] relationship between signifier and signified is a main locus of art ... But in film, the signifier and signified are almost identical: the sign of cinema is a short-circuit sign. A picture of a book is much closer to a book, conceptually, than the word 'book' is ... A picture bears some direct relationship with what it signifies, a word seldom does. (127–128)

There are at least two lessons to be learned from this. The first is 'Read the image for itself before you look beyond to see what it means'. In some ways this is harder in film analysis than it is in literary analysis, but pausing to examine the image before looking beyond it for significance is often a very rewarding practice. To begin, you might like to turn down the sound (put the verbal to one side for a moment) and reduce your chosen scene to its visual elements. What colours are used? Where is the light? What is going on in the composition of the scene? Have you seen that shape before? Which character or object is largest in the frame? What is in the background? Why did they cast that actor? What is his or her 'look'? In what other films has that actor appeared? Sometimes you will see visual correspondences between scenes which make thematic links across the film narrative. Sometimes you will see that references are being made to images outside this film – to other films, to pictures, to books. In this essay I concentrate on ways in which *The Silence of the Lambs* fits into a *literary* Gothic heritage, but there are equally important ways in which it quotes other films, such as Hitchcock's *Psycho* and *The Texas Chainsaw Massacre*, among others. Because it is easier to reproduce literary quotations in my own written text, I have chosen here to concentrate on *literary* intertextuality (quotation, allusion), but an awareness of *visual* intertextuality is just as important to the reading of film.

The second lesson to be learned from Monaco's analysis is that the film image seems to have a more immediate connection with the 'real' and the 'non-fiction' world than does the written word. The links between film events and events off-screen seem to be easier to make and, in some ways, harder to avoid or deny. This is one of the reasons why film is so often read as 'propaganda', or art that has an effect on the world. As a consequence, cinematic representations of social phenomena tend to attract comment and censorship in a way that literary representations no longer do. Both institutions and audience seek to control the way certain films are watched and understood. For example, *The Silence of the Lambs* won several academy awards, but there were protesters outside the ceremony, pointing out that the characterisation of the serial killer in the film tended to stigmatise gay people. The film contains a *verbal* disclaimer about the status of the killer character as representative of gay people, but its use of certain stereotyped *images* (of a man acting in a stereotypically camp manner) tends to undermine the disclaimers. If it is borne in mind that the visual is very much more powerful than the verbal in film, perhaps there is room for doubting the sincerity or effectiveness of the filmmakers in seeking to overturn prejudicial representations.

Those who have watched *Scream* will know that one of the cardinal rules of the horror movie genre is that 'There has to be a sequel'. *The Silence of the Lambs* is a sequel to an earlier novel by Thomas Harris called *Red Dragon* (filmed as *Manhunter*). This novel's monster, Francis Dollarhyde, is a great fan of William Blake who is well-known for his apocalyptic poetry. Several lines of Blake's 'The Tyger' are significant in the context of *The Silence of the Lambs:*

> *Tyger Tyger, burning bright,*
> *In the forests of the night;*
> *What immortal hand or eye,*
> *Could frame thy fearful symmetry? (1–4)*

> *Did he smile his work to see?*
> *Did he who made the Lamb make thee? (19–20)*

'The Tyger' is a poem about the paradoxical morality of a creator who could conceive of both tigers and lambs, both terrible and gentle creatures. The title *The Silence of the Lambs* is not as banal as it first appears (in relation to Starling's story about the horrors of meat eating). There is a way in which *The Silence of the Lambs* can be read, like Blake's poem, as a story about a perverse and contradictory moral universe. But if it is such a tale, then who is the creator? There may be a god in this text, but not necessarily a benevolent one: 'He' may be Hannibal Lecter.

Before developing this theme it is necessary to make a few observations about the status of this film as a Gothic text. One of the ways in which *The Silence of the Lambs* may be 'read' is as a continuation, albeit cinematic, of a line of literary works. Lecter is connected with the classic European architecture of nineteenth-century literary Gothic: he draws ancient churches and he inhabits a space which takes the visitor on a trip back to the barbarities of Bedlam, to the stone dungeon of the ancient castle. However, Lecter is by no means stuck in the past. One of the processes we witness in *The Silence of the Lambs* is Lecter's learning to become a modern monster. In many ways, he learns this from his pupil/patient, Jame Gumb. *The Silence of the Lambs* refers to an old tradition of literary Gothic, but it also updates the generic conventions to meet the temper of its times.

The stylised spaces of Jame Gumb's architecturally chaotic basement, complete with ancient oubliette and ultra-modern anatomy table, make the connections between nineteenth-century and twentieth-century settings quite explicit. This place refers to the twisting and inward turning mazes inhabited by the creatures in Edgar Allen Poe's tales: creatures like Poe's Roderick Usher or the narrator of 'Ligeia', or Prospero in 'The Masque of the Red Death'. Poe's spaces, however, are altogether exotic and impossible, in a way that the spaces in *The Silence of the Lambs* are not. Where Poe's architecture refers back to a European romantic tradition of castles and dungeons, the architecture of *The Silence of the Lambs* carefully establishes the connections between the bland face of the American suburb and its dark underground life. The surreal chaos of Jame Gumb's basement is shockingly connected to the tidy exterior of his ordinary-looking house. There is an insistence, in *The Silence of the Lambs*, that the proper setting for horror is not just in the exotic, isolated places that were favoured by the authors of nineteenth century Gothic writing, but that horror can also be found in apparently clean, orderly, populated spaces we might all use every day: the courthouse, for example, in which Lecter butchers two policemen.

Jame Gumb is a distinctly American creature. His 'stage' name, Buffalo Bill, attests to the Americanness of his lineage, and this is also visually encoded in the repeated use of the United States flag in association with Buffalo Bill's crimes. The car in which Benjamin Raspael's head is found is draped in the Stars and Stripes. When Lecter makes a butterfly out of a policeman, a kind of monument to Bill's project of transformation, he makes the wings out of the red, white and blue. In Gumb's basement there is a tableau of crossed American flags, with a combat helmet. We see this after Gumb's death as a mute testament to some kind of trauma associated with war. If we never get a complete explanation of Gumb's psychosis, perhaps this hints at some of his formative influences.

The entire visual scheme of *The Silence of the Lambs* works to load red, white and blue with certain symbolic meanings. When Lecter is finally liberated on Bimini, the opportunities that setting provides for him are signified by the promiscuous mingling of colours in the scene. The American world he has left is characterised by a rigid structuring of colour, but in the Bimini street, black and white skins, red, blue and white shirts all mingle. Lecter disappears into this chaos, free to pursue his cannibal urges without interference from the rigid structures of the country he has left, symbolised by the clear colour organisation of the flag.

Red is conventionally the colour of blood, of murder, but its first use in *The Silence of the Lambs* is when the tiny Starling gets into an elevator at the FBI academy: she is cast against a solid wall of very large red-clad male cadets. A certain asymmetry of power between the sexes seems to be associated with red, here. When Chilton shows Starling the photo of the mutilated nurse, the whole scene goes red. Perhaps this is red for mutilation, but it might also be a characterisation of the violent bullying to which Chilton is subjecting Starling. The photo of Lecter's work is displayed and explained in the context of Chilton trying to assert his authority over Starling. Red is not only for blood, here. Red emerges as the colour of masculine domination. This impression is reinforced when Crawford, calling Starling from his helicopter to tell her she is to miss out on the Gumb arrest, is coloured red.

Blue is conventionally the colour of cops (witness the titles *NYPD Blue*, *Hill Street Blues*), but in *The Silence of the Lambs* the police wear black. Blue is associated rather with the cool gaze of the analyst: Starling's eyes are blue, as are Lecter's (a departure from the novel, in which Lecter's eyes are red). In the asylum, Lecter wears a blue boiler suit, strangely stitched together up the front. Starling wears grey/blue at the FBI academy. Blue is associated with intellectual activity here, with the contemplative phase of the detecting process. The active phase requires other colours, however. The instructor who points out to Starling how she might die (by failing to check behind her) wears white. Outside the asylum, in his most deadly mode, Lecter also wears white. He is dressed in white when he murders the policemen in the courthouse and when he sets out after Chilton in Bimini. White, then, is a colour associated with creeping, unexpected death, but not with all deaths.

Jame Gumb's work is green. The funeral parlour in West Virginia has a green decor. The vegetating corpse is green. Green is the colour Starling wears to go into spaces where Gumb's deadly work is found: Miss Moffat's self-storage and Gumb's cellar, which is painted green. Gumb observes his victims through night vision goggles which tint the world green. He becomes a 'green eyed' monster when looking at the skins he covets. Green is the colour of jealousy, but it is also the colour of spring, of rebirth, of growth and metamorphosis. Green does not belong in the scheme associated with the flag, but it is the colour of the combat helmet, of military fatigues.

The Silence of the Lambs characterises itself as being about American horror. In this context, allusions to the American Gothic tradition are very important. The film owes an obvious debt to Poe, and particularly his conception of the detective as one who proceeds less by methodical examination of the clues than by an almost mystical mental discipline called 'ratiocination', a process which reveals the occult truth behind apparently opaque factual surfaces. An example of 'ratiocination' which seems to have particular relevance to *The Silence of the Lambs* occurs in Poe's short story 'The Purloined Letter', when the detective Dupin divines the truth by a kind of psychic mirroring: he puts himself in the shoes of the villain (who may be his brother) and works out what he would do. Something similar occurs in modern dramatic representations of the FBI 'Profiler', a detective who exploits psychological models, and psychic insight, to predict the behaviour of the criminal. The films *Millennium*, *Profiler* and *Murder Call* all rely on this characterisation of the pseudo-science of detection.

In *The Silence of the Lambs* Lecter, the miraculously omniscient 'profiler', trains Starling to stand in the shoes of her quarry, to understand his motivations. This psychic symmetry is also a feature of *Red Dragon*, in which Starling's predecessor is said to have caught Lecter because of a disturbing mental resemblance between detective and criminal. This whole idea appeals to the Gothic convention of the double, and its exploitation is announced in the opening scenes of the novel. In the film *The Silence of the Lambs*, Clarice is first seen negotiating an obstacle course at Quantico. She is climbing one rope, but another, beside her, is conspicuously unoccupied. Implied is the absent other, her potential twin. This imagery of symmetry and synthesis is completed at the end of the film when Starling breaks down Jame Gumb's darkened windows, revealing a mobile that depicts the fusion of two butterflies into one, larger creature.

The suggestion that Starling and Gumb, the lamb and the tiger, might have anything in common is startling, to say the least. Only a very 'fearful symmetry' indeed could encompass such an outrageous conjunction, let alone suggest a synthesis of two such dissimilar creatures. The whole idea is worthy of the adjective 'grotesque'. Grotesques are hybrid creatures, representative of something that does not occur in the 'real' or the 'natural' worlds. One conventional function of the 'grotesque' is to use physical deformity to point to the existence of a less visible moral or psychic deformity. Flannery O'Connor says:

> To be able to recognise a freak, you have to have some
> conception of the whole man ... The novelist with [moral]
> concerns will find in modern life distortions which are repugnant
> to him, and his problem will be to make these appear as

*distortions to an audience which is used to seeing them as
natural; and he may well be forced to take ever more violent
means to get his vision across to this ... audience ... For the hard
of hearing you shout, and for the almost-blind you draw large and
startling figures. (Quoted by Alther 5–6)*

Jame Gumb is such a figure, particularly in the scene where he
tries on his half-completed woman suit. He dresses up and dances for
the camera, tucking his penis between his legs, as if wishing it did not
exist. Bill's problem is that he hates his maleness, and seeks to elim-
inate it, without having a satisfying, coherent alternative ready to
replace it. He manages to turn himself into a bizarre composite
creature: part-man, part-woman, part-moth. The point here is not
that his body is wrong, although he thinks it is. The point is that his
psyche is diseased. That disease is the unique result of the pressures of being male at the end of the twentieth century, a time when
male powers and privileges are under attack. Buffalo Bill cuts up old
bodies to make a new one, in much the same way as Frankenstein
did, but the monster he is creating is a distinctly modern creature: a
man in revolt against masculinity. Lecter tells us this in his courthouse installation. He makes a spectacle of the policeman's corpse,
which is disembowelled and suspended from the bars of the temporary cell, making a shape like one of Bill's moths. The body so posed
also creates a visual echo of the scene in which Bill strips for the
cameras. The policeman is hung in front of the American flag, deliberately displayed as an emblem of American accomplishments in
the serial murder stakes. This lovingly displayed corpse becomes a
kind of 'angel of death in pain', put up by Lecter to 'give men pause'
(Gifford quoted in Hoberman 8). This figure is organised so as to
attest to what Lecter does (he gets inside people), and to comment
on the implications of what Bill is doing: crucifying American masculinity.

One of the shocking things about *The Silence of the Lambs* is the
film's sympathetic approach to the notion that serial murder is,
somehow, an art form. Immediately after clubbing the policeman
into submission, and before gutting him for display, Lecter is seen listening with obvious appreciation to classical music. He is surrounded
by his art and his books. This is an artist at work. He shows us that
which is both terrible and beautiful. Here, perhaps, is the eye that
frames the fearful symmetry of *The Silence of the Lambs*.

The scene in the funeral parlour, in which Starling and her colleagues examine one of Bill's victims, further illustrates the point

about the display of death as art. If Bill is a large and startling figure, some grotesques are more subtle, like the girl on the slab in West Virginia. She is covered with the detritus of the river bed: mud, leaves, green slime. There is a realistic explanation for her appearance, but the way in which the picture of her hand is composed for the camera suggests something else: that she is caught in the act of turning into a vegetable form, like the speaker in Emily Dickinson's Poem #470:

> I am alive – I guess –
> The Branches on my Hand
> Are full of Morning Glory –
> And at my finger's end –
>
> The Carmine – tingle warm –
> And if I hold a Glass
> Across my Mouth – it blurs it –
> Physician's – proof of Breath –

This allusion is underlined when the corpse seems to sigh on releasing the chrysalis. Starling's initial response to the spectacle on the slab seems to indicate that she is reading this corpse for the pain it represents, the suffering involved in the 'wrongful death'. This compassionate response is quickly sublimated to a more professional way of looking at the corpse: Starling's job is to examine the corpse for signs of criminal behaviour. I would argue, however, that cinematic spectators are encouraged to adopt a third way of looking at this body – not as a representation of pain, or of law-breaking, but as the work of an interesting, if deranged, mind. This corpse is approached as a horrid sort of wonder: the vegetating hand; the way the corpse seems to exhale when it gives up the Death's Head moth. Somebody has taken care in the presentation of this corpse; somebody loved the work. This is a way of looking where response is aesthetic, rather than ethical or empathic. In this way it can be seen that *The Silence of the Lambs*, while presenting itself as a 'realist' film, presses the surface of that realism to reveal a symbolic life that has a great deal to do with art appreciation, and little to do with a moralising response.

As objectifying as this approach to feminine death may seem, *The Silence of the Lambs* does work in defiance of conventional ways of presenting the female body in art. Particularly, this film critiques the conventional presentation of the nude. Characteristically, the nude is posed with her face averted, so that nothing challenges or upsets the privacy of the voyeur, the spectator who looks without being seen. This approach is seen in the photos Starling finds in Fredrica Bimmel's music box: Fredrica coyly hides her face from the camera/voyeur. In the pictures taken on the river bank, by contrast, Bill's victims stare into the camera, challenging the onlookers. This critique of the conventional way of looking in *The Silence of the Lambs* has won the film qualified support from some feminist critics. *The Silence of the Lambs* is very specific about how such deaths fit into a continuum of exploitative and/or abusive masculine behaviours, a continuum which links the most violent men, men like Gumb, to men who are just conducting themselves 'normally', like Chilton and Crawford. The policemen in the Virginia funeral home, who subject Clarice to some very hard stares, are different in degree, but not in kind, to men like Miggs.

So *The Silence of the Lambs* may be seen to trade on the conventional exploitation of women, but also to offer a critique of that exploitation. Problematic as this contradictory manoeuvre may be, there are even more complex problems surrounding the film's characterisation of its cross-dressing serial killer. One of the questions to be asked is whether feminist politics benefit at the expense of other marginalised groups in this film. It is not without reason that *The Silence of the Lambs* attracted vocal gay protest when it was featured at the academy awards. The film stands against a cultural background in which homosexuality, transsexuality and homicidal sadism have frequently been equated. The famous Leopold and Loeb case, about two homosexual 'thrill killers', has been filmed at least twice: once as Truman Capote's *In Cold Blood*, and more recently as *Swoon*. *The Silence of the Lambs* came out in the wake of the heavily publicised prosecution of the real life serial killer Geoffrey Dammer, who abducted, tortured and killed men and boys.

Against this background, it would be difficult for any film dealing with transsexual serial killers to avoid the stereotyped association of gayness with sick sex and danger. Both the film and the novel of *The Silence of the Lambs* contain specific denials that Gumb is representative of any 'real' transsexual or gay person, but such denials are on fairly shaky ground. The assertion that Gumb is 'not a real transsexual' implies that there is someone (in this case the medical personnel at Johns Hopkins) who has the right to say once-and-for-all what a 'real' transsexual is. The other problem with this denial is that it must continually compete for the spectator's attention against the fact that Gumb is played *very* camp in the film. Demme gives his strongest tool (the image) to the stereotype of the murderous pervert, while the critique of that stereotype is given a weaker device (the verbal qualification). Some have seen the apparent incoherence of Gumb's characterisation as a result of the tension between the desire to present the stereotyped pervert/murderer, and a desire to censor that presentation. One might attempt to make sense of all the conflicting messages Gumb sends, but I think Halberstam is sensible in pointing out that the very attempt to 'force a coherent pattern' on to this characterisation of psychopathology is problematic. There is no telling what Jame Gumb 'really' is. He does not fit comfortably into a stereotypical male sex/gender pattern, and his attempts to fit into a feminine one are grotesque: he cannot do better than to pinch his nipples and scream in mimicry. If *The Silence of the Lambs* does not quite succeed in challenging the conventions governing feminine or gay stereotypes, it does succeed in destabilising the masculine identity which forms the 'norm' against which women and gay men are traditionally found wanting.

In his project of metamorphosis, Bill reveals himself to be a very twentieth-century monster: he is obsessed with changing the *surface* of the body to conform to superficial appearances. For him, identity is all about the externals. When he captures Catherine Martin, his greatest concern is the condition of her skin: in the back of the van he exposes and inspects it; he demands that Catherine use the lotion to maintain it. This superficiality contrasts with the rather more old fashioned approach taken by Hannibal Lecter, who likes to look into the interior psychology of his subjects for material on which he can feed. For the nineteenth century monster, the mutilation of the body is only a way of getting at what is presumed to be inside: an essential self. Both Bill and Starling reveal an understanding of identity at odds with Lecter's. Both Lecter's pupils use costume as a means of altering identity: Bill makes a girl suit, and Starling uses a good bag to disguise her class deficiencies. Lecter initially sneers at these skin-deep attempts at self transformation, preferring to plumb the psyche for evidence of buried sexual trauma. However, neither Bill nor Starling offers very good material for this kind of analysis: there is no evidence that the trauma Bill suffered was sexual. War is darkly hinted at, but no details are available. Starling explicitly denies that there was a sexual element to her childhood suffering. She says the rancher who butchered lambs was 'a very decent man'.

As the drama proceeds, Lecter embraces the methods of his pupils. He engineers his escape by wearing a face mask made from the skin of the second policeman. This may be seen as a comment on his victimisation by Chilton, who makes Lecter wear a muzzle, but it is also evidence that Lecter learns from Bill a lesson about the power of superficial appearances. The young policeman who finds Lecter's prone body is momentarily stunned in contemplation of the horrific surface of the face, unsure what to make of it. This, as it turns out, is a more sensible approach than that of his commanding officer, who leaps straight to a conclusion about who is inside: 'It's Jim Garrity, damn it. Talk to him.' Of course, it is not Jim Garrity. This episode serves to underscore the dangers of looking through the surface of things for an interior that 'really' matters. Sometimes it is the surface that matters.

But if Lecter is prepared to use Gumb's approach in appropriating a superficial identity as a gimmick, his preferred approach to the exploitation of other people is of a fundamentally different kind. Where Gumb gets under his victims' skins, Lecter takes his victims into his own body. In so doing, Lecter reveals the disorder of his own sense of self: he has no stable boundaries. Bakhtin says:

> *Eating ... [is] one of the most significant manifestations of the grotesque body. The distinctive character of this body is its open unfinished nature, its interaction with the world ... [In the act of eating, the] limits between man and the world are erased ... (281)*

This lack of personal boundaries is less a problem for Lecter than it is for those around him. Crawford warns Starling about Lecter's habit of psychic invasion: 'You don't want Lecter inside your head'. Lecter is capable of transgressing even the most solid looking barriers: he murders Miggs without ever touching him, and he does manage to reach across the toughened glass front of his asylum cell to get inside Starling's head. The moment of transition is seen during one of the 'Quid pro quo' exchanges, when Lecter's face appears next to Starling's head, reflected in the glass, but on the same plane, in the same visual space.

If Lecter eats, he also feeds: while practising as a psychiatrist he nurtured Bill, and we see Lecter feed Starling. He gives her hints; he shows her signs. In Starling's case, feeding takes the form of teaching her to read. He teaches her to ask critical questions of her texts, her suspects. He annotates her case file, not so as to tell her the answer, but so as to teach her how to find it. Lecter fattens Starling's resume, feeds her appetite for advancement, by giving her Buffalo Bill. Lecter's teaching, of course, is not without its sinister undertones. There is an allusion to the figure of Renfield in *Dracula*, who collects flies and feeds them to spiders, and then collects spiders to feed them to birds, eventually eating the birds himself. Notice that although Starling is repelled by the killing inherent in the consumption of the lambs, she indirectly benefits from Lecter's manipulation of an equally violent economy of consumption. Lecter makes Starling break her own moral rules.

Is there a God in *The Silence of the Lambs*? By the standards of good and evil with which many viewers start watching this movie, Lecter is not a nice man. By the time Chilton disembarks from the plane in Bimini, under Lecter's gaze, many may well have decided that whatever Lecter plans to do to Chilton it is probably richly deserved, if not strictly for the best. What could cause such a shift in allegiances? How does Lecter make those of us who cheer him on break our own rules? First, anyone who identifies with Starling as a moral touchstone may be seduced by Lecter, as she is. Second, Lecter is characterised as a charismatic tutor: we are exposed to the power and elegance of the way he thinks. He shows us things that are both terrible and beautiful, prises stories out of people that fascinate and disturb. Third, Lecter is positioned, in many ways, as a god. This is probably most clearly evident in the scene in which he interrogates Starling about the lambs: behind him is the bright white light; behind her, a darkness that requires his illumination. While Starling herself is mystified by the significance of the tales she encounters (even some of the tales she tells), Lecter knows everything there is to know: he has an omniscience worthy of a god. Lecter sees patterns and makes plans which entirely confound the more pedestrian minds around him, and the viewer is in on the secret. Further, it is seen that Lecter is, in some ways, the creator of the whole mess: he is a prime mover in the development of Bill's psychosis, and he becomes the force that brings together such powerfully opposed creatures as Bill and Starling. An emblem of the way in which Starling is 'made' by Lecter is seen in the moment when he hands back her case file to her: their index fingers meet at the moment of the exchange in a gesture reminiscent of the inspiring touch God gives Adam in Michelangelo's famous fresco on the Sistine Chapel ceiling. To sit at the right hand of a god in this way is intoxicating, even if the god's motivations are somewhat murky.

This moral ambivalence is underlined by the movie's unusual strategy of closure. On one hand, the detective narrative is brought to a satisfactory conclusion: Bill is caught. On the other hand, the fact that Hannibal Lecter remains at large at the end of the story is troubling. Lecter's final call to Starling interrupts her graduation and cuts across the moment of her triumph, returning the viewer, with a jolt, to a moral position more akin to the one with which he or she might have begun to watch the drama. There is a double ending here: one ending helps restore moral order while the other decisively returns to the initial disorder. This is a most unusual strategy for a Hollywood feature film; such formal openness to sequel is more characteristic of the TV series. The conspicuous failure to maintain or restore moral order flies in the face of the 'rules' of melodrama (the dominant mode of Hollywood film) as described by Lang:

> *The melodramatic imagination is profoundly moral; the melodrama does not simply stage a battle between good and evil ... but rather tries to establish that clear notions of good and evil prevail, that there* are *moral imperatives. (18. Lang's emphasis).*

Perhaps the point here is not to foster complacency about the inevitability of the triumph of virtue, but to shake up the audience's well-cultivated faith in the happiness of endings. Perhaps, this fearful symmetry is Demme's way of answering Blake's question:

> *& what art,*
> *Could twist the sinews of thy heart? (9–10)*

Works Cited

Bakhtin, Mikhail. *Rabelais and his World.* Trans. Hélène Iswolsky. Cambridge, Massachusetts: Massachusetts Institute of Technology Press, nd.

Blake, William. 'The Tyger' in *The Norton Anthology of Poetry.* 4th ed. Eds. Margaret Ferguson, Mary Jo Salter and Jon Stallworthy. New York: WWW Norton, 1996: 680–681.

Johnson, Thomas H., ed. *Emily Dickinson: The Complete Poems.* London: Faber and Faber, 1970.

Monaco, James. *How to Read a Film.* New York: Oxford UP, 1977.

Halberstam, Judith. 'Skinflick: Posthuman Gender in Jonathan Demme's *The Silence of the Lambs'. Camera Obscura* 27 (Sept 1991): 37–51.

Harris, Thomas. *Red Dragon.* London: Transworld/Corgi, 1989.

——. *Silence of the Lambs.* London: Heinemann Mandarin, 1989.

Hoberman, J. 'Sacred and Profane'. *Sight and Sound* 1.10 (Feb 1992): 8–11.

Lang, Robert. *American Film Melodrama.* Princeton: Princeton UP, 1989.

O'Connor, Flannery. *A Good Man is Hard to Find.* With introduction by Lisa Alther. London: The Women's Press, 1980.

Poe, Edgar Allan *Selected Tales*. Oxford: Oxford UP, 1980.

Shelley, Mary. *Frankenstein or the Modern Prometheus*. Eds. James Kinsley and M.K. Joseph. Oxford: Oxford UP, 1980.

Stoker, Bram. *Dracula*. Ed. Maud Ellman. Oxford: Oxford UP, 1998.

Films

In Cold Blood. Dir. Richard Brooks. 1967.

Manhunter. Dir. Michael Mann. 1986.

Psycho. Dir. Alfred Hitchcock. 1960.

The Silence of the Lambs. Dir. Jonathan Demme. 1991.

Scream. Dir. Wes Craven. 1996

Swoon. Dir. Tom Kalin. 1992.

The Texas Chainsaw Massacre. Dir. Tobe Hooper. 1974.

TV Series

Hill Street Blues. NBC. 1981–1987.

Millenium. Fox Broadcasting Company. 1996 to present.

Murder Call. Channel 9 & Southern Star Productions. 1997 to present.

NYPD Blue. ABC (Amer). 1993 to present.

Profiler. NBC/Three-putt Productions. 1997 to present.

Further Reading

Bordwell, David and Kristin Thompson. *Film Art: An Introduction*. 4th edition. New York: McGraw-Hill, 1993.

Clover, Carole. *Men, Women and Chainsaws: Gender in the Modern Horror Film*. Princeton NJ: Princeton UP, 1992.

Creed, Barbara. 'Dark Desires: Male Masochism in the Horror film'. *Screening the Male: Exploring Masculinities in Hollywood Cinema*. Eds. Steven Cohan and Ina Rae Hark. London: Routledge, 1993: 118–133.

Corrigan, Timothy. *A Short Guide to Writing About Film*. US: Harper Collins, 1989.

Gatens, Moira. 'A Critique of the Sex/Gender distinction'. *A Reader in Feminist Knowledge*. Ed. Sneja Gunew. London: Routledge, 1991: 139–157.

Mulvey, Laura. 'Visual Pleasure and Narrative Cinema'. *Screen* 16.3 (Autumn 1975): 6–18.

Young, Elizabeth. '*The Silence of the Lambs* and the Flaying of Feminist Theory'. *Camera Obscura* 27 (Sept 1991): 5–35.

Television Gothic:
The X-Files

M a n d y   T r e a g u s

This examination of *The X-Files* will concentrate on three main areas: narrative, genre, and gender as they occur on the television show *The X-Files*. It will be concerned with *The X-Files* as a television series, rather than the movie, though much of it may also apply to the movie. In particular I shall discuss episode 2, 'Squeeze', which features the character Eugene Tooms, who also appears in the twentieth episode, 'Tooms'.

Narrative and Genre

One of the things that becomes obvious when studying the stories told in different places and times is that such stories are just as reflective of a culture as its material products and its history. In fact, it is impossible to separate narrative from culture. Peter Brooks has described narrative as 'one of the large categories in which we think' (323). It is possible to see narratives that arise at specific historical moments as out-workings of issues significant to the culture at that moment. One can also see the creation and existence of particular genres as means by 'which we think', as they are preoccupied with different issues in human life. The fact that genres exist over centuries does not negate this; over time, most aspects of being human only undergo variation rather than complete change, so some issues remain constant. What changes is how issues are dealt with, and it is often the variation in the expression of a genre that tells us most

about the thinking of a particular time and place. It is possible, therefore, to trace both similarities and differences in the treatment and
use of the Gothic genre over the span of a couple of hundred years,
and we can often read those changes and similarities in terms of
politics: that is, in terms of relations of power between individuals
and groups in a society. In the nineteenth century the novel was the
dominant form of narrative. In the late twentieth century this is no
longer true; now it is the Hollywood movie, the sit-com, or the crime
show in which our culture does some of its more obvious thinking.
Maybe it is even in the plot that is revealed over four quarters of football that we think, or at least experience a variety of emotions.
Perhaps these emotions keep us from thinking. Whatever the case, in
every activity, we express, as a culture, our values. We also produce
and reproduce such values, and question or challenge them.

While not ignoring the show as entertainment, this examination of
The X-Files will consider its narratives in terms of the thinking our
culture is doing through them. This does not detract from its value as
entertainment; the most compelling narratives are those that engage
us on the most levels so there is much at stake for us and for our
society. The Gothic genre engages with certain fears and uncertainties
and challenges and reinscribes notions around what it is to be human,
gendered and functioning in a partially known world. *The X-Files* certainly has these same preoccupations, but also expresses some of the
specificities of the age and society from which it has come.

Watergate, Paranoia, Genre

Chris Carter, the creator of *The X-Files* and writer of many of the
episodes, has referred to an event in US political history as 'the most
formative event of my youth' (Lowry in Graham 56). This was
Watergate, the name given to the events and revelations surrounding
the impeachment of President Nixon in 1973. What was so significant
about Watergate in terms of the nation's psyche was that it revealed
to the American public that the symbol of their nationhood, the
President, could not be trusted. Secret tapes, illegal phone bugging
and a President who swore to excess came as a great disillusion-
ment to the nation as a whole. Government could no longer be seen
as having the best interests of the nation at heart. Carter makes
direct reference to this era in the show; one of *The X-Files*' characters
has the same name as the chief Watergate informant, Deep Throat,
and there are abundant references to the conspiracy films of the
70s, such as *Three Days of the Condor* and specifically *All the
President's Men* (Graham 55–56).

However, while the conspiracy genre is a factor, so too are the science fiction films of the 50s. They were made at a time when most of the world was engaged in the Cold War, that scary 'mine is bigger than yours' game played by the US and the USSR. It was scary because it was played with nuclear weapons and the threat of complete world annihilation. At this time, the enemy was 'out there', but it was also within. All kinds of difference were persecuted in the name of keeping the US from the evils of communism and much of this persecution was carried out by the FBI under J. Edgar Hoover, persecutor of homosexuals by day, drag queen by night as we now know. Communism was the stated enemy at home and abroad, though this functioned as a label for difference or just an excuse to persecute. People were trained 'to suspect friends and family of "subversive leanings"' (Graham 59). Science fiction movies from the era, which tend to be hilarious from a technical perspective, are preoccupied with invasion from the skies, the earth or from the mistakes of scientists. Though these two issues (the proliferation of science fiction movies, and the anti-American witch hunts of the McCarthy era) may seem unrelated, both are connected by the kind of threat they posed. Both 'earthly and unearthly monsters operated according to one principal: infiltration' (Graham 60). Infiltration is a major theme of *The X-Files*, though a confusing one. If the truth is out there, it is hard to find in any consistent way in this show.

The conspiracy plots of *The X-Files*, which all involve the notion of infiltration, become apparent in the narrative life of the series, rather than necessarily in individual episodes. At this stage there have been about ninety-six episodes made (*Who* 28–57). Of these, approximately two thirds are concerned with single cases and have largely self-contained plots. They function like most shows in a TV series do. You can miss a few but it does not really matter. 'Squeeze' is an example of this kind of plot. The other third of the shows forward another kind of narrative: that which develops over the life of a series in 'plot arcs' as Carter calls them. These are the shows that promote a sense of conspiracy. Sometimes they are largely self-contained, sometimes they are in groups of two or three. Sometimes 'To be continued' comes up at the end of a season, and is a great way of hooking the audience into the next series.

The pivotal event in Mulder's life (revealed under hypnotherapy) is the abduction of his eight-year-old sister by aliens when he was twelve. Aliens come in all kinds of shapes and sizes, and are not necessarily harmful but often are. Nothing is very clear about them, except that some of them seem to have a cooperative relationship with a group of older men (the Syndicate) who apparently control 'the Western world from a smoky, badly lit HQ on West 46th Street in New York ... They have links to the US government – especially the CIA and the military', as well as with others around the world (*Who* 21). They have done all kinds of horrible things since World War II, but 'aliens are their grandest passion' (*Who* 21). The Syndicate works with some of the aliens in a project that seems to involve the creation of a master race. In order to achieve this they do four things. Firstly, under the guise of providing smallpox examinations, everyone born in the US since 1954 is injected with a tiny DNA tag which is linked up with the Social Security System. Secondly, humans are used for endless experiments, including placing tracking devices or memory collectors in their gums, nasal passages and necks. These humans do not know if they have been in contact with aliens or humans. Thirdly, the ova of any women abducted are collected and mixed with extra-terrestrials. This involves such high doses of radiation that the women will develop brain cancer. Fourthly, the results are cloned.

Carter has said that he 'would like to think that because we can never truly know all the answers in life, that the show might follow that same route' (*Who* 21). He seems to have succeeded. It is very difficult to work out the overarching plot, and especially why the Syndicate tolerates Mulder and Scully, even feeding them pieces of information. Dead characters reappear. But even though details sometimes seem contradictory, in a sense the details do not matter. It is the general air of paranoia pervading the show that is the notable thing, together with the blending of two kinds of obsessions: one with all things alien, the other with the firm belief that the government and military bureaucracies are hiding momentous things from the public.

Because of infiltration, it is hard to know who can be trusted in this show, especially in the FBI hierarchy. As viewers, we get down to the small group of two trustworthy characters, Mulder and Scully. They provide our identification point, though sometimes even Mulder and Scully act in inexplicable ways.

Horror

Episode Two, 'Squeeze', does not feature any of the conspiracy plot details, though its sequel, 'Tooms', does feature the unexplained presence of the Cancer Man in Boss Skinner's office. Cancer Man works for the Syndicate and, though he thwarts Mulder, seems to be the reason why the Syndicate does not do away with him. Interestingly, when Tooms is finally disposed of at the end of the sequel and Skinner asks Cancer Man whether he believes the report submitted by Scully and Mulder, he replies, 'Of course I do', thereby endorsing the two agents' belief in the paranormal to their FBI chief. The viewer needs no convincing, having seen the evidence. 'Squeeze' is about horror, and also about establishing the working relationship between Mulder and Scully. Horror is treated in fairly conventional ways. Trained as we are in viewing such things, we know the significance of editing so that when we see a close up shot of the storm water drain in the opening moments we know that this is a source of some threat. When we are directed back to it within seconds, we are waiting for the evil to emerge, but all we see at this stage is a pair of yellow eyes. These eyes function as the symbol of transformation in the monster throughout the show. Tooms's eyes are normally brown, but when he anticipates an attack, they are yellow or green.

Full revelation of the monstrous is withheld in time-honoured fashion right up until after the first murder. We follow the unknown business man into the office; he is slightly humanised by his phone call, but really it is not of much consequence to us when he dies. In this scene, tension is built up by our lack of knowledge about what exactly is going on. We see the screws turning in the air-conditioning duct; we do not see who or what turns them. What we do see is the violence of the attack on the business man as it impacts on the door. Even after the attack, we are not quite sure what has occurred. All we get is a few shots of dripping blood and the reflection of the body with a bloodied neck. It is only afterwards that we hear the details; the liver has been ripped out without the use of implements. We also hear that the victim's name is George Usher. In this evocation of Poe's 'The House of Usher', we are reminded that sometimes buildings can seem to be living things themselves, and that they can hold secrets and concealed spaces which may prove menacing. The implication is that a threat can come from the inanimate as well as the animate, adding to a general sense of horror. Alfred Hitchcock has demonstrated that really effective thrillers do not necessarily show us what is going on. Apart from the technical difficulties graphic violence might present to the director, this acknowledges the role of the viewer's imagination, and its capacity to link any threat on the screen with whatever fear lurks in the human brain. By the time we actually see the monster, all we really know is that he probably has ten-inch fingers.

The moment of viewing the monster in any horror show is generally climactic. Here we have the build up, the wait while he emerges from the air-conditioning duct, and then an appearance that is anticlimactic. The baby-faced Tooms does not look like a monster, though he has a creepy air. Of course, it is much cheaper and easier to have a monster who looks completely human as well, and this *is* a TV show, not a big budget movie. However, his appearance suggests a human rather than a monster. The initial suspense of waiting for the monster to emerge is replaced by the suspense of waiting for him to kill, and finally by the suspense of his attack upon Scully. This is enhanced by the display of his monstrosity, his Otherness and non-humanness, in acts such as climbing a brick wall using his bare hands, squeezing through narrow spaces (air-conditioning ducts and chimneys) and changing his shape. Tooms's monstrosity is accentuated by his journey into unclean spaces. We see him in drains, chimneys, and in the sequel, in the toilet plumbing. The final scenes show him covered in yellow bile. He also participates in unclean acts apart from the murders, such as licking the juice of a dead rat from his fingers while carrying out his job of collecting dead animals. All of these things add to his monstrosity. When he attacks the second victim we are allowed to see more than the first time as we watch and hear him dislocate his joints in order to go down the chimney. However, our voyeurism, should we have a taste for such things, is not completely satisfied: we do not see the murder. We are offered the rather tired symbol of the flame going out in the fireplace instead of watching the victim die. Withholding satisfaction of the viewer's gaze is part of the reason for this, but the fact that it is much cheaper and easier to film as well is a consideration that should not be overlooked.

Tooms's monstrosity occupies middle ground as far as monsters go. He is not so different that we cannot consider him to be human, although he is different enough to be a form of freak. The role of aliens and freaks is similar; they mark borders for humanity, showing us what we are not. But they also muddy borders, showing us what we could be, and possibly are. The show is explicit about this issue, especially through the role of the retired police investigator who links Tooms with other acts of human evil, specifically the Nazi death camps and so-called 'ethnic cleansing' in the former Yugoslavia. He does not attempt to place Tooms in the realm of the Other so much as in the realm of Us; he is us: what we are capable of. This idea is reiterated at various points in the narrative by the retired investigator, though it does not seem to be Mulder's view. Rather, Mulder views Tooms as a genetic mutant acting on a 'biological imperative'. We are left to contemplate whether this places other human evil in the same category. Can it be helped, or is it innate? How driven are we as humans? Do we really have 'biological imperatives'? The series features a number of genetic mutants: one feeds off cancerous growths, another eschews liver in favour of sucking the fat from his victims. While blood is the focus of many horror shows, the liver can be seen as a better symbol for life in an age of infectious blood. Scully reads it this way in her criminal profile, describing it as a means of purification and cleansing for her imagined obsessive killer.

Monsters have always raised questions about humanity. What distinguishes a human from a machine, an animal, an experiment? Such questions seem to be stimulated by developments in science which are then worked out in narrative. Many of the plot directions of this series are directly related to new scientific possibilities, especially genetic ones. But how different are these questions from those raised by *Frankenstein* or *Dr Jekyll and Mr Hyde*? Not very, I would suggest, at their most basic. So the representation of the monster, or the freak, creates a scenario in which the limits and boundaries of the human can be defined but also blurred; it also allows us to explore the conundrum of human evil. One of the reasons why *The X-Files* is not so different from these earlier works is that it borrows from them ceaselessly. The writers of *The X-Files* are happy to cannibalise anything from any remotely related genre – and they do.

Gender

Because so few of the characters in the series are treated sympathetically or can be trusted, we as viewers have our attention focused almost entirely on the two investigators, Mulder and Scully, and their interactions with each other. *The Silence of the Lambs*, predating *The X-Files*, has provided the show with the role model for Scully as well as for the fixation of Tooms (human liver consumption) and the setting of the action (Baltimore in both instances). Scully's debt to Starling was even more obvious in the pilot episode, in which Gillian Anderson was made up to look like Jodie Foster, especially in her hairstyle (Wilcox and Williams 103). This was subsequently changed for the series. While popular culture is littered with male FBI agents, there is a distinct lack of female agents. Even in *The X-Files* Scully is the exception. So it is not surprising that Starling should serve as a model, though in Scully she has been modified in telling ways. Mulder's character, especially his methods, also has a precedent in investigator Dale Cooper from *Twin Peaks* (Malach 64; Wilcox and Williams 104).

Every representation produces gender in some way; where there are shared male and female leads, the negotiations of gender roles are likely to provide one of the more interesting entries for analysis. While the average crime show tends to have a more masculine focus, actively cultivating a male audience, a show featuring a male and female lead can be read as seeking a mixed audience. This means that the representation of gender is likely to be even more finely nuanced than otherwise. The way gender is represented varies depending on the genre of the show. A close analysis of soaps has shown that male characters tend to be softened in comparison with those from action shows; they discuss their feelings and relate closely to female characters (Brown 4). Likewise, female characters in soaps are more likely to have professional jobs and reflect positions of relative power (Brown 4). The Australian soap *Neighbours* exemplifies this trend. All the males are very domestic, and have a strong focus on family and activities such as preparing food; all the women work or have very similar relative power to the male characters. The makers of *The X-Files* have projected their own particular representations of gender. While they do not quite equate with those of soaps, they are not the same as the average investigative genre *The X-Files* in part reflects. As an aside, the show's genre has been described as being 'akin to one of its own mutant characters, with its own eclectic genetic heritage; part police procedural, part suspense thriller, part action adventure, part medical drama, part science fiction and part horror' (Vitaris in Lavery 17). Accordingly it does its own thing with gender.

There are many instances in *The X-Files* in which there is an apparent reversal of gender stereotypes in the investigative approaches of Mulder and Scully. Traditional western thought has linked the feminine with intuition and the irrational, generally in a negative way. The masculine has been linked with the rational, the logical, and with control. In Mulder and Scully, these are apparently reversed. Scully, who by now has seen more alien abductions and supernatural phenomena than any other person living, still manages to roll her eyes in scepticism every time Mulder comes up with a 'spooky' explanation. She stands for the rationalism of science. There is a scientific explanation for everything; we just have to find it. Carter has said of science: 'That it has definitely usurped religion and can explain everything now', so it has an important place in his worldview (*Who* 50). Mulder on the other hand stands for an opposing view. Science is inadequate when it comes to explaining everything; sometimes, things are beyond what has been seen traditionally as rational. What would the show have been like had Scully been the intuitive and Mulder the rationalist? I do not think it would have worked; we would not have found it convincing. The weight of explaining the show's plots lies with Mulder. In our culture, the male is still invested with far more authority than the female. Watch the Channel 7 News any night and see who reads the hard news stories and who does the fillers. In order to give these cranky stories some authority, it is imperative that Mulder be the kook. Though Scully questions and adds her own theories, it is nearly always Mulder who clinches the issue and cuts through to the truth of a situation. He has Tooms figured out within minutes of being exposed to the case, while Scully keeps trying to find normal explanations. In its negotiation of gender then, though it plays with the stereotypes and makes Mulder more traditionally feminine than most investigators in TV shows, and Scully more rational, it does not do this to the point of upsetting gender patterns completely. Mulder is still dominant. The fact that most viewers know that Gillian Anderson is paid half of David Dochovny's fee only adds to this. The show's producers are fully aware of gender relations in our culture.

In many ways, then, the representation of gender in *The X-Files* is quite traditional. That great skill of investigators, ratiocination, is a skill both Scully and Mulder have, but even in this, Mulder seems supreme. It is often not his intuition that leads to his success, but his openness to different explanations of the evidence: his superior skills in ratiocination in fact. Scully also has these skills, but arguably relies more on her training in science and specifically as a doctor to arrive at her conclusions which are usually only part of the puzzle. In Edgar Allan Poe's investigative stories, the character with the greatest power of ratiocination, Dupin, can function as God in a text. *The Silence of the Lambs* shows this also, in that Lecter appears to hold all the keys to what is going on. Knowledge and especially the ability to think is power and Lecter has it. While Mulder is not God in the series, he knows more than most. If there is a god pulling the strings, it is probably the Syndicate, and Mulder knows more about them than anyone else.

As with any investigative pair, Mulder and Scully have to 'bounce off' each other. The ways in which they do this evoke Sherlock Holmes and Watson, for while Scully is not as thick as Watson, she is still often the only audience for Mulder's theories. Mulder is very much an illustration of Holmes's dictum: 'When you have eliminated the impossible, whatever remains, however improbable, must be the truth' (Doyle in Wilcox and Williams 106). Ratiocination, that very masculine process, is part of Mulder's repertoire. As Wilcox and Williams assert, 'Mulder is more than capable of masculine ratiocination, but he chooses difference in his ways of knowing, chooses ideas considered nonrational and Other/feminine' (106).

Scully differs from many representations of the female in that she is not primarily represented as 'body'. She does conform to the dominant view of how a woman in popular culture should look though. The very red and pouting lips in particular are meant to be read as sexual. However, Scully is not just there to be looked at; she is active. In particular, she acts upon bodies herself. Many episodes feature Scully performing autopsies, accessing the knowledge that bodies hold, in a position of mastery that has traditionally been seen as masculine. Outside the series and in contrast to it, Gillian Anderson is unashamedly promoted as sexual object. This means that the view the camera takes of her in the show can be coloured by the publicity surrounding it. She can be read as sexual even when the camera does not place the viewer to read her in this way.

In the attack scene in 'Squeeze', there are some mild but nevertheless erotic moments that build on a common sexualisation of the female victim in both high and low culture. As viewers we know that Scully will be the next victim from the moment her necklace is taken. The way in which this is prevented from happening provides us with an example of the delicate way this show negotiates notions of gender as far as plot lines go. Initially the scene is quite conventional, in that the potential female victim is inside unaware of being observed from without by her attacker. Scully's first hint of danger is the blob of bile that drops from the duct in the ceiling. She was the one who recognised the smell in the first place and so she knows immediately what is going on. Like Starling she is resourceful and has that other sign of phallic power, the ability to use a gun, though significantly she drops it. Her powers of ratiocination mean that she knows Tooms will emerge from a vent. However, he has superhuman strength and still surprises her. It is a classic scene: woman in peril, male hero (Mulder) racing to save her. However, this scene resolves in some non-traditional ways. It is not as strong as the climax of *The Silence of the Lambs*, in which Starling is entirely responsible for her own rescue, but Scully is no passive female either. Her weakest moment is when Tooms has her on the ground and is about to perform his crude surgery on her. At this point she is most strongly inscribed as traditional female. Not only is she flat on her back to an attacker, but her midriff is exposed in a way that we did not see in any of the other victims. In fact, the reflection of the first victim showed his white shirt and we did not have a view of the second. Thus exposed, she looks like a rape victim. Mulder needs to burst in when he does in order for her to be rescued. However, Scully fights back too. When Tooms goes for Scully again, Mulder clips on one side of the handcuffs. Tooms's response to this, lunging at Mulder, allows Scully to clip the other half of the cuffs to the plumbing. Ultimately they save each other, though we are fairly sure she would have died on her own. The show evokes the stereotypes, but moderately subverts them in order to produce a modified gender order. Two episodes after this, Mulder is in a similar position. He lies on the ground with a beast woman, the Jersey Devil, over him and the only reason he escapes is because Scully saves him.

While this scene captures their approximate gender equality in narrative form, this is most often expressed in their consultations with each other. Their 'reciprocal look' (112) as Wilcox and Williams describe it is not a prelude to sexual contact; rather it is part of a consultation: '"What do you think?" is a question asked on *The X-Files* perhaps more than on any other series in television history' and we also see this look in their consultations during 'Squeeze' (Wilcox and Williams 105). It implies mutual respect. As Mulder comments to Scully during 'Squeeze': 'You may not always agree with me, but at least you respect the journey'.

The other thing that is notable about Mulder and Scully is the way in which they are both marginalised by the normal patriarchal apparatus of the FBI. To an extent, this feminises both of them in terms of their colleagues. There are several scenes in which highly unlikeable agents joke about how weird Mulder is and then also Scully. Mulder plays with this as well, easily outsmarting the other agent in his investigative techniques and taunting him with their potential rivalry as well as his stupid jokes about aliens. The show is also very 'looksist'; you can pick a creep by how unappealing he looks.

One of the reasons *The X-Files* has been so successful is that it demonstrates a respectful relationship in which the male is still dominant but in which the female is valued and important. It pushes the gender boundaries of other investigative shows without totally upsetting the dominant gender order. There is also an underlying sexual tension that is brought to the fore at certain strategic moments. UST (Unresolved Sexual Tension) is an important ingredient in many shows which feature a male/female lead. We all know that a show dies when the UST is released; nobody is interested any more. The viewer has the opportunity to make much of this, and can read it in every exchange. The show also uses many of the other techniques that have made soaps so appealing to the female audience. These techniques, such as numerous close-ups of the two leads' faces, in order to allow the viewer to read them for meaning themselves, differentiate it from most other action shows. Another significant and notable factor is the narrative. Action shows customarily have a very linear narrative. The action is usually propelled by the hero or heroic team who attempt to solve some dilemma. Action builds to a climax, and the threats to equilibrium are contained within the space of one show. The ending is almost always closed. Soaps, on the other hand, have many plot strands. These develop over a period of time, resolve or not, but tend to present as a series of mini-climaxes that never really close. If one narrative line finishes, others are left open, so there are multiple plot lines. While *The X-Files* does not display this level of multiplicity, it is quite complex in terms of its ongoing conspiracy plots. The episode 'Squeeze' is quite linear, but it does have an ending that is open enough to allow for a sequel. Some episodes leave so many threads hanging that they are unsatisfying if one wants a closed ending. Sometimes it just seems to stop after the regulation forty minutes. This willingness to leave things hanging is a narrative characteristic shared by soaps.

The other overriding element of *The X-Files* is its apparent paranoia. What does it say about the human condition in the late twentieth century? Obviously in some respects, not much has changed since *Frankenstein*. We are still trying to work out humanity, especially in the light of current challenges to the boundaries of what is human. However, there is also a mood in the US and increasingly in our own culture that links all human fear into a single focus. There has always been human fear and the search for meaning, and they have generally been linked in some kind of religious expression. That is not the case here. However, this show does not suggest that nobody knows what is going on and that there is no meaning. It suggests, rather, that somebody does know what is going on, but they are not telling. In many ways one can read this as a desperate attempt to assert that things are not out of control. If someone knows, it is better than nobody knowing. Even the aliens are under control if the Syndicate has a deal with them. The enlistment of general paranoia, and the apparent attempt to incorporate potential threats to human life as we know it are a major part of this series, and as such serve to link *The X-Files* to earlier and more conventional manifestations of the Gothic genre.

Works Cited

Brooks, Peter. *Reading for the Plot: Design and Intention in Narrative*. New York: Alfred A. Knopf, 1984.

Brown. Mary Ellen. 'The Politics of Soaps: Pleasure and Feminine Empowerment'. *Australian Journal of Cultural Studies* 4.2 (1987): 1–25.

Graham, Allison. '"Are You Now or Have You Ever Been?": Conspiracy Theory and *The X-Files*' in *Deny All Knowledge: Reading The X-Files*. Eds. David Lavery, Angela Hague and Marla Cartwright. London: Faber and Faber, 1996.

Malach, Michele. '"I Want to Believe . . . in the FBI": The Special Agent and *The X-Files*' in *Deny All Knowledge: Reading The X-Files*. Eds. David Lavery, Angela Hague and Marla Cartwright. London: Faber and Faber, 1996.

'Squeeze'. *The X-Files: File 2 Tooms*. Videocassette. Dir. Harry Longstreet. Created by Chris Carter. Written by Glen Morgan and James Wong. With David Duchovny and Gillian Anderson. Twentieth Century Fox, 1996.

Who Extra with Entertainment Weekly: The X-Files. Ed. Hazel Flynn. *Time Inc Magazines, 1998.*

Wilcox, Rhonda and J.P. Williams. '"What Do You Think": *The X-Files*, Liminality, and Gender Pleasure' in *Deny All Knowledge: Reading The X-Files*. Eds. David Lavery, Angela Hague and Marla Cartwright. London: Faber and Faber, 1996.

Further Reading

Fiske, John. *Television Culture*. London: Routledge, 1987, especially chapters 10 and 11 on 'Gendered Television'.

Lavery, David, Angela Hague and Marla Cartwright. Eds. *Deny All Knowledge: Reading The X-Files*. London: Faber and Faber, 1996. Contains other useful readings on *The X-Files* not cited here.

Girl Culture; or, Why Study the Spice Girls?

Catherine Driscoll

Girls and Modern Culture

This essay considers new ways of approaching the roles of young women in representations of modern culture and cultural production. The 'modern' here means 'modernity' as opposed to the 'Classical' period. Modernity is the period of Western history that, most broadly, focuses on 'the person' as the knowing centre of the world, and it is usually dated as beginning with the eighteenth century philosophies now called 'the Enlightenment', although certain texts of the Renaissance period are also modern in this sense. Across the broad span of modernity, girls and young women have become increasingly visible in public life. The most visible figure of the girl in public life has been the daughter, although modern history has also seen an increasing diversity in the public roles that girls take. Before beginning my discussion of the late modern phenomenon of 'girl culture', I want to suggest some of these changes, considering how the figure of the daughter has entered into a more expansive understanding of girlhood.

The significance of daughters in canonical texts of literature in English is often neglected. For example, while there is an extensive range of criticism and commentary dealing with gender in Shakespeare's texts, very little of it recognises the importance of girls and daughters to Shakespeare's plays. Shakespeare's androgynous girl-boys and brides raise a range of questions about the role of the daughter in cultural reproduction. References to Shakespeare's girls often note the practice of employing boys to act their parts, but this does not address the significance to Shakespearean texts of the transitional social positions which centuries later became the roles of modern feminine adolescents. Shakespeare's young women are emblems of the future, whether as pastoral promise, social disintegration, or something more ambiguous. Social order, the plays make clear, requires order among young women, while the collapse of patriarchal systems exposes the unstable containment of Cordelia, Ophelia or Miranda.

While the girls in Shakespeare's plays emblematise both the desirable continuity of society and the desire for social change, later representations place the girl as less a symbol of society than an example of it. This is true of the girls and daughters of Jane Austen's fiction, who continually question what a daughter's or a girl's role might be. The distinctions between Jane, Elizabeth, Lydia and Mary Bennett in Austen's *Pride and Prejudice* (1813) are exemplary moral positions in relation to an increasingly modern world. They also evidence the increasing specialisation of the modern girl's role in relation to culture. While fashion and other distracting pleasures were sometimes moral issues in Shakespeare's plays, by Austen's time these are closely linked to failings and opportunities which are seen as increasingly specific to girls. This exemplary moral role for girls is often represented by bridal motifs. The girl's desire for a place in the world through the figure of the bride or the idea of marriage is a central convention of romantic and of Gothic fiction. In much eighteenth and nineteenth-century fiction young women strive to establish an acceptable role in life which might be compatible with their own desires, such as in Charlotte Brontë's *Jane Eyre*. Or else, this bridal figure is a more or less mute symbol of cultural coherence, and of the imaginative reproduction of the world by Romantic heroes, as in Mary Shelley's *Frankenstein*.

In the late nineteenth and early twentieth centuries, changes to compulsory education for girls and other legislation concerning the proper development of girls, such as age of consent laws and new divorce laws, signal the degree to which the centrality of the girl to thinking about how society and culture are reproduced had become a public discourse. The new feminist movements of this time also suggest this newly public role for, and responsibility of, the 'modern girl'. Some of the tensions this produced are evident in the turn of the century literature like Miles Franklin's *My Brilliant Career*, which is awkwardly balanced between the conventions of romance fiction and the classic realist novel of development (the *bildüngsroman*), which usually focuses on the processes of the protagonist's growing up. Texts in this genre tend to be about boys, or men, not because there were no novels written about girls growing up, but because a novel about a girl's development tended to be romance fiction – how she grows up and into love, and is made by love. In the impossible satisfactions of romance in *My Brilliant Career*, or in the unrealisable ideals of girls in James Joyce's collection of short stories, *Dubliners*, we might see a foreshadowing of the difficulty of the late modern girl's relation to her opportunities and limitations *as a girl*.

Both the increasing 'adolescence' of representations of young people during the end of the nineteenth and the beginning of the twentieth centuries, and the increasing feminisation of 'adolescence' during this period, are evident in *Dubliners*. *Dubliners* presents frustrated men and desperate feminised adolescents, and invokes the 'unattached' woman as a paralysed separation: at best a form of stasis like Eveline's waiting at the window, Polly's waiting on the bed. Girlhood here is a displaced and transitional identity distinguishable from the solidity of childhood or of a Womanhood fixed by maternity: Polly is probably pregnant, Lily might be – but what will happen to them is yet unknown. In *Dubliners*, girls are mostly present out of focus, unless in the soft focus of romantic interest or the spotlight of desire, but they continue to be absolutely central to narratives about becoming a person and identifying a cultural location. Later twentieth-century texts have continued to underline the importance of the girl to explaining the difficulty of the modern self, particularly the contradictory roles and images offered for modern women entwined with an escalation of mass-produced representations of modern life. These texts often emphasise the impossibility of becoming a woman, detail problems with defining girlhood as a state of dependency, or trace histories of the girl and the unattached woman as narratives of tension, instability, difficulty and promise.

Girls are products and performances of the long history of Western discourses on gender and identity, but girls in the sense we use the word – encompassing no specific age group but rather an idea of mobility which precedes the stability or fixity of Womanhood and implying an unfinished process of personal development – are specific to late modernity and the product of these changes. I wanted to introduce this essay through a survey of the daughter's role in some influential literary texts in English in order to give more context for what, at the end of the twentieth century, seems to be an escalation of the ways in which girls themselves represent being girls. The establishment in the early twentieth century of the category of 'feminine adolescence', which newly permeated increasingly diverse images of girls, used this existent set of discourses on girls in new ways, including representations of the girl as a crucial marker of and market for popular culture. The study of popular cultural texts is relatively new as a component of university studies in the humanities, but the new discipline which has mostly engaged this study, cultural studies, provides an opportunity to look not only at, for example, the representations of and by girls in popular culture, but to consider their significance to the everyday lives of late modern girls. I want to suggest here that no satisfactory understanding of relations between girls and cultural reproduction has yet been produced by modern theories of subjectivity or identity, or by distinctions between 'high' and popular culture, and in this context my essay is part of a larger project on girls and feminine adolescence in popular culture and cultural theory.[2]

This essay will introduce some terms crucial to the discipline of cultural studies and, more particularly, ask about the relation between the idea of 'girl culture' and images of politically radical popular culture. It considers the relations between some recent forms of popular culture which represent girls and are, at least predominantly, directed toward girls – specifically, the Riot Grrrls movement and the Spice Girls. I want to consider here some of the dynamics of conformity and resistance that constitute these popular cultural forms; their relations to audiences of various kinds, including each other; and I want to raise some questions more generally concerning the roles assigned to and produced by girls in relation to popular culture in the 1990s. Finally I want to ask whether contestation over the meanings of girl culture and 'girl power' surrounding and pervading these groups have produced any kind of new relationship between popular culture and girls.

Girl Culture – The Spice Girls and Pop Music

The 1997 MTV awards began with a monologue by the host Chris Rock, in which he quipped that, despite their massive sales, he couldn't find anyone who would admit to having bought a Spice Girls album. In fact the Spice Girls were the running joke of the telecast, consistently derided as not musical, not artistic, not political, and all around not sensible. Not only was their talent at issue, but that question flowed over on to dismissal of their claims to have a political agenda. So who buys the Spice Girls?[3] While generic expectations, media commentary, and the releases of Virgin Records place Spice

Girls consumers in the eight to eighteen age bracket, predominantly female, this continues to be a set of expectations. It does not say anything in itself about use of or identification with the Spice Girls – it does not say anything about what meanings can be or are made of the Spice Girls. More telling, I think, are the forms in which the Spice Girls are marketed and merchandised. These indicate that, whoever is actually buying the Spice Girls, they are being marketed as for girls, and within the codes of girl culture already established by, for example, pop groups and girls' magazines.

It is girls, mostly, who buy sticker books or do girls' magazine or pop music magazine quizzes on 'girl power'. The *SPICE* liner notes ask who 'your' favourite Spice Girl is, and show off the gold rings inscribed 'Spice' on the outside and 'Girls' on the inside. Their official website features a 'Which Spice Girl Are You Most Like' quiz, and also the Spice Girls 'pencil case' containing gossip, advice, pictures and more. Finally, Australian MTV's late 1997 '6th Spice' competition, in conjunction with the 'Portmans' chain of boutiques, directly invoked the Spice Girls as conforming, if at a more affluent level, to expected roles for the 'ordinary' girls presumed to be their fans. The prizes included hairstyling, make-up, a personal trainer, and a trip to Rome for the European MTV awards to 'hang with the Spice Girls'. These are conventional 'girl' prizes, invoking identification with and as a Spice Girl. While marketers apparently anticipated that the Spice Girls Action Figures (1998) might sell to boys, they are designed not to be new girly GI Joes, but to be action figures rather than dolls for girls.[4] The leaflets included in *SPICE* CDs (1997), posterbooks, and video cassettes like *One Hour of Girl Power* (1997), all inviting consumers to respond directly to the Spice Girls, do not exclude the possibility that those consumers are boys, but the questions and the format are based on girls' magazines and 'star' magazines which are marketed mainly to girls, sharing similar calls for connection and identification between the consumer and the girl-as-star.

Such appeal to identification has long been associated with girls' consumption of popular culture.[5] And the Spice Girls are presented in their fan material as 'every girl':

> *they're the mirror of Every Girl who's out there slaving away in school or at a boring job, sick of being trodden on, waiting for the evening or the weekend to roll around so they can go out and have fun. They dress in the fashions ... that people buy every day from the High Street stores, the clothes Every Girl sees when she goes shopping at lunch time. (Golden xiv)*

Most responses to the relation between the Spice Girls and their audience come down to asserting that this everygirlness, this 'pop' conformity, is a phase, and that girls who like the Spice Girls will grow out of it. But such invocation of popular cultural 'identification' is not as simple as girls wanting to be pop stars. The promotional material insists that Spice Girls fans are themselves Spice Girls, while also asserting that Spice Girls fans wish they were Spice Girls. This is not a contradiction within the terms of girl culture. Girls who like the group know that they are not the same as the Spice Girls, and are not ever likely to be Spice Girls, and yet they are also responding to statements that the Spice Girls are just like them. The Spice Girls are figured, moreover, as performing in the place of all the girls who cannot be Spice Girls – this is part of what is at stake in the Spice Girls kicking over tables in a social club in the 'Wannabe' video clip.

A great deal has been written on the Spice Girls at this point. For a 'manufactured' pop band they have provoked a lot of specific, rather than generally derisive, commentary.[6] But this commentary has not adequately placed the group and its success within a broader context of 'girl culture', culture produced by and amongst girls, and not just for sale to girls, let alone contextualised girl culture within the twentieth-century arena of global popular culture with which girls have always been associated.

First it is worth reprising some established readings of girls as fans of pop music, all of which invoke the idea that girls strongly *identify with* the popular culture they consume – that is, they see themselves as closely named by and related to the stars and characters of popular cultural texts. Stuart Hall and Paddy Whannel have claimed that the pop stars girls admire 'are not remote stars, but tangible idealisations of the life of the average teenager' (35). This kind of analysis asserts in part that girls tend to over-invest in objects, reflecting a fear of separation and difference that is specific to a 'feminine' kind of adolescence, and even asserting as typical among girls a search for 'non-threatening' role models and objects in relation to which a moderately more independent self might be produced. According to these readings, girls' consumption of pop music is bound into a transitory freedom between childhood and the impending future of becoming wives, mothers and responsible adults (Chambers 39–40). Sheryl Garratt argues, representatively, that 'Falling in love with posters can be a way of excluding real males and of hanging on to that ideal of true love for just a little longer. It is a safe focus for all that newly discovered sexual energy, and a scream can often be its only release' (401). The difficulty of applying this model to the Spice Girls indicates, I think, some of the assumptions about identification and development it employs, but in this context I am more concerned with the way in which it privatises that development, constructing girls' identification with popular culture as belonging exclusively to a familiar, domestic (and even specifically bedroom), setting.

This model of pop music consumption is situated in a domestic girl space informed by privatised discourses on heterosexual reproduction, and represented as entirely distinct from the technically informed, participatory relation to music belonging to more independent forms of 'youth culture'. A reply to this presumption might be most readily found in 'alternative' forms of girl culture, like the Riot Grrrls or the cybergirls, who often question what girl space might be while the Spice Girls seem more amenable to the sometimes limited range of spaces allowed to girls. The Spice Girls might, particularly in comparison, constitute an acceptable interest and means of grouping amongst girls. But are they more than that, something more like the productive self-interest Garratt suggests when she argues that for pop music fans 'Our real obsession was with ourselves; in the end, the actual men behind the posters had very little to do with it' (402)?

Since its early twentieth-century establishment (though there were nineteenth-century precursors), the 'Youth' market has utilised images of both non-conformity and the popular, the 'non-conformist' being one of its regular marketing labels. The marketing of 'girl culture', in particular, has always utilised relations between conformity and non-conformity. The 'teenybopper' figure so often cited in studies of girls and popular culture exemplifies representations of girl culture as both conformity and resistance, perhaps even as something like a conformist mode of resistance – a set of consumption practices which carve out a space of excess within established limitations on the girl's everyday life: within the good girl's life.

Recognition of a girl audience for mass culture seems to have usually led to more or less direct claims that girls are easily deluded. With reference to the Spice Girls, enough people explain Spice Girls fandom as a kind of delusion to necessitate someone questioning why such fandom is delusional. If this is conceived as more completely a product of 'market conformity' than, for example, wearing Nike or drinking Coke, this claim takes much of its force from Spice Girl fandom being perceived as a girl thing. The more considered of these accounts of Spice Girl delusion claim that the real desires of girls have had little outlet and are thus understandably if regrettably projected on to a commodity invented by marketers – an explanation which seems as dismissive as the less thoughtful claim that girls are naturally susceptible to delusion. In fact, consumption of pop music, like other popular culture products, is a means for individuals to engage with their cultural contexts and to articulate identities and communities. The Spice Girls are often thought about as belonging to a demographic wrapped up in negotiating their own power and powerlessness through consumption. But this intimacy with consumption is also presumed to be the main problem with the Spice Girls: they are popularly represented as defined, delimited and extinguished by consumption, and in this they are intimately connected to a long history of employing girls as exemplary consumers, and even as representative of what consumption means.

Alternative Girls

How do the supposedly alternative forms of girl culture relate to this widespread conception of girls as mainstream, and of 'girl culture' as a culture of consumption? Do 'alternative' girl cultures employ different modes of marketing or deploy different forms of consumption? Or are they defined by something other than consumption – perhaps even by production, to which consumption is usually opposed in cultural theory? If the Spice Girls are a market conformity offering some expression of girls' desires but encouraging passive conformity in the long term, what are the alternative forms of girl culture that are being evoked in comparison? And, how is it that the machinery that produces the Spice Girls seems hostile to and destructive of some real girl culture, a vague realm of authenticity which is mostly opposed to any kind of popular culture when it is described at all, while 'alternative' girl culture can still produce music, art, literature and politics via those same systems?

The Spice Girls claim to be what girls want, and they have been very successful at it. The usual grounds for dismissing this claim is that they are just a glossy prepackaged commodity. The usual story of their origins, that they were brought together by managers through an advertisement in a theatre magazine, is a principle reference. *The Spice Girls: The Uncensored Story Behind Pop's Biggest Phenomenon* – a book designed to explain the Spice Girls to Americans – relays this story in detail, insists upon its irrelevance, and then qualifies it (in fact they left that management to pursue their own vision for the band). It also explicitly addresses the question of the girls' image as manufactured, contrived and concocted:

*When you get right down to it, does it really matter that someone
else brought the Girls together? ... By the time the world first saw
them, in June 1996, they were already raw, loud, blunt, bold and
in-yer-face – in other words completely themselves ... So how
could this be the new manufacturing process for pop stars?
(Golden xii).*

In response to their reputation as talentless package the Spice Girls
embarked on a world tour – which was not halted by accusations
that their performances were inadequate, by the illnesses of several
members, or the mid-tour departure of one of the five members of the
group – and also launched a film, *Spice World*, parodying their own
manufactured images and image as manufactured. The film had
several possible titles in planning, including *Five* and *Spice Girls: the
Movie*, but was always conceived with the tag – 'They don't just sing'.

The Spice Girls' claims to authenticity invoke the experience and
passion of girls unrestrained by being good girls, and also invoke
various related claims to show how things really are for girls now – or
how they could be. These are claims to display a truth that can be
acknowledged, and bought, by girls, and boys. Andrew Goodwin
summarises much commentary on the 'subcultural' musical forms to
which the Spice Girls might be compared when he argues that 'perceived authenticity derives in no small measure from ... [an]
antipathy to popular culture' supposedly based on 'both its sounds
and its sentiments' being opposed to, as Goodwin puts it, 'commer-
cialism' (109). The Spice Girls' own thematisation of authenticity
includes their music, dance and lyrics, but not as an aesthetics to
which all other aspects of their appeal are subsidiary. Receiving the
1997 MTV New Talent award, the Spice Girls, speaking through Scary
Spice, announced they were proud to receive that award for 'Pop
Music. Yeah, I can say it – Pop Music!'.

Manufacture, fads and popularity are deployed in public discourse on the Spice Girls as accusations, but these do not in themselves account for the broad dismissal of the Spice Girls, which also
takes up debates over what constitutes feminist politics or comment,
and over the ways girls might identify with girlstars or, more unusu-
ally, with politicised slogans. Take the following description of the
Spice Girls from the British magazine *Melody Maker*: 'High Street
glamour, cartoon feminism, and shouting. Now that's what we call a
pop group' (in Golden xvi). The questions that dominate arguments
over the Spice Girls are more than the usual debates over whether a
manufactured pop group does or could produce 'good' music.

Instead, the questions also include: Can merchandised relations to girls be authentic? Can anything feminist be so prominently popular, even for a short time? Can feminism be a mass-produced, globally distributed product? I cannot answer these questions here, but I can approach them through one comparison – between forms of girl culture labelled conformist, in part because they are massively popular, and forms of girl culture labelled *avant-garde* because they neither conform to dominant representations of pop music nor are amenable to dominant representations of girlhood. I am going to use the Spice Girls and the 'Riot Grrrl' movement to make this comparison, and I want to use the comparison to ask what the distinction between popular and *avant-garde* means within the field of girl culture.

Avant-garde means cutting edge and is traditionally a description of aesthetic innovation. But it also means something more than that, implying a degree of authenticity in a work of art because it can be seen to be opposed to popular culture. *Avant-garde* art, then, despite any commercial success, can be seen as opposed to dominant cultural norms, and even as sub-cultural. More than twenty years ago now, Angela McRobbie and Jenny Garber suggested that the invisibility of girls in some subcultures, and the marginality of them to others, might suggest that 'Girl' subcultures had become invisible because the very term subculture 'has acquired such strong masculine overtones' (114). I think the question remains whether girl culture can be thought of as subcultural. Are any forms of girl culture a separate self-recognising (and self-articulating) group spectacularly outside of the mainstream? Perhaps the Riot Grrrls fit that description, but it might also be worth asking why subcultural in this sense is equated with resistance, and whether resistance is the right term for evaluating girl culture. Also long ago now, Dick Hebdige recognised the role of subcultures in articulating the boundaries of dominant culture. Subcultural groups form, he says, 'a diverting spectacle within the dominant mythology from which [they] in part [emanate]' (94). They are not, then, necessarily opposed to the interests of 'dominant culture'.

Riot Grrrls and Rebellion

Despite their own strategies and slogans, the Spice Girls are widely discussed – in the mass media, in specialist music and political publications, and in a variety of public forums – as having no kind of authenticity at all, and in this they are aligned to many other groups of girls. Prominent references are to Go Go Girls or Bond Girls. But any girl reference will do, even to the Riot Grrrls – girls spelt with a growl and not an I. The American cover of *Rolling Stone* made that reference with 'Pop Tarts: Spice Girls Conquer the World' (Riot Grrrls sometimes call themselves Pop Tarts or even Media Sluts). But comparisons between the Spice Girls and the Riot Grrrls are especially interesting because they are often made in order to condemn one of them. While Riot Grrrl zines and sites decry such pop phenomena as the Spice Girls, some of the Spice Girl fan material describes the Riot Grrrls as dull and dour, whining, self-pitying and sexless – which are, interestingly enough, some of the same accusations Riot Grrrls have levelled at 'second wave' feminism.

Riot Grrrls are easier to define than such loose girl culture scenes as 'teenyboppers', despite heated debates over their interests, allegiances, and even how to spell them. There are 1, 2 and 3 r versions of the girl that riots, mostly defined in relation to girl bands influenced by punk. The most influential Riot Grrrl band is Bikini Kill, who I am going to use as exemplary, but also on the list are Cold Cold Hearts, Sleater-Kinney, The Third Sex, Babes in Toyland, Hole, 7 Year Bitch, and Bratmobile. Riot Grrrls are not as difficult to define as many 'movements' because of the repeated attempts by Riot Grrrls to define and even enumerate themselves, particularly in small circulation zines, and electronic or e-zines, but the definition is still across a field of debate. The two r grrls accuse the three r grrrls of claiming a superior badness: 'maybe that third "r" is like a proud scarlet letter, a matter of haute transgression and baaadddddness stumbled over, a door slammed, a curse hurled'. This is from the original 'Pop Tart' home page, where the owner claims: 'It's actually [sic] pretty cool that grrrl/grrl/grl has entered the language as such. Nobody "owns" it, ya know' (Kile). But ownership is the explicit focus of the antagonism between forms of riot-grrrlness as well as between Riot Grrrls and pop girl groups like the Spice Girls. The *Riot Grrl* e-zine changed its name from three to two rrs in order to get a patent on the term, prompting a surge of internet outrage which seems telling concerning the parameters of Riot Grrrlness (and its distinction from cybergirls, a form of girl culture which often overlaps with Riot Grrrl, but which, unfortunately, I do not have space to consider here).

Riot Grrl the zine has on its front page the slogan 'Riot Grrl changes lives!' It features stories, competitions, quizzes, games – like 'Feed the Supermodel – Feed her now!' – letters to the magazine, and lists for exchanges with other Riot Grrls, a format derived directly from girls' magazines. While Riot Grrrls war over representing themselves in any way, the track 'Rebel Girl' by Bikini Kill is often discussed as the Riot Grrrl Anthem. 'Rebel Girl' is probably the most generically mainstream track on the *Pussy Whipped* album. And neither is it obvious, despite their opposition in girl culture debates, that the Kill's lyrics – 'Rebel Girl you are the queen of my world' – are more radical than those Riot Grrrl bands who are represented as more mainstream, like (Courtney Love's) Hole – 'I wanna be the girl with the most cake'; or even than the lyrics of the Spice Girls – 'I'll tell you what I want, what I really really want'. Certainly the groups differ in their musical influences, and derive a lot of their distinctions from one another from those influences: punk, grunge, and dance music respectively. But Bikini Kill are supposedly more radical than the Spice Girls first of all because they interrogate the popular representation of girls. In this comparison, the visual representation of the Spice Girls' songs as popular narratives (and as funkily dressed narratives too) seems important to the kinds of identification that comprise being a Spice Girl fan. But the idea and the marketing concept of 'girl power' is also part of this visualising system, and it too must be seen. The back of the *Spice Girls' Hour of Power* video exclaims: 'We don't only talk about girl power, we live it! Just watch!' It would be a mistake to downplay the role of MTV in this distinction between the accessibility and coverage of the Spice Girls and groups like Bikini Kill. But much of the dominant late 1990s girl-band aesthetic in fact draws on Bikini Kill, Hole and other punk-influenced groups. As one fanzine notes, Riot Grrrl bands not only produced feminist texts, but also 'inspired a new type of dress, short, little girl dresses as well as Hello Kitty pocketbooks and backpacks' as part of their resistance to a perceived desexualisation of girls among feminists. A careful consideration of the continuities and discontinuities between what the Spice Girls and Bikini Kill resist, and what they lay claim to, would, I think, go a long way toward mapping the contemporary parameters of girl culture.

In opposition to the global circulation of Virgin records, Bikini Kill are associated with what is sometimes called DIY girl culture. But is this different aestheticisation of music industry production any basis for excluding or diminishing the Spice Girls? Kathy Bail makes this introduction to her collection on *DIY feminism:*

> *Riot grrrls, guerilla girls, net chicks, cyber chix, geekgirls, tank girls, super-girls, action girls, deep girls – this is the era of DIY feminism. For young women, rather than one feminism there are a plethora of feminisms going under new and more exciting tags ... This change is allied with a do-it-yourself style and philosophy characteristic of youth culture. (Bail 3)*

Riot grrrl thus re-articulates the tension between group identity and individualism which characterises twentieth-century feminism more widely. Bikini Kill are The Bikini Kill. They often refer to themselves as a group noun which also insists on being comprised of individuals – just like the Spice Girls, who supposedly fired their first management team for not respecting their individuality and their equality within the group. As I suggested above, comparison between the Spice Girls and Bikini Kill raises the question of whether any involvement in mass produced culture is a form of conformity. Can you merchandise a revolution?

The cultural distinction between Bikini Kill and the Spice Girls depends more on accessibility and their responsiveness to fans. Rather than hanging with and getting together with their fans, Riot Grrrls cohere loosely by opposing aspects of their social context, including the idea of the girl audience – the Riot Grrrl group Bratmobile, for example, have a song with the double-edged title 'Fuck Your Fans'. The Spice Girls and Riot Grrrls both question whether girls have a special need for expression specific to them. But the Spice Girls direct their slogans and appeals very broadly, certainly with the intention of including 'domestic' or home-oriented teenagers or preteens, while Bikini Kill has primarily a college/university or adult audience, and market themselves with specific reference to this delimited rather than general audience – market themselves, that is, as their punk ancestors taught them, as subcultural. The crossover points and variations on these audiences are also worth noting, however, and while fewer girls would have a space to listen to Bikini Kill rather than the Spice Girls, the Spice Girls are unlikely to be consumed in any homogeneous fashion.

Girl audiences are not adequately understood by dividing popular music up into hierarchies of popularity, or lyrical or musical innovation, or of resistance. What does constitute the mainstream in the context of middle-class grunge looks, and Riot Grrrl fashion lines? The generic conventions of pop and punk music rather than political content distinguish the Spice Girls from Bikini Kill, and this comprises as well the language in which they speak (a statement about their expected audience). So, rather than simply attributing a subcultural edge to the less commercial form of girl cultures we might, for example, think about the processes of intimate identification between girls and music to which the politics of both Bikini Kill and the Spice Girls are attached. This doesn't require homogenising all forms of music addressed to young women. As Holly Kruse points out 'as much as the word "identification" seems to imply a sense of

belonging, perhaps even more it describes a process of differentia-
tion ... Senses of shared identity are alliances formed out of opposi-
tional stances' (34). The similarities between these forms of girl
culture might be just as interesting as their opposition, even though
Bikini Kill's claims to authentic girl experience rely on an opposition
to pop music.

Both these feminist modes of girl culture are also sexy prolifera-
tions of images, but the Riot Grrrls do not appeal to dominant narratives of what is sexually appealing in a girl like the Spice Girls do.
Are the Spice Girls marketed as different flavours of sexual opportunity–versions of what a girl would be like in bed? They certainly
could, I would even say surely do, appeal to many forms of voyeurism
and desire. But does that exclude the possibility that 'Girl Power'
describes more than one set of images and practices, even with reference to girl sexuality? Both the Spice Girls and the Riot Grrrls
produce mixed messages concerning their eroticism: not the sexy-
dangerous mix (Scary Spice or Rebel Girl), which is nothing new,
but an assertion that 'our sexiness is part of our politics'. What, if
any, effects does this have on their circulation of the label 'feminism'? What, if any, effects on dominant understandings of what girls
want and how they behave do such feminist slogans have? On the
terrain of international multiple-platinum selling pop music articu-
lated as by and for girls, no revolutionary claims are necessary to
argue that this presents a fascinating event in the paradigms of girl
culture.

Girl Culture (Feminist Cultural Studies)

Studies of popular culture are crucial to feminism in terms which I
can easily appropriate from Meaghan Morris's discussion of what
cultural studies does. Morris points out that cultural studies is 'an
investigation of particular ways of using culture, of what is available
as culture to people inhabiting particular social contexts, and of
people's ways of *making* culture' (43). Feminist criticism is unavoid-
ably interested in the way people inhabit and make gendered culture
and gendered cultural identities. In this light it seems to me not only
patronising but ultimately pointless to assume that conformist girls
like the Spice Girls while more radical (more intelligent) ones like
Bikini Kill. Taste is not in the least independent of culture industries
or the globalisation of entertainment, of course, but this is not an
even field of choice in which distinctions between products equal distinctions between consumers. At the very least, we can not make
assumptions about how girls like the Spice Girls, or whether 'polit-

ical' slogans have anything to do with this. Moreover, when personal agency is evaluated according to ideas of resistance it is inevitable that the agency of some people or groups – the ones with least access to modes of cultural production for example – will seem less independent and less individual than others. Choosing Bikini Kill or their version of 'resistance' would not be equally possible for all girls, or even equally empowering.

The Riot Grrrls interrogate dominant discourses on femininity – they aim to, as they put it, 'smash the mask'. They interrogate patriarchal and feminist gender roles and both American society and international recording industries, but they continue to rely on the dominant economic system they are attacking. Riot Grrrls are presumed to belong by choice – activism – rather than by the consumption of any products; their products in fact constrain any articulation of Riot Grrrlness. This assumption pretends that processes of consumption are not at all productive – that consumption is not a valid means of forming identities and communities and relations to both dominant and alternative cultural fields. But some girls, many girls, buy things. This is what girl culture most obviously consists of for late modern girls, and girl culture inherits and foregrounds this attachment to consumption from the 'problem' of reproducing girls across centuries as discussed above. Girl culture circulates the things girls can do, be, have and make. This circulation of things – this economy of girl culture – produces the unresolvable tensions of 'alternative' girl culture's problems with incorporation and distribution within the globalised recording industry just as certainly as it does debates over the authenticity of the Spice Girls. To actually embrace the communities these different forms of girl culture imagine requires complicity in systems with which they claim to be incompatible, and they both produce legitimated models of identity and agency within the systems they say exclude them.

'Girl power' was always open about its limitations and constraints, and there is something productive about girls acting on the world in ways that are widely accessible to the everyday lives of their audience. If this everydayness does conform to generic expectations for girl music, or even for girls, does that define these forms of cultural production as conservative or reactionary, or might it be (instead or as well) a vivid recognition of, and an accessible commentary on, the way power and identification work to name girls, and work for girls? I have no projections for the Spice Girls' longevity, for their millenial significance, or for their potential inclusion on courses introducing English, or even Cultural Studies. But the Spice Girls do belong to a long history of relations between girls and debates over cultural reproduction, and to a twentieth-century history of relations between girl culture and feminism, and they produce both girls and feminism in ways that seem worthy of more subtle consideration than they have as yet inspired.

Notes

1. This larger project is a book on *Girls: Feminine Adolescence in Popular Culture and Cultural Theory*, to be published by Columbia University Press in 2000, which considers the historical, theoretical and popular constitution of girls and adolescent women since the late nineteenth century. This essay is drawn from several conference papers on this subject, and a longer form of this argument directed to the relations between feminism and 'girl culture' appears in *Australian Feminist Studies*, 1999.

2. As I am revising this work, the Spice Girls have undergone a major change with the departure of Geri Halliwell, generally described as 'the most vocal' and as the oldest of the Spice Girls. Whether or not this change will affect the Spice Girls' popularity or change their apparent agendas discussed below remains unclear, but predictions of the Spice Girls' immanent disappearance as yet remain unfulfilled.

3. The Official Spice Girls Page <http://c3.vmg.co.uk/spicegirls/>

4. For relevant work on girl consumption see Sheryl Garratt's 'Teenage Dreams' in *On Record: Rock, Pop and the Written Word*. Eds. S. Frith and A. Goodwin. London: Pantheon, 1990; Angela McRobbie's 'Shut Up and Dance: Youth Culture and Changing Modes of Femininity'. *Cultural Studies* 7.3 (Oct. 1993); and the work of Ehrenreich, Hess and Jacobs on 'Beatlemania: A sexually defiant consumer subculture?' in *The Subculture Reader*. Eds. K. Gelder and S. Thornton. London: Routledge, 1997.

5. For example, Susan J. Douglas, 'Girl power puts a new spice into feminist debate'. *The Nation*, August 25–September 1 1997: 29.

Works Cited

Bail, Kathy, 'D.I.Y.Feminism' in *DIY Feminism*. Ed. K. Bail. Sydney: Allen and Unwin, 1996: 3–17.

Bikini Kill. 'Rebel Girls', *Pussy Whipped*. Kill Rockstars, 1993.

Chambers, Iain. *Urban Rhythms: Pop Music and Popular Culture:* Houndmills: Macmillan, 1990.

Sheryl. 'Teenage Dreams' in *On Record: Rock, Pop and the Written Word*. Eds. S. Frith & A. Goodwin. London: Pantheon, 1990: 395–411.

Golden, Anna Louise. *The Spice Girls: The Uncensored Story Behind Pop's Biggest Phenomenon*. London: Ballentine Books, 1997.

Goodwin, Andrew. 'Popular Music and Postmodern Theory' in *Cultural Theory and Popular Culture: A Reader*. Ed. J. Storey. Hemel Hempstead: Harvester Wheatsheaf, 1994: 414–427.

Hall, Stuart and Paddy Whannel. 'The Young Audience' in *Cultural Theory and Popular Culture: A Reader*. Ed. J. Storey. Hemel Hempstead: Harvester Wheatsheaf, 1994. 69–75.

Hebdige, Dick. *Subculture: The Meaning of Style*. London: Methuen, 1979.

Hole. 'Doll Parts', *Live Through This*. Geffen Records, 1994.

Joyce, James. *Dubliners*. H. Levin, ed. *The Essential James Joyce*. London: Grafton Books, 1988: 21–73.

Kruse, Holly. 'In Praise of Kate Bush' in *On Record: Rock, Pop and the Written Word*. Eds. S. Frith and A. Goodwin. London: Pantheon, 1990: 450–465.

McRobbie, Angela. 'Shut up and Dance: Youth Culture and Changing Modes of Femininity'. *Cultural Studies* 7.3 (1993): 406–426.

McRobbie, Angela and Jenny Garber. 'Girls and Subcultures' in *Feminism and Youth Culture: from 'Jackie' to 'Just Seventeen'*. Ed. Angela McRobbie. London: Macmillan, 1991: 1–15.

Morris, Meaghan. 'A Question of Cultural Studies' in *Back to Reality?: Social experience and cultural studies*. Ed. Angela McRobbie. Manchester: Manchester UP, 1997: 36–57.

Spice Girls. 'Wannabe'. *SPICE*. Virgin Records, 1996.

Further Reading/Viewing

Douglas, Susan J. 'Girl Power puts a new spice into feminist debate'. *The Nation*, August 25–September 1 1997: 29.

Ehrenreich, Barbara, Elizabeth Hess and Gloria Jacobs. 'Beatlemania: A sexually defiant subculture?' in *The Subculture Reader*. Eds. K. Gelder and S. Thornton. London: Routledge, 1997: 523–536.

Harpold, Leslie. 'Courtney Love=RiotGrrl'. Riotgrrl, <http://www.riotgrrl.com/archive/fem10.htm>

Kile, Crystal. Poptart Home Page <http://ernie.bgsu.edu/~ckile/ckile.html>

One Hour of Girl Power: The Spice Girls. Virgin Video, 1997.

CONTRIBUTORS

Philip Butterss teaches in the English Department at the University of Adelaide. He is co-editor of *The Penguin Book of Australian Ballads* (1993) (with Elizabeth Webby), and editor of *Southwords: Essays on South Australian Writing* (Wakefield, 1995). He is currently working on masculinity in contemporary Australian film.

Catherine Driscoll's research and teaching engages widely with feminism, cultural theory, popular culture, modernism and youth studies. Her recent publications include the essays 'Becoming Bride', in *UTS Review*, and 'Locating Everyday Life', in the *South Atlantic Quarterly*. Among a number of forthcoming publications is a book called *Girls: Feminine Adolescence in Popular Culture and Cultural Theory*, to be published by Colombia University Press in 2000.

Megan Fyffe completed a first class Honours degree in English at the University of Adelaide in 1998. Her Honours thesis on Emily Dickinson is entitled *'I dwell in possibility': Emily Dickinson and the Concept of Home*.

Sue Hosking is a Senior Lecturer in English at the University of Adelaide. Her particular research interests and areas of publication activity include contemporary Australian fiction and literature which reflects the interaction of Aboriginal and non-Aboriginal cultures. She is currently collaborating with South Australian Aboriginal elder Clem O'Loughlin, who has lived and worked between cultures, to produce his autobiography.

Joy McEntee is an Associate Lecturer in the English Department of the University of Adelaide. Her research interests include American literature and film, and Renaissance drama.

Rosemary Moore teaches courses in Women's Writing and has published in this field. She has an ongoing interest in the relations between feminist literary theory and psychoanalytic theory. She is an elected member of the prestigious Australian Centre for Psychoanalysis in the Freudian Field.

Amanda Nettelbeck teaches English I and Australian literature at the University of Adelaide. She is the editor of *Provisional Maps: Critical Essays on David Malouf* (1994), author of *Reading David Malouf* (1995) and co-editor (with Heather Kerr) of *The Space Between: Australian Women Writing Fictocriticism* (1998). With Robert Foster and Rick Hosking she is preparing a book manuscript on myths of the South Australian colonial frontier.

Lucy Potter is working on her doctoral thesis entitled *Political Aesthetics and the Redefinition of Marlovian Tragedy*. She has presented papers on early Modern English drama at conferences in New Zealand, Melbourne and Cambridge. Her essay on *Hamlet* in this collection is the result of three years working with Year 12 students in the classroom. Aspects of the essay "Re-reading *Hamlet*" were first published in a focus edition of *Australasian Drama Studies* (October 1998) under the title '*Hamlet* and the Scene of Pedagogy'.

Dianne Schwerdt is a Senior Lecturer in the Department of English at the University of Adelaide. Her teaching and research interests include post-colonial literature and theory, particularly in relation to the works of Ngugi, Achebe, Armah and other African writers. The author of a number of articles on African literature, she is currently writing a book on Ngugi and is editor of the *CRNLE Reviews Journal*.

David Smith teaches English at the Unviversity of Adelaide. He has published on left-wing writers, nineteenth-century fiction and modern drama. He is currently exploring the use of space in literature and the visual arts.

Mandy Treagus is the Lecturer-in-charge of English I at the University of Adelaide. She also teaches Australian popular culture and Victorian fiction. Recent publications include articles on Jimmy Barnes and the Spice Girls. She is currently undertaking research on the rise of female sport in the late nineteenth century.

Marc Vickers is a postgraduate student at the University of Adelaide, writing a PhD on the relationship between the works of Joseph Conrad and Impressionist and Post-Impressionist painting.

Philip Waldron is a graduate of Wellingon, New Zealand, and Harvard, U.S.A., who taught in Universities in New Zealand and Scotland before settling in the Department of English at the University of Adelaide.

INDEX OF NAMES, TERMS AND TITLES